The Product Manager Interview

167 Actual Questions and Answers

LEWIS C. LIN

With Teng Lu

ALSO BY LEWIS C. LIN

Career

Be the Greatest Product Manager Ever

Interview Preparation

Case Interview Questions for Tech Companies

Decode and Conquer

Interview Math

The Marketing Interview

Secrets of the Product Manager Interview

Negotiation

71 Brilliant Salary Negotiation Email Samples

There are three types of people: winners, losers and winners that haven't learned how to win yet.
LES BROWN

Published by Impact Interview, 115 North 85th St., Suite 202, Seattle, WA 98103.

This book contains several fictitious examples; these examples involve names of real people, places and organizations. Any slights of people, places or organizations are unintentional.

The author and publisher have made every effort to ensure the accuracy and completeness of information contained in this book. However, we assume no responsibility for errors, inaccuracies, omissions or any inconsistency herein. This book is sold without warranty, either expressed or implied. The authors, the publishers, distributors, or other affiliates will not be held liable for any damages caused either directly or indirectly by the instructions contained in this book.

This book uses trademarked names in an editorial fashion and to the benefit of the trademark owner, with no intention of infringement of the trademark. Hence, we do not indicate every occurrence of a trademarked name.

Corporations, organizations and educational institutions: bulk quantity pricing is available. For information, contact lewis@impactinterview.com.

FOURTH EDITION / Third Printing

Lin, Lewis C.
The Product Manager Interview: 167 Actual Questions and Answers / Lewis C. Lin.

Table of Contents

CHAPTER 7 ANALYTICS: DATA SCIENCE 95

CHAPTER 8 ANALYTICS: PRICING NEW PRODUCTS 100

CHAPTER 9 ANALYTICS: PRICING EXISTING PRODUCTS 105

CHAPTER 10 ANALYTICS: ROI 110

CHAPTER 11 PRODUCT DESIGN: CUSTOMER JOURNEY MAP EXERCISES 114

CHAPTER 12 PRODUCT DESIGN: PAIN POINT EXERCISES 119

Chapter 1 Introduction

The product management (PM) interview is hard. Just consider the following questions, recently reported by Google, Facebook, and Uber candidates:

Estimations	Estimate how much Gmail costs for Google per user, per year.
Product Design	What is the best decision tree for Facebook or LinkedIn's "People You May Know" feature?
Metrics	There was an 8 percent drop in hits to google.com. Larry Page walks into your office. He asks you to list what the reasons might be.
Go-to-market strategy	How would you start Uber operations in a city with no precedent?
Technical	Design a simple load balancer for google.com. What data structures would you use? Why? Define access/delete/add order of complexity for each data structure and explain your choices. Design an algorithm to add/delete nodes to/from the data structure. How would you pick which server to send a request? Why? Why not?

Why PM interviewers ask seemingly impossible questions

Hiring managers are getting increasingly risk-averse. They are afraid of making bad hires. Bad hires:

- Under-produce
- Affect team morale
- Devour excessive coaching resources
- Consume additional time and effort to identify replacements

As a result, it is not enough to *tell* the employer what you can do. Hiring managers ask that you *show* them what you can do. In the last few years, the "show me, not tell me" trend has accelerated. More employers are demanding that candidates now:

- Complete a take-home assignment, as part of the interview process
- Sign on as a temporary employee first, perhaps as a contractor or intern, before giving a full-time offer

Fortunately, not all employers have these requirements. However, there is a double-edged sword. In lieu of take-home assignments or temporary employment, interviewers ask interview questions that simulate work projects instead. We call interview questions, based on hypothetical work scenarios, case questions.

These questions cannot be reasonable

Candidates feel case questions are difficult and unfair, whereas interviews see them as sensible. Do keep in mind that every case question, asked in a PM interview, is typically part of a product manager's day-to-day responsibilities. Consider:

- *Estimations.* The PM provides a forecast to the supply chain manager so that the supply team can buy an appropriate number of servers for a new cloud service.
- *Product Design.* The PM provides not only UX feedback but also product vision for the UX team, who executes on that vision and feedback.
- *Metrics.* The PM is the spokesperson for the product. They need to explain and investigate changes in business performance to executives.
- *Go-to-market strategy.* The PM is the quarterback of the launch team, which can include marketing, sales, operations, support and legal. The launch team expects the PM to bring leadership and detailed product knowledge.
- *Technical.* Engineers build the product; the PM provides the product vision, roadmap, and prioritized backlog. Engineers are less likely to consent to a PM's vision if the PM is not confident with technical details.

In the technology industry, many believe the product manager is the mini-CEO or general manager for a feature or product. As the mini-CEO, the product manager interacts with different functions from engineering to design to marketing. To interact, influence and lead effectively with these different groups, the product manager needs to speak their language. Speaking a functional language is easier when one has domain expertise. That is what the PM interview is about: testing your domain knowledge. In real-time. Just like real life.

What this book is about and how it is organized

This book offers over 160 PM interview practice problems, with sample answers.

I have organized the questions by type. There are different question categories including product design, analytics, and technical questions.

I have also created detailed preparation plans for Google, Facebook, and Amazon – the three most desirable companies. Keep in mind that companies assess talent differently. Furthermore, their assessment methods may change over time. To use your preparation time wisely, research, either on the Internet or with a friend at your target employer, the kinds of questions a company is likely to ask.

How to use the book

By yourself

If you are using this book correctly, you should attempt the problems on your own and then compare *your* answer with the sample.

I never intended for you to tote this book on your next European holiday. In fact, I intentionally made it difficult to do so. There is no Kindle version; there is no audiobook. I intended for you to place this large book, on a table, alongside your notebook.

I've created blank pages for the first 10 questions. Use them to show your work. After that, I hope you get the idea: attempt the problems on your own. No cheating.

With others

You can also practice questions, in this book, with others.

Dedicated practice can lead to the perfect job. A reader completed an astonishing 102 mock interviews on my interview practice community: bit.ly/PMInterviewGroup. It paid off. As a student from a top 400 US university, he beat the odds and got his dream job as a Google product manager. It is remarkable considering that his peers will be graduates from Stanford, MIT, and UC Berkeley.

Who should read this book

Over the years, readers of my first product management book, *Decode and Conquer: Answers to Product Management Interviews*, have asked, "Where can I find a big bank of practice interview questions?" For all my readers who have supported me over the years, this book is that bank of questions.

Sure, you can find plenty of questions on the Internet. But they don't have sample answers. This book has meticulously detailed answers. Lots of them.

Why I am confident you will get better

In 2015, I released a similar book called, *Interview Math: Over 50 Problems and Solutions for Quant Case Interview Questions*. *Interview Math* is targeted to aspiring management consultants applying at top-tier firms like McKinsey, Bain, and Boston Consulting Group. It includes the following types of questions:

- Estimation
- Profitability
- Breakeven
- Pricing

As readers made their way through every problem, they gained remarkable proficiency, including readers who believed they were not born to do math.

With *The Product Manager Interview*, you will be empowered in the same way. You may be terrified of product design, metrics, and technical interview questions now. And that's normal. We do not practice these interview questions every day. Nevertheless, I am positive that if you dedicate yourself, you will see a significant 10 to 15X improvement in your PM interview skills.

Have these books and frameworks within an arm's reach

Many of you have read my previous books. This book has brand new questions and sample answers.

If you have not read my previous books, you will want to get them so you can refer to the frameworks I recommend for solving each PM question. Here is a summary of books I would recommend:

- *Decode and Conquer* has explanations to PM-related frameworks including the CIRCLES Method™, AARM, and DIGS.

- *Interview Math* has great introductory material and provides more methods on how to tackle estimation, market sizing, ROI and lifetime value questions, especially if you find the harder analytical questions in this book too intimidating.
- *Case Interview Questions for Tech Companies* has even more practice questions and answers. In addition to PM questions, you will find non-PM case questions for the tech industry, including questions for marketing, operations, finance, and business development roles. If you are looking for more PM practice problems or if you are considering non-PM roles, you will want to look at *Case Interview Questions for Tech Companies*.

How to get the most out of this book

Many of you will appreciate that this book has sample answers. However, do not get tempted into reading the answers as if you were reading a novel!

Instead, I recommend that you:

- Try solving the practice question(s) on your own.
- Then compare your response with the sample answer.

With consistent and deliberate practice, you will:

- Get comfortable answering questions that most candidates find difficult.
- Absorb the concepts more deeply.
- Create an efficient feedback-learning loop, deducing when and where your response underperformed or outperformed the sample answer.

Email me

I would love to hear your feedback, comments, and even typos. Contact me at lewis@impactinterview.com.

Lewis C. Lin

Chapter 2 Finding Practice Partners and Bonus Resources

To help further your learning, I have made it easy for you to find PM interview practice partners and provided several bonus materials, listed below:

Find PM Practice Partners

Practicing with others is incredibly beneficial. It will:

- Give you a fresh perspective.
- Provide moral support.
- Keep you accountable.

To make it easy for you to connect with others who are preparing for the PM interview, I created a special Slack community for all of you. Enter the following in your Internet browser: bit.ly/PMInterviewGroup

Here is what people have said about the PM Practice partner community:

"Thanks for starting this community. It's pretty awesome." – A.P.

"Hey Lewis, you already know this, but you've built something amazing here. I've done a few practice interviews now and most folks have been welcoming and really helpful. You should be proud ☺ Congrats." – S.G.

"Hey Lewis, awesome group you got going here! A few of us loved your presentation at Berkeley Haas this past weekend and will be using your resources to get a few study groups together to work on cases. Looking forward to interacting with everyone here." – J.Z.

Interview Evaluation Sheets

I interviewed PM hiring managers and interviewers, and I asked them what they considered a strong response for design, estimation and behavioral questions.

I created these interview evaluation sheets, based on that research. The evaluation sheets will make it easier to provide feedback to your practice partner.

Interview Evaluation Sheet: Product Design

	Rating 1-5 1 = Not like the candidate at all 5 = Very much like the candidate	Interviewer's Explanation
Goals & Metrics Did the candidate define objectives before answering? Were the candidate's selections reasonable?		
Target Persona & Pain Points Did the candidate choose a target persona? Did the candidate explain the persona's pain points to the extent that demonstrated true consumer insight?		
Prioritization Did the candidate demonstrate the ability to prioritize competing use cases or pain points convincingly?		
Creativity Did the candidate show creativity? Or were the ideas a replica of competitive products and features?		
Development Leadership When asked, did the candidate reasonably explain how to implement a proposed feature?		
Summary and Next Steps Did the candidate summarize their main argument at the end, including clear next steps?		

Interview Evaluation Sheet: Estimation

	Rating 1-5 1 = Not like the candidate at all 5 = Very much like the candidate	Interviewer's Explanation
Problem Solving Skills Did the candidate take an unfamiliar problem and develop a plan to solve it?		
Communication Skills Did the candidate communicate his or her action plan to the interviewer? Easy-to-follow? Or did the interviewer have to ask an excessive number of clarifying questions to unravel the candidate's thoughts?		
Comfort with Numbers Did the candidate confidently calculate numbers by hand? Or was the candidate hesitant? Did the candidate rely on using a calculator or computer to crunch numbers? Or did the candidate oversimplify calculations by needlessly rounding numbers?		
Judgment Did the candidate choose reasonable assumptions, backed by logical thinking? Or was the candidate sloppy in choosing assumptions, believing that reasonable assumptions do not matter?		

Interview Evaluation Sheet: Metrics

	Rating 1-5 1 = Not like the candidate at all 5 = Very much like the candidate	Interviewer's Explanation
Understanding Metrics Did the candidate have an understanding of product metrics? Did the candidate provide a comprehensive and relevant list?		
Evaluating Metrics Did the candidate articulate which metrics are better than others, backed with sound logic and evidence?		
Diagnosing Metrics How was the candidate's diagnosis? Did the candidate provide an issue tree depicting drivers that affect that specific metric?		
Affecting Change on a Metric Did the candidate offer a plan on how to influence positively a metric, primarily through product changes but perhaps through other levers, including marketing and business development initiatives?		

Interview Evaluation Sheet: Behavioral

	Rating 1-5 1 = Not like the candidate at all 5 = Very much like the candidate	Interviewer's Explanation
Owner vs. Participant Did the candidate play a primary or marginal role?		
Good vs. Great Achievement Was the achievement impressive? Were the results largely due to the candidate's impact? Or would the results have occurred, even without the candidate's involvement?		
Communication Skills Is the candidate's story easy-to-follow and memorable? Was it a struggle to extract information from the candidate?		

Interview Evaluation Sheet: Other Question Types

	Rating 1-5 1 = Not like the candidate at all 5 = Very much like the candidate	**Interviewer's Explanation**
Communication Skills Did the candidate provide a response that is well organized and easy-to-follow? Or was it boring and disorganized?		
Thoughtful Insights Did the candidate provide thought-provoking insights? Did you feel smarter after talking to the candidate?		
Creativity Did the candidate show vision and imagination?		
Problem Solving Skills Did the candidate take an unfamiliar, unambiguous question, problem or situation and provide a plan as well as compelling leadership?		

PM Interview Cheat Sheet

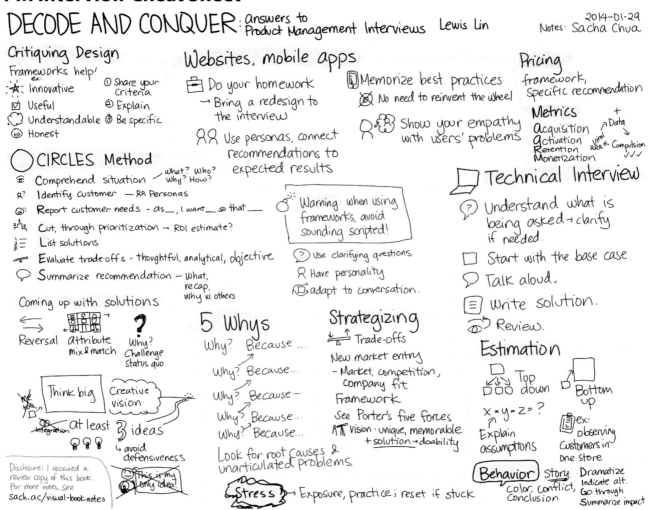

DECODE AND CONQUER: Answers to Product Management Interviews — Lewis Lin

Notes: Sacha Chua — 2014-01-29

Critiquing Design

Frameworks help!

ex:
- ⭐ Innovative
- ☑ Useful
- ☁ Understandable
- 🙂 Honest

① Share your criteria
② Explain
③ Be specific

◯ CIRCLES Method

- 💼 Comprehend situation — What? Who? Why? How?
- 👤 Identify customer — 👥 Personas
- 👁 Report customer needs - as ___, I want ___ so that ___
- Cut through prioritization → ROI estimate?
- ☰ List solutions
- Evaluate trade-offs - thoughtful, analytical, objective
- 💬 Summarize recommendation — What, recap, why vs others

Coming up with solutions

Reversal   Attribute mix & match   ❓ Why? Challenge status quo

Think big   Creative vision

At least **3** ideas
↳ avoid defensiveness

"This is my only idea!"

Disclosure: I received a review copy of this book. For more notes, see sach.ac/visual-book-notes

Websites, mobile apps

💼 Do your homework
→ Bring a redesign to the interview

👥 Use personas, connect recommendations to expected results

Warning: when using frameworks, avoid sounding scripted!

- ❓ Use clarifying questions
- 👤 Have personality
- adapt to conversation.

5 Whys

Why? Because...
Why? Because...
Why? Because...
Why? Because...
Why? Because...

Look for root causes & unarticulated problems.

Stress → Exposure, practice; reset if stuck

Strategizing

⚖ Trade-offs

New market entry
- Market, competition, company fit

Framework
See Porter's five forces

Vision: unique, memorable + solution → doability

Memorize best practices
🚫 No need to reinvent the wheel

Show your empathy with users' problems

Pricing

framework, specific recommendation

Metrics   +

- Acquisition   Data
- Activation   viral
- Retention   👥 ← Compulsion
- Monetization   ✓✓✓

💻 Technical Interview

- ❓ Understand what is being asked → clarify if needed.
- ☐ Start with the base case.
- 💬 Talk aloud.
- ☰ Write solution.
- 👁 Review.

Estimation

Top down   Bottom up

$x \times y \times z = ?$

Explain assumptions

ex: observing customers in one store

(Behavior) Story: Dramatize, Indicate alt, Go through, Summarize impact
Color, conflict, Conclusion

Screenshot / Lewis C. Lin

I created a PM Interview Cheat Sheet just for you: bit.ly/PMInterviewCheatSheet

It includes frameworks for product design, pricing, metrics, strategy, and technical questions. If I could only bring one sheet of paper for an upcoming PM interview, I would bring this one.

Two-Week PM Interview Plan

Task Item	Topic	Resource	Deadline	Minutes to study	Minutes studied	% Complete
	Product Design Questions					
	Practice brainstorming		5-Dec	40	15	36%
	Define a list of 10 problems. Brainstorm 10 solutions to each problem without any time constraints.	Thinkertoys / SCAMPER brainstorming framework	4-Dec	20	10	50%
	Define a list of 10 problems. Brainstorm 10 solutions to each problem. This time, apply a 60-90 second time constraint.	Thinkertoys / SCAMPER brainstorming framework	5-Dec	20	5	25%
	Practice customer empathy		6-Dec	20	20	100%
	Define a list of customer problems. Practice "ranting" on why that problem is terrible.		6-Dec	20	20	100%
	Lead the end-to-end product design discussion using CIRCLES Method™	Decode and Conquer	7-Dec	180	60	33%
	Practice 10 questions leading the end to end discussion		7-Dec	180	60	33%
	Build UX vocabulary by reviewing common design patterns for web and mobile	Web UI Design Patterns & Mobile UI Design Patterns	8-Dec	30	10	33%
	Practice wireframing	Guide to Wireframing	8-Dec	45	15	33%
	Metrics Questions					
	Pick 3-5 products		10-Dec	180	45	25%
	Brainstorm top metrics for each one of those products	Decode and Conquer, AARM Method™	9-Dec	60	15	25%
	Explain which metric is the most important, starting with a balanced pros and cons table	Decode and Conquer, Metrics Section	10-Dec	60	15	25%
	Discuss one potential feature for each product and explain why you should ship / no-ship	Decode and Conquer, Metrics Section	10-Dec	60	15	25%
	Estimation Questions					
	Read chapter 3: Assumptions	Interview Math, Starting from Page 17	11-Dec	20	20	100%
	Complete the following exercise problems		11-Dec	20	20	100%
	BMW Dealerships	Interview Math, Page 22	11-Dec	10	10	100%
	Airports	Interview Math, Page 24	11-Dec	10	10	100%
	Read chapter 4: Estimation	Interview Math, Starting from Page 26	11-Dec	10	10	100%
	Complete the following exercise problems		12-Dec	50	50	100%
	Chinese Diaper Market	Interview Math, Page 32	12-Dec	10	10	100%
	Women's Rain Boot Market	Interview Math, Page 34	12-Dec	10	10	100%
	TV Ads	Interview Math, Page 51	12-Dec	10	10	100%
	Subway's Sales	Interview Math, Page 56	12-Dec	10	10	100%
	Netflix Subscription Sales	Interview Math, Page 64	12-Dec	10	10	100%
	Lifetime Value Questions					
	Read chapter 8: Lifetime Value	Interview Math, Starting from Page 143	13-Dec	90	45	50%
	Complete the following exercise problems					
	Starbucks' Lifetime Value	Interview Math, Page 145	13-Dec	15	5	33%
	AT&T New iPhone Promotion	Interview Math, Page 147	13-Dec	90	45	50%
	New York Times Website	Interview Math, Page 157	13-Dec	90	45	50%
	Behavioral Questions					
	Read Winning the Behavioral Interview	Decode & Conquer, Page 193-202	13-Dec	15	5	33%
	Write down responses for Common Behavioral Interview Questions	Decode & Conquer, Page 193; Stories Sheet: http://bit.ly/1CJarRB	13-Dec	90	45	50%
	Minimum stories: 5		15-Dec	120	120	100%
	Include your written responses to "Tell me about yourself" and "Why do you want to work for this company?"					
	Verbally rehearse written responses		16-Dec	90	45	50%
	Technical					
	Read How to Approach a Technical Question	Decode & Conquer, Page 88	17-Dec	10	10	100%
	Review Big O notation	Wikipedia / http://bigocheatsheet.com / How to Ace the Software Engineering I	17-Dec	20	0	0%
	Review data structures: arrays	Wikipedia / How to Ace the Software Engineering Interview	17-Dec	20	0	0%
	Review data structures: linked lists	Wikipedia / How to Ace the Software Engineering Interview	17-Dec	20	0	0%
	Review data structures: stack & queues	Wikipedia / How to Ace the Software Engineering Interview	17-Dec	20	0	0%
	Review data structures: trees	Wikipedia / How to Ace the Software Engineering Interview	18-Dec	20	0	0%
	Review data structures: heap	Wikipedia / How to Ace the Software Engineering Interview	18-Dec	20	0	0%
	Review data structures: trie	Wikipedia / How to Ace the Software Engineering Interview	18-Dec	20	0	0%
	Review data structures: graphs	Wikipedia / How to Ace the Software Engineering Interview	18-Dec	20	0	0%

Download this spreadsheet to make your own customized interview preparation plan, filled with my suggestions: bit.ly/PMPrepPlan

Common assumptions to know and memorize

Here are some common assumptions that would be helpful to know and memorize before the interview.

Population: United States

United States	323M
New York City	8.4M
Los Angeles	3.9M
Chicago	2.7M
San Francisco	806K
Seattle	687K

Population: Outside the United States

World	7.4B
Europe	739M
Asia	4.4B
South America	423M
Africa	1.2B
China	1.4B
India	1.3B
Japan	126M
UK	65M

Other Useful Assumptions for the United States

Life Expectancy	80 years
People per Household	2.5 people
Median Household Income	$53K
GDP	$16.8T
GDP Growth	2%
Corporate Tax Rate	35%
Smartphone Penetration	70%
Percent with Bachelor's Degree	30%
Percent Married Adults	52%
Percent Under the Age of 18	23%
Percent over the Age of 65	13%

Number of Internet Users
Key Regions

Global	3.2B
North America	320M
Asia	1.8B
Europe	636M
Africa	353M
LatAm	385M
Middle East	141M

Key Countries

USA	286M
China	731M
India	462M
Japan	118M
Brazil	139M

Smartphone Facts
Smartphone Install Base

Global	2.8B
USA	226M
China	717M
India	300M
Japan	63M
Brazil	79M

Mobile OS Market Share

	Global	US
Android	86.8%	61.7%
iOS	12.5%	36.5%

Social Network Facts

Users, by Geography

Americas	599M
Europe	412M
Asia Pacific	1.5B
Africa	170M
Middle East	93M

Users, by Platform

Facebook	1.8B
Snapchat	300M
WhatsApp	1.5B
WeChat	1B
Instagram	1B
Twitter	321M
Pinterest	291M
QQ	899M

Online Advertising Facts

Industry Metrics

CTR for Google Search Ads	2%
CTR for Google Display Ads	0.35%
CPM for Display Ad	$2.80
CPM for Video Ad	$12.80
Average CPC on Google Search Ads Overall	$2.14
Average CPC on Display Network	<$1
Avg CPM for iOS Banners	$0.20-$2.00
Avg CPM for Android Banners	$0.15-$1.50
Avg Conversion Rate Search Ads	2.70%
Avg Conversion Rate Display Ads	0.89%

Annual Ad Revenues, Key Players

Google	$79.4B
Facebook	$26.8B
Twitter	$2.5B
Snapchat	$404.5M

eCommerce Facts

# of Users Purchasing via E-commerce - Global	1.61B
Total Online Sales - Global	$1.915T
Total Online Sales - USA	$390B
Average Annual E-Commerce Revenue per User - Global	$1,189
Parcel Shipped Volume - USA	10B

Enterprise Software Facts

Cloud Infrastructure Spending	$36B
Traditional Data Center Infrastructure Spending	$61B
Total IT spending on Enterprise Software	$351B
Global ERP Software Revenue	$34B
Global CRM Software Revenue	$26.3B
Global IT SaaS Spending	$246B

Streaming Services - Paid Subscriber Base

Spotify	100M
Netflix	148M
Apple Music	56M
Pandora	6.8M
Hulu	27M
HBO NOW	8M

Other Relevant Internet Facts

Average Time Spent per Day on Mobile - US	3.7 hours
Mobile Share of Web Traffic - Global	50.30%
# of YouTube Videos Watched Every Day	5B
Total iOS Apps in the App Store	2.2M
Total Android Apps	2.6M

Chapter 3 Study Guides for Coveted Tech Firms

The PM interview is already difficult as it is. There is no need to overwhelm you with another to-do: constructing your own preparation guide. Therefore, I have put together a sample preparation guide for the following companies:

- Google
- Facebook
- Amazon

I have also made suggestions on how to create a preparation guide for Uber and LinkedIn roles.

Every candidate is unique; skills, experiences, and timelines will differ. Tailor the suggested preparation guides to your situation.

30-Day Google PM Study Guide

Day 1. Getting familiar with Google's PM Interview

Tasks

- Read Google's official preparation note to its PM interview candidates: bit.ly/GOOGPMIntNote
- Search Google for Lewis' blog post and read: "Google Product Manager Interview: What to Expect and How to Prepare"

Goal

Know the scope and nature of the Google PM interview.

Day 2. Getting familiar with the product design interview

Background Reading

- Read about the CIRCLES design method in *Decode and Conquer*.
- Review the product design examples from *Decode and Conquer* to see how CIRCLES is applied.

Exercises

Do the following pain point exercises in *The Product Manager Interview*:

- Child's 1st Birthday Party
- Best Handyman
- Job Search Pain Points
- Finding Someone to Do Taxes

Do the following customer journey map exercises in *The Product Manager Interview*:

- Expedia Journey

- Airbnb Journey
- Job Search Journey
- Home Improvement Journey
- Customer Service Journey
- Online Course Journey

Goals

- Learn about product design questions.
- Understand the product design framework, CIRCLES.
- Observe how others answer interview questions with CIRCLES.
- Practice two parts of the CIRCLES framework:
    a. Listing (brainstorming) solutions.
    b. Reporting customer needs (customer journey map).

Day 3. Putting product design questions together with the CIRCLES Method™

Exercise

Do the following product design exercises in *The Product Manager Interview*:

- Improving Google Hangouts
- Disney Experience with Your Phone

Goals

- Like a wine connoisseur, detect and deduce how your response differs from the sample. As you become more aware of the differences, your responses will improve.
- For now, do not worry about response quality or speed. Getting started, by practicing, is half the battle.

Day 4 to 10. Practice one product design question per day

Exercise

Complete one example a day for the next seven days, choosing from the list of questions from *The Product Manager Interview*, below.

1. Improving Google Play Store
2. Monetizing Google Maps
3. Mobile App Design for Nest
4. Favorite Product
5. Favorite Website
6. People You May Know
7. Car for the Blind
8. ATM for the Elderly

Goals

- Easily explain why CIRCLES leads to better interview responses.
- Understand when, how, and why one should adapt CIRCLES.

Day 11-13. CIRCLES in Real-life

Exercise

Improve your product design skills further by applying the CIRCLES Method™ to real-life. For each one of the next three days:

1. Walk around the neighborhood.
2. As you walk, use the CIRCLES Method™ to improve everyday items. Here are some design problems you can ponder:
   - How to improve sidewalks?
   - How can street lamps be more effective?
   - Build a product to solve the dog poop problem.
   - What new products can prevent flat tires in cars or bikes?
   - What innovation can make gardening less of a chore?
   - What innovative new product can make park gatherings more social, with strangers?

Goal

Acculturating a product design mindset 24 hours a day, both at the interview and in your everyday life.

Day 14*. Find a practice partner for product design

Exercise

Sign up for the product management interview practice group on Slack: bit.ly/PMInterviewGroup

Post a request for a partner or partners in the #req-practice-ptr channel.

Take turns during your practice session. That is, Partner A (interviewer) gives a case to Partner B (interviewee). Then, swap roles.

Coordinate in advance which case each person will receive; to simulate the interview environment, the interviewee should do an unfamiliar case. The interviewer should take time to acquaint themselves with the question and the sample answer.

Repeat the partner practice activity as often as you would like. The best candidates will have practiced at least 20 product design cases.

Goal

Master the product design interview. It is the number one reason why candidates fail the Google PM interview. If you have committed yourself to thoughtful practice, you should be an expert when it comes to tackling product design questions. Use the guidelines below to gauge your product design proficiency:

- A novice suggests the obvious or copies competitive features. An expert suggests novel and memorable ideas. An expert suggests ideas that make the interviewer go, "Hmm, I wish I thought of that; maybe I should build a company based on that idea."
- A novice mentions shallow user insights. The novice does not take interest in users or their motivations. The novice is deficient in user empathy. The expert is a lifelong learner of human psychology and behavior. An expert continually asks questions about what people do and why they do it. As a result, an expert easily points out insights that are urgent, relevant and surprising.
- A novice follows the CIRCLES Method™ step-by-step, like a home cook trying to make a sophisticated soufflé for the first time. The novice is afraid of making mistakes and clings tightly to a prescribed framework. The novice is so busy trying to recall the different steps of the CIRCLES framework that the novice's responses sound robotic and textbook. The expert understands that a framework is a checklist, not a recipe. The expert understands that CIRCLES is there to prevent errors of omission. CIRCLES is there to help ensure that the listener's experience is complete, satisfying and possibly even entertaining.

Day 15. Getting familiar with the metrics interview

Background Reading

- Read about the AARM framework in *Decode and Conquer*.
- Read metrics examples in *Decode and Conquer* to get familiar with metrics questions in an interview setting.

Exercises

Do the following metrics brainstorming exercises in *The Product Manager Interview*:

- Metrics for eCommerce
- Metrics for Two-sided Marketplaces
- Metrics for SaaS
- Metrics for Mobile Apps
- Metrics for Publishers
- Metrics for User-Generated Website
- Metrics for Support Tickets

Do the following metrics prioritization exercises in *The Product Manager Interview*:

- Most Important Metric: eCommerce
- Most Important Metric: Two-Sided Marketplace
- Most Important Metric: Mobile App

Goal

Get more familiarity in coming up with and identifying good metrics.

Day 16. Diagnosing metrics problems

Exercises

Complete the following examples in this book, on your own or with a partner:

- Shopping Cart Conversions
- Mobile App Ratings
- Reddit Posts

Goals

Gain proficiency in brainstorming a complete and exhaustive list of issues when troubleshooting a metric.

Day 17 and 18. Putting the metrics problem together

Exercises

Complete one example a day for the next seven days, both on your own and with your practice partner, from this book.

- Your Favorite Google Product
- Drop in Hits
- Declining Users
- Metrics for Uber Pick-up
- Slow Download on Kindle
- Pinterest Metrics
- Go-to-Market and Success

Goals

Build proficiency in identifying, prioritizing and diagnosing metrics issues.

Day 19. Getting familiar with the estimation interview

Tasks

- Read about estimation questions in *Interview Math*.
- Read the following estimation examples in *Interview Math* to get familiar.
  - Women's Rain Boot Market
  - Smartphone Case Market
  - Subway's Sales

- o   Netflix Subscription Sales

Goals

1. Learn about estimation questions.
2. Learn how to set up estimation questions using issue trees.
3. Learn how to make assumptions.
4. Try the following estimation questions:
   a.   Cars in Seattle
   b.   How Many G Suite Users
   c.   Revenue from YouTube Red

Day 20. Practice estimation questions

Tasks

Complete one example a day, from this book, for the next seven days.

1. Planes in the Air
2. Gmail Ads Revenue
3. Google Buses
4. Gmail Costs
5. Driverless Car Purchases 2020
6. Storing Google Maps
7. Facebook's Ad Revenue

Goals

Master estimation questions. Not only is response quality important, but also you should complete most estimation questions in about 10 to 15 minutes.

Day 22. Learn more about strategy questions

Tasks

Read the following chapters in *Decode and Conquer*.

- Strategizing: Tradeoffs
- Strategizing: New Market Entry
- Strategizing: CEO-Level Issues

Goals

- Learn about common strategy question types.
- Figure out how to approach strategy questions using frameworks.
- See how to apply frameworks to common strategy questions.

Day 23. Practice strategy questions

Tasks

Practice the following strategy questions, in this book, either on your own or with your practice partner:

1. Google's Cable TV Service
2. iPhone Exclusive Partnership

Goals

Provide a response that is thoughtful, logical and addresses the company's objectives. For more examples of thoughtful strategy responses, refer to the popular blog, stratechery.com.

Day 24. Learn more about pricing questions

Tasks

Read the "Pricing" chapter in *The Marketing Interview*.

Goals

- Learn about pricing questions, including the difference when pricing new vs. existing products.
- Figure out how to approach pricing questions using frameworks.
- See how to apply pricing frameworks to popular questions.

Day 25. Practice pricing questions

Tasks

Practice the following pricing questions, either on your own or with your practice partner:

- Pricing New Products
  - Google Driverless Car Pricing
  - Google and Teleportation
- Pricing Existing Products
  - Kindle Pricing at Target
  - AWS Price Reduction

Goals

1. Google's Strategy
2. Google vs. Microsoft
3. Google Moonshot Projects
4. Google Maps in Mongolia
5. Google Store

Day 26. Traditional and behavioral questions

Tasks

- Read the "Winning the Behavioral Interview" chapter in *Decode and Conquer*.
- Draft and polish your answers to the following questions:
    - Tell me about yourself.
    - Why Google?
    - Influencing your team
- Practice and get feedback from your practice partner

Goals

While Google has an affinity for case questions, you should spend some time preparing for traditional and behavioral questions. Google interviewers usually ask traditional icebreaker questions like "Tell me about yourself" and "Why Google?" However, behavioral interview questions like "Tell me a time when you influenced a team" are a newer occurrence. Google's HR department, since 2013, has asked its PM interviewers to ask more behavioral interview questions.

Day 27. Getting familiar with technical interview questions

Tasks

Review the technical topics suggested in: bit.ly/PMPrepPlan

Goals

Gain familiarity with technical concepts and questions. Google reserves technical interview questions for on-site interview candidates, especially those who answered product design, analytics, and strategy questions well.

Day 28. First try at technical interview questions

Tasks

Attempt the following technical interview questions:

- Racing 15 Horses
- Reducing Bandwidth Consumption

Goals

Try some technical interview questions, with a focus on calming your nerves and approaching questions with open curiosity. "Racing 15 Horses" question is an example of an algorithm question. "Reducing Bandwidth Consumption" is an example of a technical architecture question.

Day 29-30*. Second try at technical interview questions

Tasks

Attempt the following technical interview questions from *The Product Manager Interview*:

- Load Balancer for google.com
- Dictionary for Scrabble
- Google Search Service
- Bayesian vs. AI

* Repeat the technical interview practice activity, as necessary.

Goals

Build confidence tackling technical interview questions.

How to Modify the Google PM Prep Guide for Uber and LinkedIn

Unlike Google, most companies do not ask difficult technical interview questions at the PM interview. At most, these companies may ask you to explain a technical concept such as:

- What happens when you type facebook.com into a Google Chrome browser?
- Tell me a time when you had to assess a technical tradeoff.

At most hiring companies, PM candidates will not be asked whiteboard coding or technical architecture questions. Thus, to modify the Google PM prep guide for Uber and LinkedIn, simply do the following:

- Cut out technical interview prep
- Read Lewis' overviews of Uber and LinkedIn PM interview processes.
    - o Uber Product Manager (PM or APM) Interview: What to Expect and How to Prepare: bit.ly/uber-pm-int-tips
    - o LinkedIn Product Manager Interview: What to Expect and How to Prepare: bit.ly/lnkd-pm-int-tips
- Instead of Google-centric practice questions, swap in Uber and LinkedIn examples, as appropriate.

30-Day Facebook PM Study Guide

Day 1. Getting familiar with Facebook's PM Interview

Tasks

Read Lewis' blog post: "Facebook Product Manager Interview: What to Expect and How to Prepare" bit.ly/fb-pm-int-tips

Goal

Know the scope and nature of the Facebook PM interview.

Day 2. Product Sense Interview: Getting familiar

Background Reading

- Read about the CIRCLES design method in *Decode and Conquer*.
- Review the product design examples from *Decode and Conquer* to see how CIRCLES is applied.

Exercises

Do exercises from:

- Chapter 12, Product Design: Pain Point Exercises
- Chapter 11, Product Design: Customer Journey Map Exercises

Goals

- Learn about product sense questions.
- Understand the product sense framework, CIRCLES.
- Observe how others answer interview questions with CIRCLES.
- Practice two parts of the CIRCLES framework:
    - c. Listing (brainstorming) solutions
    - d. Reporting customer needs (customer journey map).

Day 3. Product Sense: Putting questions together with the CIRCLES Method™

Exercise

Do the following product design exercises in *The Product Manager Interview:*

- Improving Facebook for the Web
- Improving Facebook Mobile

Goals

- Detect and deduce how your response differs from the sample. As you become more aware of the differences, your own responses will improve.
- For now, do not worry about response quality or speed. Getting started, by practicing, is half the battle.

Day 4 to 10. Product Sense: Practice one question per day

Exercise

Complete one example a day for the next seven days, choosing from the list of questions from *The Product Manager Interview*, below.

1. People You May Know
2. Instagram UX
3. Improving Facebook Login
4. Favorite Product
5. Favorite Website
6. Car for the Blind
7. ATM for the Elderly
8. Physical Product

Goals

- Easily explain why CIRCLES leads to better interview responses.
- Understand when, how and why one should adapt CIRCLES.

Day 11-13. Product Sense: CIRCLES in Real-life

Exercise

Improve your product design skills further by applying the CIRCLES Method™ to real-life. For each one of the next three days:

3. Walk around the neighborhood.
4. As you walk, use the CIRCLES Method™ to improve everyday items. Here are some design problems to ponder:
   - How to improve sidewalks?
   - How can streetlamps be more effective?
   - Build a product to solve the dog poop problem.
   - What new products can prevent flat tires in cars or bikes?
   - What innovation can make gardening less of a chore?
   - What innovative new product can make park gatherings be more social, with strangers?

Goal

Acculturating a product design mindset 24 hours a day, both at the interview and in your everyday life.

Day 14*. Product Sense: Find a practice partner

Exercise

Sign up for the product management interview practice group on Slack: bit.ly/PMInterviewGroup

Post a request for a partner or partners in the #req-practice-ptr channel.

Take turns during your practice session. That is, Partner A (interviewer) gives a case to Partner B (interviewee). Then, swap roles.

Coordinate in advance which case each person will receive; to simulate the interview environment, the interviewee should do an unfamiliar case. The interviewer should take time to acquaint themselves with the question and the sample answer.

* Repeat the partner practice activity as often as you would like. The best candidates will have practiced at least 20 product sense cases.

Goal

Master the product sense interview. It is a common reason why candidates fail the Facebook PM interview. If you have committed yourself to thoughtful practice, you should be an expert when it comes to tackling product design questions. Use the guidelines below to gauge your product design proficiency:

- A novice suggests the obvious or copies a competitor's features. An expert suggests novel and memorable ideas. An expert suggests ideas that make the interviewer go, "Hmm, I wish I thought of that; maybe I should build a company based off of that idea."
- A novice mentions shallow user insights. The novice does not take interest in users or their motivations. The novice is deficient in user empathy. The expert is a lifelong learner of human psychology and behavior. An expert continually asks questions about what people do and why they do it. As a result, an expert easily points out insights that are urgent, relevant, and surprising.
- A novice follows the CIRCLES Method™ step-by-step, like a home cook trying to make a sophisticated soufflé for the first time. The novice is afraid of making mistakes and clings tightly to a prescribed framework. The novice is so busy trying to recall the different steps of the CIRCLES framework that the novice's responses sound robotic and textbook. The expert understands that a framework is a checklist, not a recipe. The expert understands that CIRCLES is there to prevent errors of omission. CIRCLES is there to help ensure that the listener's experience is complete, satisfying and possibly even entertaining.

Day 15. Execution Interview: Getting familiar

Introduction

Interviewers are testing your judgment in choosing a reasonable goal, along with your ability to defend your opinion.

Example

Imagine you are the PM in charge of Reactions on Facebook - the new way to interact with posts by using "love", "haha", "wow", "sad", and "angry" reactions. Your gut tells you that the average number of these reactions per post will be less than the current average number of likes per post. What would success look like in terms of the number of non-like reactions per post at launch and how do you come up with this? Would this number differ by the reaction? Why or why not?

How to Approach

1. Brainstorm a list of metrics.
2. Identify a shortlist of 2 to 3 potential metrics you'd consider as the "success" metric. Discuss the strengths and weaknesses of each.
3. Make your final recommendation.

Exercises

Do exercises from:

- Chapter 15, Metrics: Brainstorming Exercises
- Chapter 16, Metrics: Prioritization Exercises

Goal

Get familiarity in coming up with and identifying good metrics.

Additional Background Reading

- Read about the AARM framework in *Decode and Conquer*.
- Read metrics examples in *Decode and Conquer* to get familiar with metrics questions in an interview setting.

Day 16 to 18. Execution Interview: Diagnosing problems

Introduction

Tests your ability to diagnose and explain a drop in a critical metric.

Examples

- Weekly active usage dropped on Android. Why?
- Facebook signups dropped. Why?

How to Approach

1. Build an issue tree (aka diagnostic map).
2. Systematically explore each issue.
3. Deduce the issue by process of elimination.

Exercises

Do exercises from:

- Chapter 17, Metrics: Diagnose Exercises

Goals

Gain proficiency in brainstorming a complete and exhaustive list of issues when troubleshooting a metric.

Day 19 to 21. Execution Interview: Solving a problem with a metric

Introduction

Tests your ability to diagnose an issue and suggest a solution.

Examples

You are the PM of Facebook Ads. The clickthrough rate has gone down 5%. What do you do?

How to Approach

1. Build an issue tree (aka diagnostic map).
2. Systematically explore each issue.
3. Deduce the issue by process of elimination.
4. Brainstorm a list of at least 10 ideas to solve the issue you've root caused.
5. Describe the pros and cons of your top 3 solutions. Top 2 is okay if you're short on time.
6. Recommend a single solution out of your top 2 to 3.

Exercises

Do exercises from:

- Chapter 18, Metrics: Putting it Together

Goals

Build proficiency in solving metrics problems, along with identifying, prioritizing and diagnosing.

Day 22 & 23. Execution Interview: Giving your strategic opinion

Introduction

Sometimes interviewers ask for your strategic opinion to test your ability to reason out a course of action.

Example

What are the tradeoffs between having advertisements vs. no advertisements on Facebook?

Exercises

Do exercises from:

- Ch. 19 - Hypothetical: Opinion
- Ch. 20 - Hypothetical: Problem Solving
- Ch. 23 - Strategy: Other

Goals

- Demonstrate that you comprehend the situation, including appropriate goals, constraints, and risks.
- Develop a plan or criteria for evaluating the issue.
- Provide analysis.
- Make a recommendation.

Day 24 to 26. Execution Interview: Crunching Numbers

Introduction

Facebook is looking for product managers who are data-driven in their approach. That means making executive decisions *backed with data*. The two question examples below do not beg for a quantitative approach, but my debriefs with Facebook hiring managers indicate that they want candidates to *support* their recommendation with a *back-of-the-envelope calculation*.

Example

- How would you decide between showing more ads on the Facebook News Feed vs. showing a People You May Know recommendation widget?
- We've outsourced a critical mobile app to a third-party developer. How do we decide when to take that development in house?

Exercises

Do exercises from:

- Ch. 6 – Analytics: Estimation
- Ch. 8 – Analytics: Pricing New Products
- Ch. 9 – Analytics: Pricing Existing Products
- Ch. 10 – Analytics: ROI

Day 27 to 29. Execution Interview: Revisiting Product Sense with Execution Emphasis

Introduction

Sometimes FB interviewers will ask a question that focuses only on a product's execution (aka implementation) details.

Examples

- Interviewer says that based on the reports gathered, two-factor authentication (2FA) seems like a good first option to implement. What sort of things would I consider upon the development of 2FA to ensure that the development and adoption go well?
- Imagine you are the product manager behind launching the Safety Check feature. Walk me through the various product design and software engineering tradeoffs you had to consider when defining which features would make it to minimum viable product (MVP).

How to Approach

1. Diagram or wireframe how a feature would work.
2. Discuss strengths, weaknesses, and tradeoffs of the implementation.
3. Propose alternative solutions, if appropriate.
4. Make a recommendation on what the final development plan should be.

This is essentially the "LES" (last three steps) of the CIRCLES Method™.

Exercises

Choose exercises from Ch. 14 – Product Design: Putting it Together with either a wireframing or implementation emphasis.

Day 30. Leadership Interview: Getting familiar

Introduction

Facebook firmly believes that good PMs are strong leaders. They evaluate a PM candidate's leadership and drive by evaluating the four criteria below:

1. **Introspection**. Is the candidate self-aware, especially of their own flaws?
2. **Emotional Intelligence**. Does the candidate get along with others?
3. **Leadership & team building**. Does the candidate enjoy leading others and building teams?
4. **Vision**. Does the candidate get excited about technology? Can they set a bold and inspiring vision?

Examples

- What's a self-development area that needs improvement?
- Tell me a time when you disagreed with an engineer. How did you convince him or her?
- What's your favorite project where you played a leadership role?
- What's a technology trend that you're excited about?

Exercises

Choose appropriate exercises from Ch. 19 – Hypothetical: Opinion and Ch. 26 – Behavioral.

36-Day Amazon PM Study Guide
Day 1. Getting familiar with Amazon's PM Interview

Tasks

Search Google and read Lewis' Amazon PM interview process overview: "How to Prepare for the Amazon Product Manager Interview"

Goal

Get to know the scope and nature of the Amazon PM interview.

Day 2. Traditional and behavioral questions

Tasks

- Read the "Winning the Behavioral Interview" chapter in *Decode and Conquer.*
- Review Amazon's Leadership Principles: www.amazon.jobs/principles
- Draft and polish your answers for the following questions:
    - Tell me about yourself.
    - Why Amazon?
- Practice and get feedback from your practice partner

Goals

Of all the tech companies, Amazon is the most devoted to its corporate values, called the Amazon Leadership Principles. This devotion manifests itself heavily in their interview process. At least half of your interview questions will be behavioral in nature, focused on their 14 Leadership Principles.

Internalize Amazon's values deeply as you will have a lot of work ahead of you when preparing your behavioral interview responses.

Day 3-7. Drafting responses to behavioral questions

Task

Using the DIGS Method™, prepare behavioral interview responses for each Amazon Leadership Principle below. To make it easier for you, I have provided this template for you to draft your responses: bit.ly/AMZNInterviewStories.

AMAZON PRINCIPLE	SUGGESTED QUESTION	SAMPLE ANSWER*
Customer Obsession	Walk us through a time when you helped a customer through a difficult process and what that looked like.	Helping a Customer
Ownership	Give me an example of when you took a risk and failed.	Risk and Failure
Invent and Simplify	Tell me a time when you created an innovative product.	Creating an Innovative Product
Are Right, A Lot	Tell me about a time when you observed two business opportunities to improve ROI, and how did you determine they were connected?	Connected ROI
Learn and Be Curious	How do you find the time to stay inspired, acquire new knowledge, and innovate in your work?	Learning Outside of Work
Hire and Develop The Best	Tell me about a time when you had to deal with a poor performer on your team.	N/A
Insist on the Highest Standards	Tell me a time when you could have stopped working on something but you persisted.	N/A
Think Big	Tell me a time when you proposed a new business.	See chapter *Strategy: New Market Entry* for inspiration
Bias for Action	Describe how you would handle a busy situation where three people are waiting for help from you.	Handling a Busy Situation
Frugality	Tell me a time when you came up with a clever way to save money for the company.	N/A
Earn Trust	Tell me a time when you earned the trust of a group.	Earning the Trust of a Group
Dive Deep	Tell me about a time when you had to dive deep into data and the results you achieved.	Diving Deep into Data
Have Backbone; Disagree and Commit	Tell me about the most difficult interaction you had at work.	Most Difficult Interaction
Deliver Results	Tell me a time when you overcame an obstacle and delivered the results.	Overcoming an Obstacle

*Refer to the table of contents for the appropriate section in this book

Source / *The Product Manager Interview* and Amazon.com website

Goals

Complete drafts for each Amazon Leadership Principle.

Day 8. Get feedback to your behavioral responses

Task

Find a practice partner and get feedback on your responses. You can either present your stories in outline form or a more formal mock interview setting.

Goal

Have answers that are:

- Easy-to-understand and follow.
- Thoughtful.
- Indicate your role in the story, especially whether you were an owner vs. a participant.
- Have an impressive, not merely good, achievement.

Day 9 and 10. Get familiar with lifetime value questions

Background Reading

- Read the *Lifetime Value* chapter in *Interview Math*.
- Follow the lifetime value (LTV) example in *Interview Math*: Starbucks' Lifetime Value.

Exercises

Do the following exercises:

- In *The Product Manager Interview*
    - Apple iPhone LTV
    - Kindle Pricing Error
- In *Interview Math*
    - AT&T New iPhone Promotion
    - American Express I
    - American Express II
    - Crest Toothpaste
    - New York Times Website

Goal

- Internalize the LTV framework.
- Gain mastery in applying LTV, in detail, to a variety of challenging questions.

Day 11 and 12. Get familiar with pricing questions

Background Reading

Get familiar with the two categories of pricing questions, new and existing products, by reading the Pricing chapter in *The Marketing Interview*.

Exercises

Do the following exercises:

- Existing Product Pricing in *Interview Math*
    - Google Phone
    - Star Wars Ticket Price
    - Starbucks Coffee Latte
- New Product Pricing in *The Product Manager Interview*
    - Google Driverless Car Pricing
    - Google and Teleportation
    - Pricing UberX

Goals

- Understand that there are two types of pricing questions: new and existing products.
- Know which framework to use for each one.
- Gain proficiency in answering both types of questions.

Day 13 to 36. Follow Day 2 to 25 from the Google PM prep guide

Substitute exercises with Amazon-specific ones from *The Product Manager Interview*. Amazon interviews are unlikely to include coding or technical interview questions, so you can disregard technical interview prep if you are short on time.

Chapter 4 Abbreviations, Terms and Concepts

Abbreviations

This book will deal with large numbers in the thousands, millions and billions. To save space, I will use the following abbreviations:

- K = thousands
- M = millions
- B = billions

For instance, 10K is 10,000. 10M is 10,000,000, and 10B is 10,000,000,000.

I will also use these shorthand abbreviations:

- Q = quantity
- P = price
- R = revenue
- C = cost

Terms and Concepts

AARM metrics™

An analytical framework that defines the metrics for a product.

- **A**cquisition: Tracking customer signups for a service. The bar for signing up for a service has gotten lower and lower, thanks to the popularity of free signup and pay later "freemium" models. The typical acquisition metric to track is lazy registrations or app downloads.
- **A**ctivation: Getting users that have completed a lazy registration to register fully. For a social networking site like Google+, this may include uploading a photo or completing their profile page.
- **R**etention: Getting users to use the service often and behave in a way that helps the user or business. Key metrics include adding more information to their profile page, checking the news feed frequently or inviting friends to try the service.
- **M**onetization: Collecting revenue from users. It could include the number of people who are paying for the service or the average revenue per user (ARPU).

Before and After Analysis

A way to interview answers to consider the before and after impact of a change.

Big Picture Framework

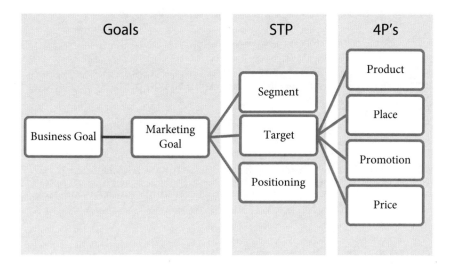

A comprehensive model that provides an effective way to answer interview questions about marketing plans and campaigns. There are three parts to the framework: Goals, STP (segmentation, targeting, and positioning) and the 4P's (product, place, promotion, and price).

- *Goals.* State the overall business objective and intermediate marketing objectives that contribute to it.
- *Segmentation.* Group buyers by attributes to identify customers that would benefit from the product.
- *Targeting.* Choose segments that would appreciate and seek out the product's benefits.
- *Positioning.* Create a product image for customer segments through the 4P's.
- *Product.* Develop new product ideas using the CIRCLES Method™.
- *Place.* Choose the distribution channel that best meets the business goal(s).
- *Promotion.* Match promotional tactics with your strategies.
- *Price.* Use breakeven analysis for existing products, and the pricing meter for new products.

CIRCLES Method™

A guideline that provides complete and thoughtful responses to product design questions.

- ***Comprehend the Situation.*** Avoid miscommunication by asking clarifying questions (5W's and H) and/or stating assumptions.
- ***Identify the Customer.*** List potential customer personas and choose one to focus on.
- ***Report the Customer's Needs.*** Provide a user story that conveys their goals, desires, and potential benefits. *As a <role>, I want <goal/desire> so that I can get <benefit>.*
- ***Cut, Through Prioritization.*** Showcase your ability to prioritize, assess tradeoffs, and make decisions. Create a prioritization matrix with estimated values for important metrics like revenue and customer satisfaction.
- ***List Solutions.*** Brainstorm at least three BIG ideas that exploit future trends in technology and customer behavior. Use the following frameworks for inspiration. 1) Reverse the situation to uncover new possibilities. 2) Mix and match product attributes to get new combinations. 3) Challenge the status quo.
- ***Evaluate Tradeoffs.*** Define your tradeoff criteria and analyze the solution through a pros and cons list.

- *Summarize Your Recommendation.* Specify which product or feature you would recommend, recap its benefits to the user and/or company, and explain why you preferred this solution compared to others.

Critical Path Dependency

A relationship where preceding tasks affect succeeding tasks in a sequence of activities. Not properly accounting for these key relationships can affect the project's end date.

DIGS Method™

To get a job offer, I believe that candidates have to do just two things: be likable and show credibility that they can do the job. DIGS Method™ is a behavioral interview framework that promotes credibility and likability in your response.

- *Dramatize the situation.* Provide context and details that emphasize the importance of your job, project or product.
- *Indicate the alternatives.* Be thoughtful and analytical by listing three different approaches to a problem.
- *Go through what you did.* Convince the listener that you were the driving force.
- *Summarize your impact.* Provide numbers and qualitative statements that validate your impact.

5Es Framework

An acronym and checklist to help brainstorm different stages of the customer experience. The 5Es framework helps you build a customer journey map effortlessly. Here are the 5Es:

- *Entice.* What event triggers a user to enter into the UX funnel?
- *Enter.* What are the first few steps in the UX funnel?
- *Engage.* What task(s) is the user trying to accomplish?
- *Exit.* How does the user complete the task?
- *Extend.* What follow-up actions occur after the user completes the task?

Increase your effectiveness in answering product design questions by building a customer journey map. Customer journey maps help you uncover product improvement opportunities easily.

Five Ws and H

A checklist of questions to get the complete facts on a situation. For example, when understanding a new product, here is what listeners want to know:

- **What** is it?
- **Who** is it for?
- **When** is it ready?
- **Where** will it be available?
- **Why** should I get it?
- **How** does it work?

Five Whys

A technique to determine the cause of a particular situation. It involves asking "Why?" in succession.

Issue Trees

A problem-solving diagram that breaks down a 'Why' or 'How' question into identifiable root causes or potential solutions, respectively. For more information: bit.ly/issue-trees

Marketing funnel

An analytical model that tracks the customer journey towards a purchase of a product or service. There are four general steps, indicated by the AITP acronym:

- *Awareness*. Bring recognition to a product brand.
- *Interest*. Stir fascination with a product (what it does, how it works, and what benefit it delivers.)
- *Trial*. Compel a prospective user to try the product.
- *Purchase*. Get the customer to buy the product.

MOB

A marketing framework that evaluates the effectiveness of a product advertisement or commercial.

- *Memorable*. Does the ad grab your attention? Is it worthy of future discussion with your friends, acquaintances and social media?
- *Oh, Product*. Is this product and brand promoted clearly and definitively?
- *Benefit*. Does the ad explain and provide evidence for the product's benefit? Is there a clear reason why the consumer should choose this product over a competitor's?

Rule of Three

A communication principle that suggests that responses that are bundled in threes are more effective and satisfying.

Pro and Con Analysis

A communication principle that states a point of view is more readily accepted if the speaker provides a balanced view that includes advantages and disadvantages.

Porter's Five Forces

A model proposed by Harvard business school professor, Michael Porter, on the competitive forces affecting a product or service. Porter's Five Forces include the following components:

- Threat of new entrants
- Threat of substitutes
- Bargaining power of buyers
- Bargaining power of suppliers
- Industry rivalry

Razor-and-Razorblade Strategy

A popular business strategy where a business sells the platform, such as a razor, at cost or less. Then the business sells complementary products, such as razor blades, at a substantial profit, offsetting the reduced profit from selling the platform.

Root Cause Analysis Tree

A hierarchical diagram that identifies the root causes of a problem and provides potential corrective actions to benefit the outcome or prevent a recurrence.

SCAMPER

A creative thinking framework used to develop innovative ideas for a topic, product or service.

- *Substitute.* What components of the topic can be substituted?
- *Combine.* What ideas, products or services can be added to the original topic?
- *Adjust.* How can the topic be altered to be more flexible and adaptable?
- *Modify.* What components can be enhanced, reduced or changed?
- *Put to other uses.* How can the topic, product or service be used in different scenarios or situations?
- *Eliminate.* What ideas or components can be removed?
- *Reverse, Rearrange.* What new approaches can be formed from the original topic?

SWOT Analysis

A structured planning method to evaluate the strategic elements of a business, industry or product to find its competitive advantage.

- *Strengths.* Attributes that provide an advantage over other competitors.
- *Weaknesses.* Attributes that provide a disadvantage relative to other competitors.
- *Opportunities.* Elements that can be utilized to maximize advantages or trends.
- *Threats.* Elements in the environment that can be an obstacle or risk to your business or product.

Chapter 5 Frequently Asked Questions

I have read the questions in *The Product Manager Interview*. I find it unrealistic to know about every single product mentioned. Every sample answer seems as if the candidate just "happened" to be extremely well versed in that subject.

You are not the only one to feel that way. You may not know:

- How corporate taxes work
- What the YouTube API includes
- What celiac disease might be

Nevertheless, what seems unreasonable without a job description can be reasonable with it. For instance, a recent MBA graduate applying for a corporate finance role should know how corporate taxes work. A seasoned product manager, applying for the YouTube API team, should not be surprised when asked about the details of the publicly available YouTube API.

That being said, there is an important reminder that goes for all interviewing situations: the interviewer has the power to ask whatever they want. They might ask a question that requires you to be knowledgeable about celiac disease, even when you have no clue or if it is irrelevant to the role.

It may feel unfair. However, in this uncomfortable position, you must react without shock, fear, frustration or anger. Instead, be honest and courageous. Do not dodge the question.

The workplace is filled with scenarios, where you feel awkward, due to your limited knowledge. The interviewer may justify the use of such questions to detect your poise and grace under pressure.

How am I supposed to react when interviewers ask me something I have no idea about?

The interview is not a police interrogation. In other words, you, the candidate, have the power to ask questions.

In one of the answer examples in *Decode and Conquer*, the interviewer asks the candidate, "You are the CEO of Yellow Cab taxi service. How would you respond to Uber?" It is hard to fathom a candidate that has not used Uber. However, in the sample answer, the candidate handles the situation gracefully by asking, "I apologize. I have never used the Uber service. Can you tell me more about it?" And the interviewer accedes, giving the information the candidate needs.

If the interviewer is being difficult and refuses to give you the context and knowledge to be successful, you need to have the self-awareness and courage to persist, despite the interviewer's resistance. Your success is at stake. Give yourself a fair chance to give the best answer possible.

How do I know when I have done enough preparation?

Do not worry about over-preparation. There is no such thing. I have spent nearly 20 years as a PM, and I still do not know it all. Every single minute you spend investing in your PM abilities is an investment in your career - whether you intend to be a PM for only a decade or several more.

Do note that when interviewers say a candidate is over-prepared, what they really mean is that a candidate comes across as robotic or is memorizing their responses. Neither is good, but it is not a symptom of over preparation. Instead, being robotic or memorizing responses is a symptom of the wrong type of preparation. So don't be a robot. And no memorizing. Chemistry and rapport, with the interviewer, counts.

How do I prepare for company X?

I have provided preparation plans for the most coveted PM roles at Google, Facebook, and Amazon. If you have a PM interview with another company, you can construct your own preparation plan by leveraging the following resources:

- **Job Description**. The job description, especially the job responsibilities section, offers clues on what categories of questions the interviewer will likely ask.
- **Glassdoor.com reviews**. Candidates share interview questions they have received.
- **Internal employees**. Find friends (or make friends with employees) at your target company or group. Ask them what questions they are likely to ask. Sebastian Sabouné, a product manager at Hive and one of our reviewers, remarked, "As an interviewer, I love having people interested in my product. So if you come prepared with ANY question about it, it will leave a good impression."

Then, based on what you have researched as probable questions, modify the bit.ly/PMPrepPlan template to create your preparation plan.

What should I do if I have less than X days to prepare?

I am a firm believer that "success comes when preparation meets opportunity."

However, life happens, and we do not always have enough time to prepare. I cannot come up with a plan for everyone's time constraints; I am sure someone will want a 15-minute study guide! Instead, I have created a table on how to best allocate your preparation time, based on the most sought-after firms. With the time you have available, allocate your preparation time based on my recommendations below.

Lastly, these recommendations are based on my research and first-hand reports from candidates. There's no way anyone can predict, with 100 percent certainty, what anyone will ask at an interview. Caveat emptor!

Google

	Product Design	Metrics	Estimation	Pricing / LTV	Strategy	Traditional	Behavioral*	Technical**
Phone	50%	10%	20%	5%	10%	2.5%	2.5%	0%
Onsite	30%	10%	15%	5%	10%	2.5%	2.5%	25%

Facebook

	Product Design	Metrics	Estimation	Pricing / LTV	Strategy	Traditional	Behavioral*	Technical
Phone	50%	10%	15%	5%	10%	5%	5%	0%
Onsite	50%	20%	10%	10%	7%	1%	2%	0%

Amazon

	Product Design	Metrics	Estimation	Pricing / LTV	Strategy	Traditional	Behavioral*	Technical
Phone	20%	10%	7%	15%	7%	1%	40%	0%
Onsite	20%	10%	7%	15%	7%	1%	40%	0%

Uber

	Product Design	Metrics	Estimation	Pricing / LTV	Strategy	Traditional	Behavioral*	Technical
Phone	50%	20%	10%	3%	14%	1%	2%	0%
Onsite	50%	20%	10%	3%	14%	1%	2%	0%

Microsoft

	Product Design	Metrics	Estimation	Pricing / LTV	Strategy	Traditional	Behavioral*	Technical**
Phone	40%	5%	15%	5%	5%	15%	15%	0%
Onsite	20%	10%	10%	5%	5%	15%	15%	20%

Include hypothetical questions as part of your behavioral preparation

** Only prepare for technical questions if you have an on-site final round interview. It is unlikely technical questions will appear in earlier rounds. If you do have an on-site interview, spend almost as much time with technical preparation as you would product design.*

Chapter 6 Analytics: Estimation

Cars in Seattle

How many cars are in Seattle?

Things to Consider

- Answer this question in less than five minutes. Most interviewers consider this a simple estimation question.
- Scope the problem correctly by clarifying with the interviewer whether it is okay to focus on consumer only, business only, or both. Also, confirm that "cars" exclude public transportation.
- Most interviewers will not give you assumptions. If you are stuck, build upon assumptions you know. For example, you might not know Seattle's population, but you do know San Francisco's is 837K. Seattle feels to be 75% the size of SF. After doing the math, you assume that Seattle's population is 628K. Seattle's actual population is 650k.

Common Mistakes

- Not having a clear plan and trying to figure it out as you go along.
- Communicating poorly, making it hard for the interviewer to understand your thinking.
- Getting scared of doing math and rounding numbers excessively. For instance, you should be comfortable multiplying and dividing numbers such as 500 / 3.

Show your work below. Make any assumptions as necessary. Answer on the next page.

Answer
Clarifications

- Consumer only, not business.
- Not counting cars at car dealerships and junkyards.

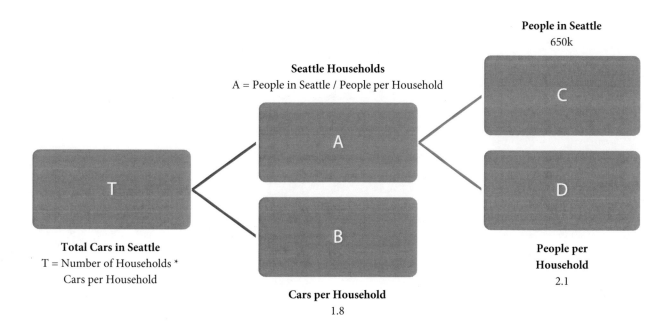

Assumptions

San Francisco's population is 837K. Assume Seattle's population is 75% of that.

If you don't know San Francisco's population, a good rule for US cities is that the largest cities have several million people such as Los Angeles, Chicago, and New York City. Large cities such as Washington DC, San Francisco, San Diego, and Portland tend to have between 500k and 1.5M people. Seattle's true population is 650K people. Most interviewers would deem any assumption between 500K and 750K as reasonable.

The average household in the USA has 2.6 people.

A rough way to derive this number is to remember that there are about 300 million people in the USA and 100 million households. 300M/100M = 3. The city of Seattle reports the average household size to be 2.06 in 2010.

Assume # of cars in Seattle to be in the 1.5 to 2.5 range.

CLRSearch reports 1.80 vehicles per Seattle household in 2012, while the US average was 2.4. Therefore, most interviewers would consider any assumption between 1.5 and 2.5 to be reasonable.

High Level Formula

Total Cars in Seattle = Households in Seattle * Cars per Household

Answer, using exact values

A= 650K / 2.1 = 309.5K

T = 309.5K * 1.8 = 557.1K

Calculations with estimated values

Low bound: 500K / 2 = 250K * 1.5 = 375K

High bound: 750K / 3 = 250K * 2.5 = 625K

Gmail Costs

Estimate how much it costs to run Gmail per user, per year.

Show your work below. Make any assumptions as necessary. Answer on the next page.

Answer

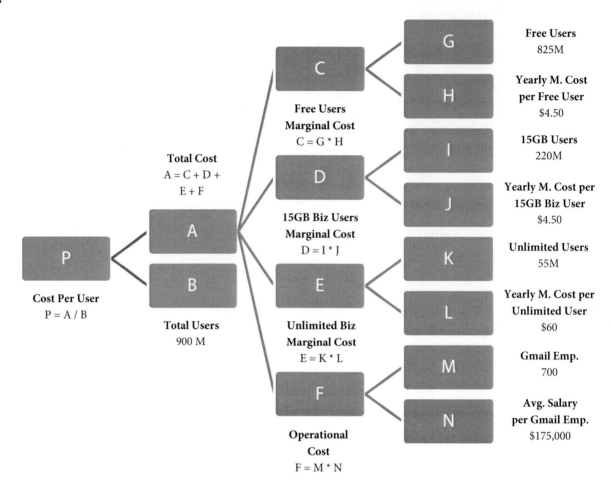

Assumptions

- Global users.
- Monthly costs per user, for storage and bandwidth, is roughly $0.05, based on Amazon Web Services data.
- Assume 1.1 billion active users.
- Split users into three tiers: free users, business users on a 15GB plan, and business users on an unlimited plan with a 75%, 20%, and 5% share respectively.
- Assume free and 15GB plan business users use roughly 7.5GB on average whereas unlimited plan business users use roughly 100GB.
- Only operational costs are employee salary, not including anything else.
- Around 70,000 employees at Google. Assume Gmail team is probably 1% of Google, which is ~700 people. Average annual salary is about $175,000.

Legend & Marginal Cost Calculations

Free Users, Marginal Cost

G: # Free Users = Total Gmail Users * % Free Users = 1.1B * 75% = 825M

H: Marginal Cost per Free User = $.05 / GB / month * 7.5 GB * 12 months = $4.50 per year

Business Users, 15GB Plan, Marginal Cost

I: # 15GB Biz Users = Total Gmail Users * % 15GB Biz Users = 1.1B * 20% = 220M

J: Marginal Cost per 15GB Biz User = $.05 / GB / month * 7.5 GB * 12 months = $4.50 per year

Business Users, Unlimited Plan, Marginal Cost

K: # Unlimited Biz Users = Total Gmail Users * % Unlimited Biz Users = 1.1B * 5% = 55M

L: Marginal Cost per Unlimited Biz User = $.05 / GB / month * 100 GB * 12 months = $60 per year

M: Total Number of Gmail Employees (700)

N: Employee Average Annual Salary ($175,000)

Calculations

C = 825M * $4.50 = $3.71B

D = 220M * $4.50 = $990M

E = 55M * $60 = $3.3B

F = 700 * $175,000 = $122.5M

A = $3.71B + $990M + $3.3B + $122.5M = $8.12B

Answer

P = $8.12B / 1.1B active users = $7.38 per user, per year

Revenue from YouTube Premium

YouTube Premium is a premium YouTube service without ads. Assume that 1.5% of the initial YouTube user base signs up for the new service.

What's the lifetime revenue that Google generates from those users?

Show your work below. Make any assumptions as necessary. Answer on the next page.

Answer

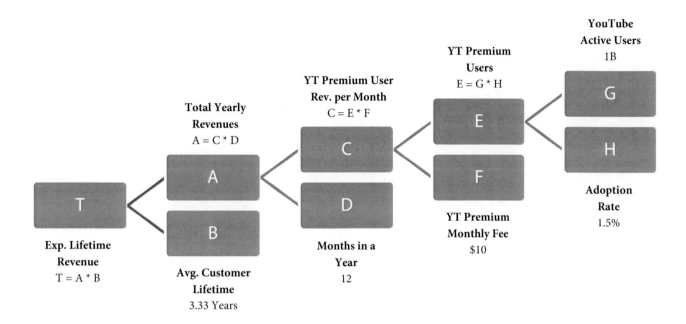

Assumptions

- Although YouTube Premium is currently only available in Australia, New Zealand, and the United States, assume that the service is available worldwide.
- Assume that churn is 30%. Customer lifetime = 1/(Churn Rate) = 3.33 years.
- Assume that this is top-line revenue. That is, the calculation does not factor in any costs including content acquisition costs (aka revenue share with content creators).

Calculations

E = 1B * 1.5% = $15M

C = 15M * $10 = $150M

A = $150M * 12 = $1.8B

Answer

T = $1.8B * 3.33 years = $6.0B

Storing Google Maps

How much storage space do you need for Google Maps?

Show your work below. Make any assumptions as necessary. Answer on the next page.

Answer

Assumptions

- Google Maps' aerial images only. It does not include Google Street View images. It does not include Google Earth either.
- There are three types of data being stored:
  - Image data including logos and location pictures.
    - Each location uses four pictures, which are about 2 MB in size each.
    - 25% of locations have a company logo, which takes 100 KB of storage.
  - Location data such as street names.
    - Location data takes 1000 bytes.
  - Street data such as street names.
    - Street data takes 250 bytes.
- Each major city has 1,000 streets and 50,000 locations.
- Each minor city has 250 streets and 12,500 locations.
- Around the world, there are around 2,000 major and 50,000 minor cities.

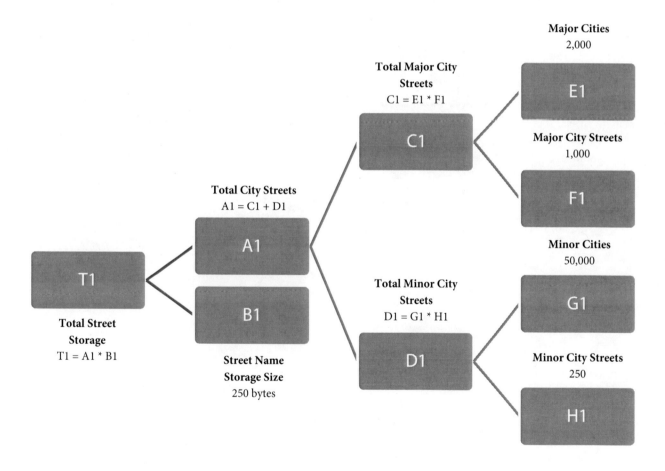

Calculations

D1 = 50,000 * 250 = 12.5M

C1= 2,000 * 1,000 = 2M

A1 = 12.5M + 2M = 14.5M

Sub-Answer T1

T1 = 14.5M * 250 = 3.625GB

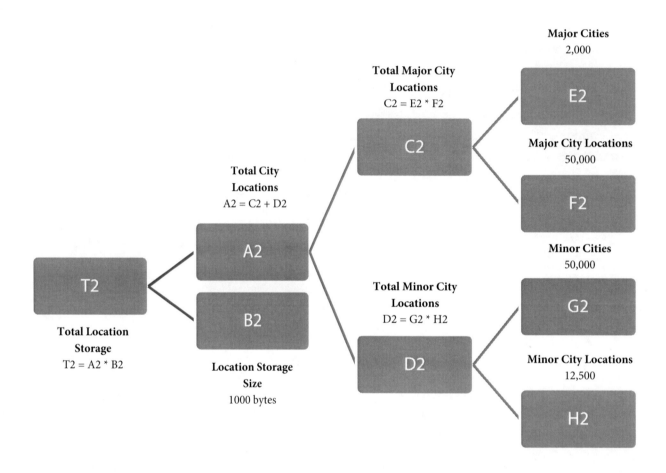

Calculations

D2 = 50,000 * 12,500 = 625M

C2 = 2,000 * 50,000 = 100M

A2 = 625M + 100M = 725M

Sub-Answer T2

T2 = 725M * 1000 = 725 GB

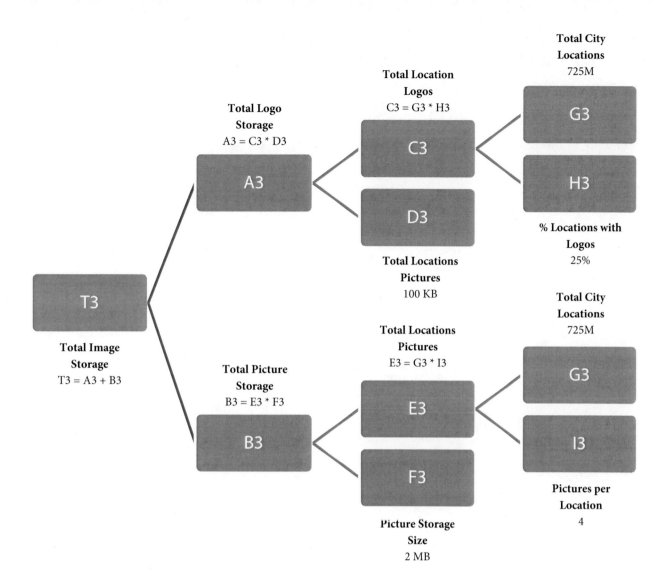

Calculations

E3 = 725M * 4 = 2.9B
C3 = 725M * 25% = 181.25M
B3 = 2.9B * 2 MB = 5.8B MB
A3 = 181.25M * 100 KB = 18.125B KB

Sub-Answer T3
T3 = 5.8B MB + 18.125B KB = ~5.82 PB

Total Answer
T = T1 + T2 + T3 = 3.625 GB + 725 GB + 5.82 PB = ~5.82 PB

How Many G Suite Users

Assume that Google makes $7 billion per year from G Suite. How many paying G Suite users are there?

Show your work below. Make any assumptions as necessary. Answer on the next page.

Answer

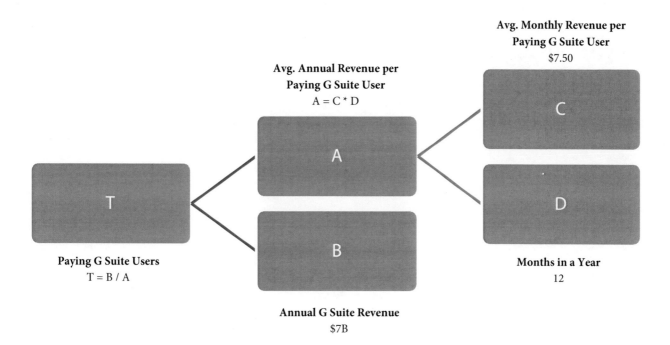

Avg. Monthly Revenue per Paying G Suite User
$7.50

Avg. Annual Revenue per Paying G Suite User
A = C * D

Paying G Suite Users
T = B / A

Annual G Suite Revenue
$7B

Months in a Year
12

Assumptions

Google has two paid versions of G Suite: a $5 and a $10 per month user. Let us assume that the paid customer mix is 50-50, which gives us an average revenue of $7.50 per monthly user.

Calculations

A= $7.50 * 12 = $90

Answer

T = $7B / $90 = 77,777,778 users

Google Buses

How many buses does Google need to transport employees between their Mountain View headquarters and the employees' Bay Area residences?

Show your work below. Make any assumptions as necessary. Answer on the next page.

Answer

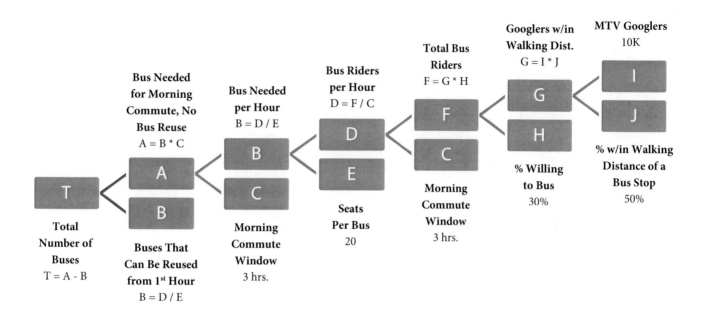

Assumptions

- Assume the morning commute window is three hrs. (6-9 am)
- Assume the buses used for the morning commute can be used for the evening commute
- Assume the buses used for the 1st hour of the commute can be used the 3rd hour of the commute because it takes about 1 hr. to travel back

Calculations

$G = 10,000 * 50\% = 5,000$

$F = 5,000 * 30\% = 1,500$

$D = 1,500 / 3 = 500$

$B = 500 / 20 = 25$

$A = 25 * 3 = 75$

Answer

$T = 75 - 25 = 50$

Gmail Ads Revenue

How much revenue did Gmail make from ads in the USA last year?

Show your work below. Make any assumptions as necessary. Answer on the next page.

Answer

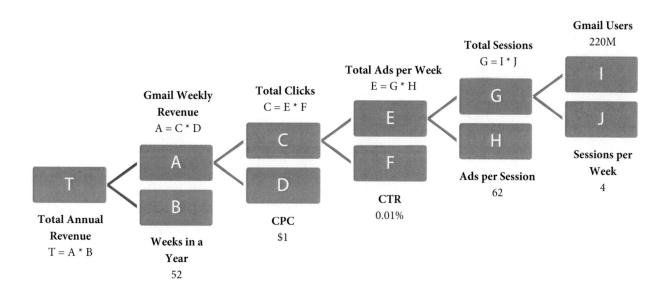

Assumptions

- There are 1.1 billion active Gmail users. US Internet users are roughly 10% of the world's Internet users, but Gmail is a service that indexes more heavily toward US usage. Therefore, we will assume that 20% of users are from the USA, making it 220 million active Gmail users.
- People open Gmail four times a week, and an average of 30 emails per day. That is two ads per email + two ads looking at the inbox = 30 * 2 + 2 = 62.

Calculations

G = 220M * 4 = 880M

E = 880M * 62 = 54.6B

C = 54.6B * 0.01% = 5.46M

A = 5.46M * $1 = $5.46M

Answer

T = $5.46M * 52 = ~$283.9M

Potential Users in Ireland

How many Dropbox accounts could there potentially be in Ireland?

Show your work below. Make any assumptions as necessary. Answer on the next page.

Answer

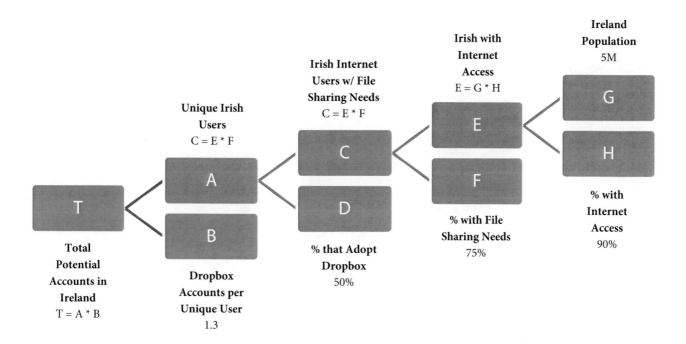

Assumptions

- World Bank reports 4.773 million people in Ireland as of 2016. Round that to 5 million.
- Ireland's central statistics office estimated that 89% of the Irish have Internet access in 2017. Round that to 90%.
- Assume 75% of Internet users need to share files.
- According to CloudRail's 2017 Cloud Storage Report, Dropbox has 47.3% market share (round to 50%), followed by Google Drive at 26.9%.
- Assume some Dropbox users have more than one account: they want more (free) storage, or they want to use an account exclusively for different purposes (e.g. work use). However, many Dropbox users do not want to deal with the hassle of having more than one account. Assume that each unique user has 1.3 Dropbox accounts.

Calculations

E = 5M * 90% = 4.5M

C = 4.5M * 75% = 3.38M

A = 3.38M * 50% = 1.69M

Answer

T = 1.69M * 1.3 = 2.2M

Dropbox in Paris

Thanks to a new partnership, Samsung pre-installs Dropbox on their smartphones.

Estimate how many new users Dropbox acquired last month in Paris.

Show your work below. Make any assumptions as necessary. Answer on the next page.

Answer

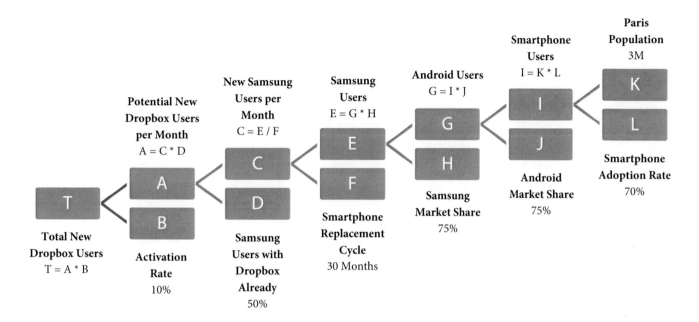

Assumptions

- Dropbox will only show up on Samsung devices sold by stores recently.
- Smartphone adoption rate is 70%.
- Android market share in Paris is approximately 75%.
- Samsung has 75% of the Android market.
- Smartphone users replace devices once every 30 months.
- 37.5% of users have Dropbox already. Of the remainder, 10% take the offer.

Calculations

$I = 3M * 70\% = 2.1M$

$G = 2.1M * 75\% = 1.58M$

$E = 1.58M * 75\% = 1.19M$

$C = 1.19M / 30 = 39.67K$

$A = 39.67K * 50\% = 19.84K$

Answer

$T = 19.84K * 10\% = 1,984$

Amazon Echo Partnership

A travel startup wants Amazon to pre-install their personal travel agent bot on existing Amazon Echos.

What is the value of the partnership to the travel startup?

Show your work below. Make any assumptions as necessary. Answer on the next page.

Answer

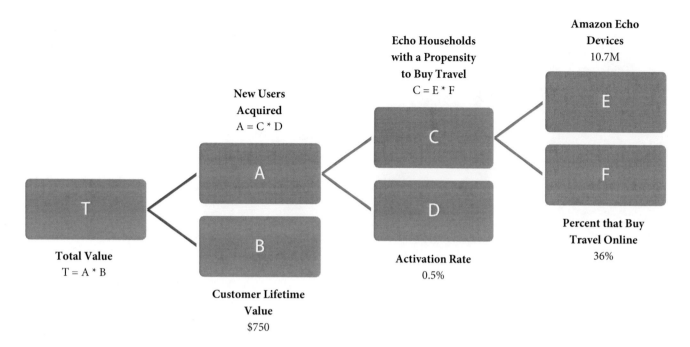

Total Value
$T = A * B$

New Users Acquired
$A = C * D$

Customer Lifetime Value
$750

Echo Households with a Propensity to Buy Travel
$C = E * F$

Activation Rate
0.5%

Amazon Echo Devices
10.7M

Percent that Buy Travel Online
36%

Assumptions

- United States only.
- In 2017, Consumer Intelligence Research Partners reports 10.7M Echo devices in the US.
- eMarketer reports that 118.1M people purchase travel online in 2017. Assuming 326M people in the US, 36% buy travel online.
- Assume a 0.5% activation rate
- Customer lifetime value = $750 for a travel industry customer according to Roomstorm.

Calculations

$C = 10.7M * 36\% = 3.85M$

$A = 3.85M * 0.5\% = 19.25K$

Answer

$T = A * B = 19.25k * \$750 = \$14.4M$

Facebook's Ad Revenue

Estimate Facebook's ad revenue.

Show your work in your own notebook. Make any assumptions as necessary. Answer on the next page.

This is the last time I will prompt you to show your work. Keep up the good practice. And no peeking at the answer; sample answers are reserved for finishers!

Answer

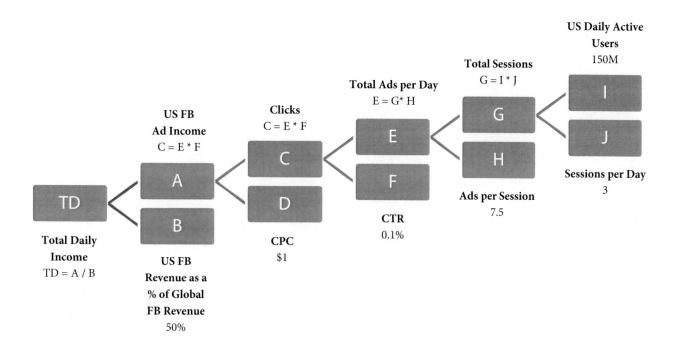

Assumptions

- Assume global ad revenue.
- Assume revenue based on ads only.
- Assume both mobile and web usage.
- Assume that Facebook shows three ads that rotate 2.5 times per session. That gives us 7.5 ads per session (H).

Calculations

G = 150M * 3 = 450M

E = 450M * 7.5 = 3.375B

C = 3.375B * 0.1% = 3.375M

A = 3.375M * $1 = $3.375M

TD = $3.375M / 50% = $6.75M

Answer

T = $6.75M * 365 days per year = ~$2.46B

Alternative Method

Rather than start with Facebook's US population and then extrapolating global revenues from a US estimate, an alternative method is to start with Facebook's global population.

Kinect Sports 2

How would you forecast the USA sales volume of a new Xbox game, Kinect Sports 2?

Answer

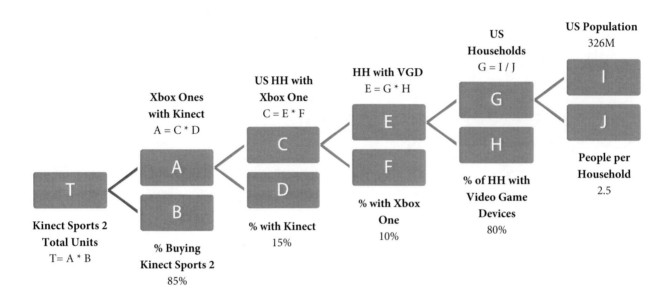

Calculations

G = 326M / 2.5 = 130.4M

E = 130.4M * 80% = 104.3M

C = 104.3 * 10% = 10.43M

A = 10.43M * 15% = 1.56M

Answer

T = 1.56M * 85% = 1.33M

Apple and Lyft Partnership

Apple and Lyft are considering a partnership where Lyft is pre-installed on new Apple iPhones in the United States.

How many users will Lyft gain from the partnership in NYC?

Answer

Assumptions

- Estimate for a single year.
- The pre-install will occur on all newly purchased Apple iPhones.

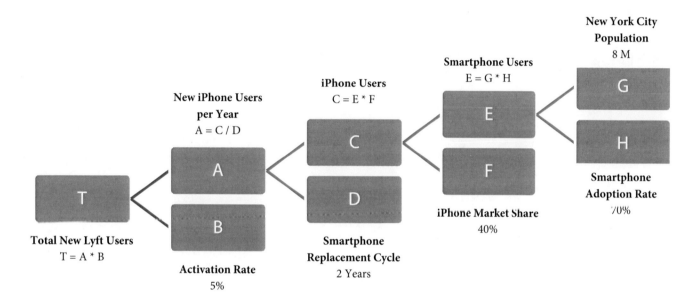

Calculations

E = 8M * 70% = 5.6M

C = 5.6M * 40% = 2.24M

A = 2.24M / 2 = 1.12M

Answer

T = 1.12M * 5% = 56,000

NYC Uber Driver

How much does an Uber driver in New York City make in a day?

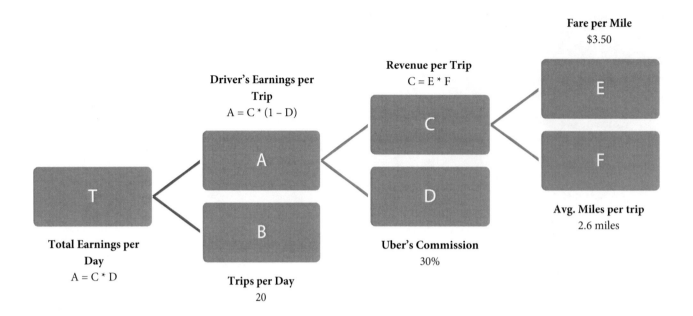

Assumptions

- $3.50 fare per mile; do not factor in surge pricing.
- Average trip is 2.6 miles.
- Uber's effective commission is 30%.
- Two to three trips per hour, which averages to 2.5 trips per hour.
- Eight hours per day.

Calculations

C = $3.50 * 2.6 miles = $9.10

A = $9.10 * (1 – 30%) = $6.37

Answer

T = $6.37 * 20 = $127.40 per day

Uber Drivers

How many drivers does Uber need to serve the Bay Area?

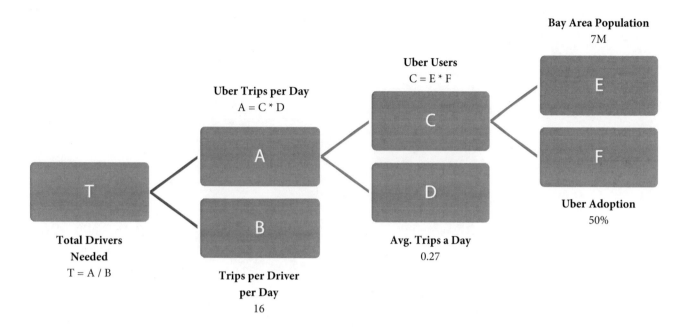

Answer

Assumptions

- *No Uber Pool.* One passenger per trip.
- *Average Trips a Day.* Assume that there are three types of Uber users: heavy, moderate and casual.
    - 20% are heavy users, and use Uber once a day;
    - 40% are moderate users, and use Uber once a week;
    - 40% are casual users, and use Uber once a month;
    - The weighted average number of trips, based on these assumptions is 0.27 trips per day.
- *Trips per Driver per Day.* Assume that an Uber driver works 8 hours a day, doing approximately two trips per hour.

Calculations

C = 7M * 50% = 3.5M
A = 3.5M * 0.27 = 945K

Answer

T = 945K / 16 = 59K drivers

Cab Ads for the Burrito Shop

You own a burrito shop and you want to advertise inside a fleet of 100 cabs in San Francisco. Only the passenger(s) will see the ad. How much are you willing to pay per month?

Answer

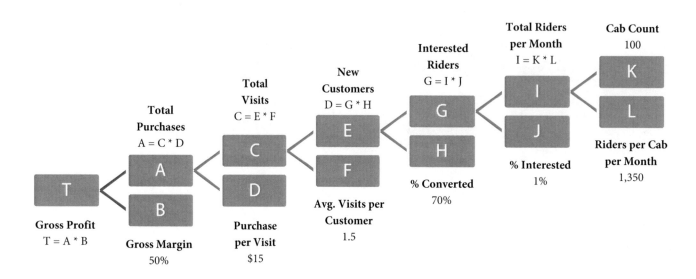

Assumptions

- *Cab Rides per Month.* Assume 30 trips a day, 30 days in a month and 1.5 riders per trip.
- *Average Visits per Customer.* Some new customers will return more than once.
- *Purchase per Visit.* A burrito is roughly $10, but some customers might buy a drink or appetizers. Other customers might buy food for others in their party such as a family member.

Calculations

I = 100 * 1,350 = 135,000 = 135,000 * 1% = 1,350

E = 1,350 * 70% = 945

C = 945 * 1.5 = ~1,418

A = 1,418 * $15 = $21,270

Answer

T = $21,270 * 50% = ~$10,635

The gross profit is the breakeven amount for the adverting campaign, so the owner should pay no more than this amount for the ad.

Driverless Car Purchases 2020

Estimate the number of driverless cars purchased by consumers in the USA in 2020.

Answer

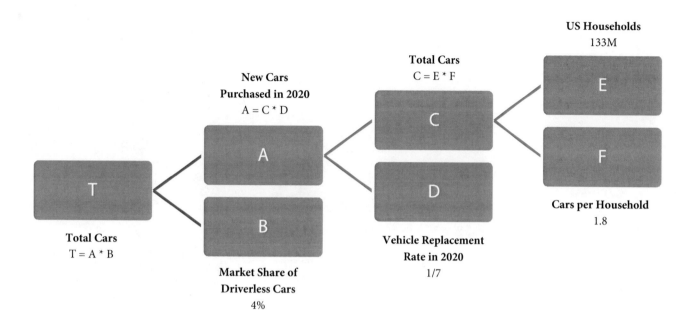

Assumptions

- Consider only consumer purchases only. No corporate purchases.
- Consumers change cars approximately once every 7 years.
- Tesla sold about 300 000 Model 3 cars which are to be delivered in 2018, this means that in 2018 we can expect ~1% of total car sales to be driverless (as Model 3 will have self-driving capabilities and Tesla will likely own most of the market at that point).
- The number of driverless cars sold doubles each year, giving 2% of total sales in 2019 and 4% in 2020.

Calculations

C = 133M * 1.8 = 239.4M

A = 239.4M * 1/7 = 34.2M

Answer

T = 34.2M * 4% = 1.37M

College Campus Bandwidth

Estimate the total annual Internet bandwidth required for a college campus.

Answer

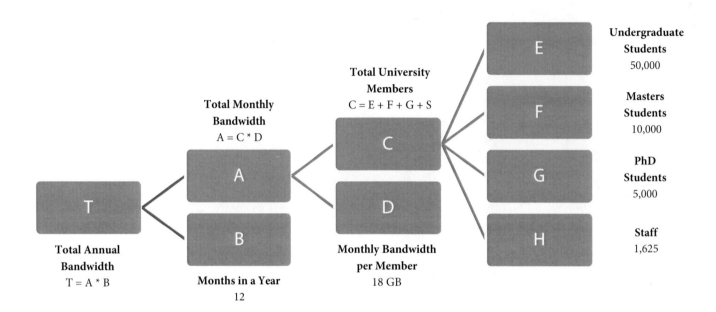

Interviewer Assumptions

- US only.
- Large public university.
- Factor in both students and staff.
- Students include undergraduate and graduate students.

Candidate Assumptions

- One professor for every 100 students.
- One and a half additional staff members per professor.
- Estimated daily bandwidth usage per user:
  - 15 minutes of low-resolution video: 15 min. * 50 MB = 650 MB
  - 2 hours of Internet browsing: 120 min. * 1 MB = 120 MB
  - 1 hour email (with attachments): 100 MB
  - Other usage: 30 MB
  - Total usage: 900 MB
- Average number of on-campus days per university member: 20 days.
- Monthly bandwidth per Member: 20 * 900 MB = 18 GB.

Calculations

Total Students = 50,000 + 10,000 + 5,000 = 65,000

College Staff = Professors + Non-Professors = (65,000 / 100) + (65,000 / 100) * 1.5 = 1,625

C = 65,000 + 1,625 = 66,625

A = 65,000 * 18 GB = 1,170,000 GB

Answer

T = = 1,170,000 GB * 12 = 14.04 petabytes (PB)

Planes in the Air

How many airplanes are in US airspace at 9 am Pacific Time zone?

Answer

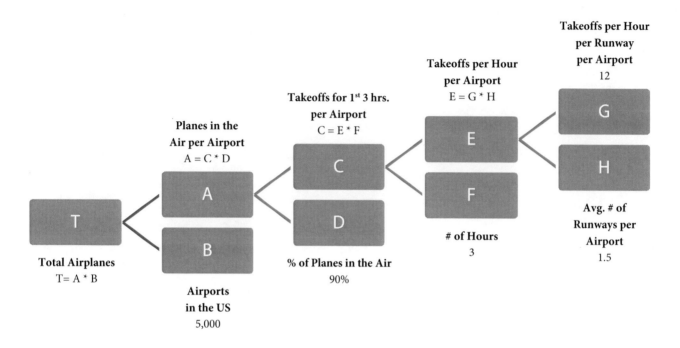

Assumptions

- The first flight leaves at 6 am. On average, a flight takes off every five minutes. Therefore, between 6 and 9 am there are three hours of takeoffs.
- 90% of flights that begin between 6 and 9 am have a duration of 3+ hours and thus still in the air. The other 10% have landed.
- There are approximately 5,000 airports in the United States with paved runways.
- Do not include non-US flights in US airspace.

Calculations

E = 12 * 1.5 = 18

C = 18 * 3 = 54

A = 54 * 90% = 48.6

Answer

T = 48.6 * 5,000 = 243,000

Monthly Reviews on Yelp

Estimate how many restaurant reviews a single user writes, on Yelp.com, each month.

Answer

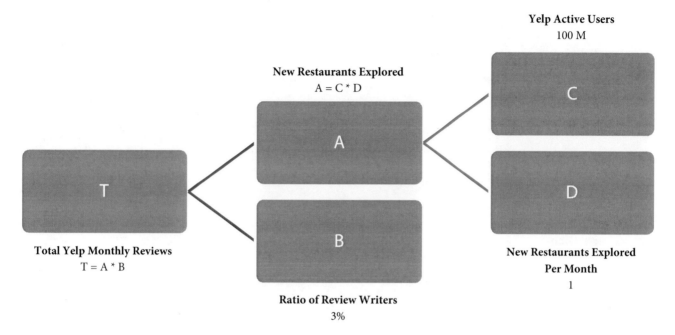

Yelp Active Users
100 M

New Restaurants Explored
A = C * D

Total Yelp Monthly Reviews
T = A * B

Ratio of Review Writers
3%

New Restaurants Explored Per Month
1

Calculations

A = 100M * 1 = 100M

Answer

T = 100M * 3% = 3M

Operational Costs for a Video Interview Application

Your CEO wants to build a video software solution. She asks you to estimate the ongoing cloud computing costs.

Usage assumptions

- Minutes per video interview: 6
  - Consisting of three questions at two minutes per question
- Playbacks per video interview: 5
- Number of candidates: 86,400
  - Assume a linear ramp up in candidates; in other words there will be an *average* of 43,200 candidates through the year
- Video storage duration, in months: 36

Cost assumptions

- Recording cost per minute: $0.02
- Playback per minute: $0.0007
- Storage per minute each month: $0.0013

Answer

Recording Costs

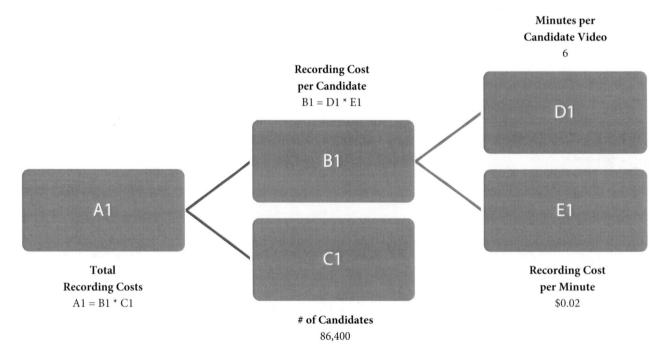

Playback Costs

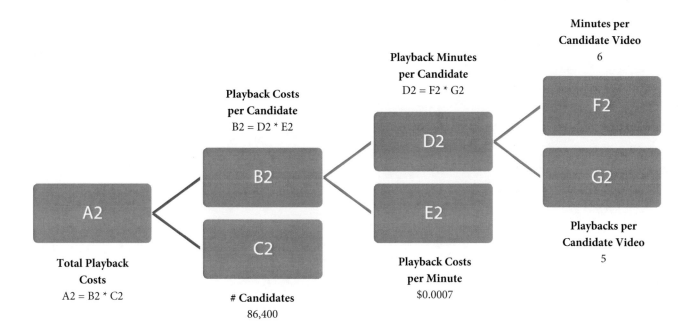

Minutes per Candidate Video
6

Playback Minutes per Candidate
D2 = F2 * G2

Playback Costs per Candidate
B2 = D2 * E2

F2

A2

B2

D2

G2

E2

C2

Total Playback Costs
A2 = B2 * C2

 # Candidates
86,400

Playback Costs per Minute
$0.0007

Playbacks per Candidate Video
5

Storage Costs

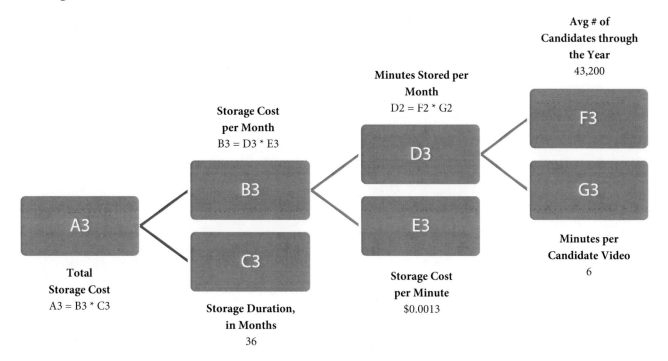

Avg # of Candidates through the Year
43,200

Minutes Stored per Month
D2 = F2 * G2

Storage Cost per Month
B3 = D3 * E3

F3

A3

B3

D3

G3

E3

C3

Total Storage Cost
A3 = B3 * C3

Storage Duration, in Months
36

Storage Cost per Minute
$0.0013

Minutes per Candidate Video
6

Calculations

Recording Costs

B1 = 6 * $0.02 = $0.12

A1 = $0.12 * 86,400 = $10,368

Playback Costs

$D2 = 6 * 5 = 30$

$B2 = 30 * \$0.0007 = \$0.02$

$A2 = \$0.02 * 86,400 = \$1,728$

Storage Costs

$D3 = 43,200 * 6 = 259,200$

$B3 = 259,200 * \$0.0013 = \$336.96$

$A3 = \$336.96 * 36 = \$12,130.56$

Total Costs

$A1 + A2 + A3 = \$10,368 + \$1,728 + \$12,130.56 = \$24,226.56$

Appointment Scheduling Software

You're the PM for an appointment scheduling software company. Quantify the time savings from adopting your company's scheduling software.

Usage assumptions

- Number of appointments scheduled per year: 1,560
- Assume appointments are scheduled via email only
    - Average number of emails to schedule an appointment: 2.5
    - Average time spent per email: 1.5 minutes
- Average time spent sending meeting reminder emails: 1.5 minutes

Software cost assumptions

- Software costs $39 per month

Answer

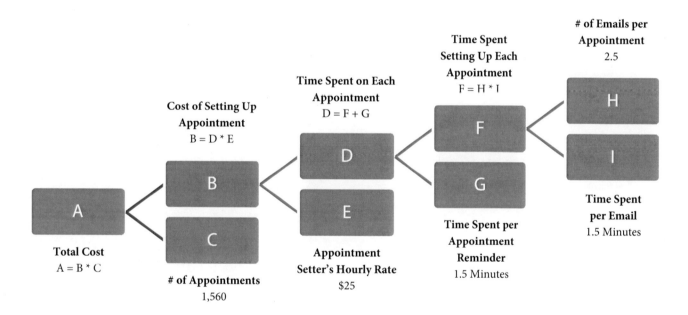

Calculations

Cost of Scheduling: Manually

$F = 2.5 * 1.5 = 3.75$ min.

$D = 3.75 + 1.5 = 5.25$ min.

$B = 5.25$ min. $* \$25$ per hour $/ 60$ minutes per hour $= \$2.19$ per appointment

$A = \$2.19$ per appointment $* 1,560$ appointments $= \$3,416.40$ per year

Cost of Scheduling Through Software

$39 per month * 12 months = $468 per year

Cost Savings

Total Savings = $3,416.40 - $468 = $2,948.40

Chapter 7 Analytics: Data Science

Tying Strings

You have a bag of N strings, and at random, you pull out an end of a string. You pull out another end and tie the two ends together. You take another two string ends and tie them together. You repeat this until there are no loose ends left to pull out of the bag. What is the expected number of loops?

Things to Consider

- Understand what the interviewer is asking. For instance:
  - Once an end is tied, is it left out of the bag?
  - What counts as a "loop?"
- Work through the simple base case and then derive a more general solution.

Common Mistakes

- Not talking and thinking aloud.
- Missing a chance to get tips from the interviewer.
- Insufficiently clarified the question to come up with an accurate answer.

Answer

CANDIDATE: To get some momentum, I will work through some simple base cases.

Analysis: Number of Open Ends

N = 1 string

- Number of open ends = 2
- After tying together, number of open ends = 0

N = 2 strings

- Number of open ends = 4
- After tying together, number of open ends = 2

N = 3 strings

- Number of open ends = 6
- After tying together, number of open ends = 4

Takeaway #1: For any N, anytime we tie an open end, we reduce the number of open ends by 2.

Analysis: Number of Loops

N = 1 string

- Number of open ends = 2
- Number of ends left after grabbing the first = 1
- Probability of closing the loop by grabbing the other end of the same string = 1

N = 2 strings

- Number of open ends = 4
- Number of ends left after grabbing the first = 3
- Probability of closing the loop by grabbing the other end of the same string = 1/3

N = 3 strings

- Number of open ends = 6
- Number of ends left after grabbing the first = 5
- Probability of closing the loop by grabbing the other end of the same string = 1/5

Takeaway #2: There are 2N string ends. Probability of closing the loop at the first attempt is $1/(2N-1)$.

Takeaway #3: The question prompt asks us for the expected number of loops, if we keep repeating. Therefore, we sum the probabilities to get the expected number of loops. Expressed in equation format:

Expected number of loops = $1/(2N-1) + \ldots + 1/5 + 1/3 + 1$

University Acceptance Rate

A university's overall acceptance rate is higher for men than women, but each department's acceptance rate for women is higher than for men. Why is that?

Things to Consider

- Work through a simple example.
- Provide a straightforward explanation without jargon.

Common Mistakes

- Letting an unfamiliar concept rattle the candidate.
- Not working out an example.
- Inability to provide a jargon-laden explanation for why the phenomenon occurs.

Answer

This example illustrates this phenomenon.

	Male Applicants	Males Accepted	Female Applicants	Females Accepted
Computer Science	90 (90%)	72 (80%)	10 (1%)	9 (90%)
Business	10 (10%)	4 (40%)	1000 (99%)	500 (50%)
Total	100	76 (76%)	1010	509 (~50%)

This is called Simpson's paradox. That is, a trend that appears in groups of data (in this case, the higher 90% female acceptance in computer science) disappears when the groups combine. In this example, Simpson's paradox occurs because a higher percentage of females applied to the more competitive business department (99%) than males (10%).

Ladder of N Steps

You have a ladder of N rungs (aka steps). You can go up the ladder by taking either one or two steps at a time, in any combination. How many different routes are there (aka combinations of one or two steps) to make it up the ladder?

Things to Consider

- Start with working out simple base cases.
- Identify the common pattern for different ladders of length N.
- Specify a formula for the N case.
- Recursion may help.

Common Mistakes

- Feeling and exhibiting stress.
- Assuming that reversed paths are equivalent. That is, 2+1 is not the same path as 1+2.

Answer

CANDIDATE: Let us work out the basic N (rungs) first to see if we can spot a pattern:

- N = 1: 1 way
- N = 2: 2 ways: 1+1, 2
- N = 3: 3 ways: 1+1+1, 1+2, 2+1
- N = 4: 5 ways: 1+1+1+1, 2+1+1, 2+2, 1+2+1, 1+1+2.

We can also think of this is going to N = 1, then picking the 3 ways of N = 3 and going to N = 2, and picking the 2 ways of N = 2. 3 + 2 = 5.

- N = 5: 8 ways. Pick N = 1, then picking N = 4 (5 ways) and N = 2 and picking N = 3 (3 ways). 5 + 3 = 8.
- …

We can then express this in this formula: Ways(N) = Ways(N-1) + Ways(N-2). This is a classic recursion algorithm.

Counting Handshakes

If in a room, there are 10 persons and if each person has to shake hands with all other. How many total handshakes will be there?

Things to Consider

- Take a moment to work through a simple base case to increase comprehension.
    - E.g. How many handshakes are there if there are two people?
    - In addition, how many handshakes if it's 3? 4?
- Check with the interviewer if he or she wants you to write the generalized solution for N number of people.

Common Mistakes

- Blurting the first answer that comes to mind.

Answer

CANDIDATE: Hmm, if there are 10 people, each person needs to shake hands with 9 other people. This means 90 handshakes. But, since when you are handshaking someone, they are also handshaking you as well, so we don't want to count that twice. So realistically, it should be 10 * 9 / 2 or 45.

INTERVIEWER: Hmm, I am not convinced that is the correct answer. How can you prove it?

CANDIDATE: Okay, let's do this incrementally. Let's say we have N people.

N = 1: 0, no handshakes since it's just one person.

N = 2: 1, they handshake with each other and we are done.

N = 3: 3 = 1 + 2. So let's say we originally had 2 people. They shook hands once and that was that. Then a new person joins, and she shakes hands with both of the people.

N = 4: 6 = 1 + 2 + 3. Let's build on the previous case. Now a 4th person is coming, and he needs to shake hands with the 3 original people.

We now see a pattern. Whenever we have a newcomer, he or she needs to shake hands with everyone else that were already here. The formula then becomes: 1 + 2 + 3 + ... + (N-1).

If we plug in 10, we have 1 + 2 + 3 + 4 + 5 + 6 + 7 + 8 + 9 = 45.

Weighing 27 Balls

There are 27 balls. One ball that is heavier than the others are. How many attempts do you need to make to find which ball it is using a seesaw?

Things to Consider

- Ask to collect your thoughts if the question prompt overwhelms you.
- Ask clarifying questions if you do not understand the situation.

Common Mistakes

- Feeling stressed and giving up.

Answer

CANDIDATE: Three. Let me explain my approach.

First, I check nine balls vs. nine other balls. We have two cases here:

- One of the two sets of nine balls is heavier, and that one contains the heavy ball.
- The ball is in the nine balls we did not check.

Either way, we checked once already, which reduces the problem to nine balls. We then use the same technique to check three balls vs. three other balls. Like the last step, we have two cases here:

- The ball is in one of the sets of three balls we checked (the heaviest).
- The ball is in the three balls we did not check.

We are now up to two checks, and we have three balls left. We then check one ball vs. another ball; there are two cases here:

- The ball is in the two balls we are checking.
- The ball is the ball we did not check.

That gives us three attempts in total.

Chapter 8 Analytics: Pricing New Products

Google Driverless Car Pricing

How much should Google charge for a driverless car?

Things to Consider

- When pricing new products, evaluate these price points:
    - **Customer Value**. Customer value refers to the customer's utility from a product or service. Customer value is synonymous with a customer's willingness to pay. For example, a haircut might cost a bride $400. However, to look good in her wedding photos, which she plans to look at for the rest of her life, is priceless. In other words, the bride's willingness to pay, in this scenario, may be much, much larger than $400.
    - **Competitors' Prices**. A company must consider competitors' prices, especially if the competitors' offer substitute goods.
    - **Cost of Goods Sold**. What does it cost to make the particular product?
- If the goal is to maximize profits, then consider pricing the product *above* the competitor's prices. It will allow you to extract extra gross margin. It is also possible to maximize profits by pricing below the competitor's prices. Doing so sacrifices margin, but you may overcome decreased margin with increased sales volume, assuming you can still be profitable.
- If the goal is to gain market share, consider pricing *below* competitor's prices. Gaining market share, sometimes at the expense of short-term profits, is a reasonable objective for winner-take-all markets.

Common Mistakes

- Proposing a pricing strategy without substantial explanation.
- Incorrectly using a price elasticity framework to solve a new pricing question.

Answer

CANDIDATE: Is Google selling the cars? Or is it selling the rides?

INTERVIEWER: Cars.

CANDIDATE: Are we talking about a one-time payment or a down payment with a pricing plan?

INTERVIEWER: A one-time payment.

CANDIDATE: Are we pricing just one car or several models?

INTERVIEWER: Just one car.

CANDIDATE: Are we working with an OEM to manufacture the cars? Or are we doing everything ourselves?

INTERVIEWER: That is up to you.

CANDIDATE: What about the demographic? Are we going for luxury cars or regular cars?

INTERVIEWER: There will be no more information given. Why don't you determine all of this and give me your rationale?

CANDIDATE: Okay. Can you give me some time to brainstorm?

Candidate takes one minute.

CANDIDATE: I feel it is better if Google manufactures and sells the car itself. It is daunting, and I know this goes against Google's past precedent. For instance, Google had an opportunity to build their own Android devices with the Motorola acquisition, and they opted to sell that division to Lenovo. But here's why I think they should manufacture the car on their own:

1. **It is in the realm of possibility**. Google may feel like they don't have the core competency to do so, but nothing is impossible. Tesla built a successful lineup of cars without prior experience.
2. **Faster time to market**. To coordinate with OEMs can take an inordinate amount of time, leading to delays.
3. **Preserve the end-to-end experience**. By keeping manufacturing in-house, Google can optimize the product and end-to-end experience. Take Apple for instance. By vertically integrating the end-to-end computing experience, from the operating system to hardware to core applications, they created a seamless, easy-to-use experience. Legions of Microsoft employees now envy Apple's computing experience.
4. **Minimizes product fragmentation**. By choosing an open ecosystem, like Android or Windows, the market can fragment quickly. In addition to the inconsistent end-to-end experience, supporting all the variants and suppliers can be overwhelming.

As for our demographic, I would start with luxury cars for the wealthy, followed by mainstream cars for the middle class. You may think that Google's brand may not represent luxury or prestige. However, I'm aware that early tech innovations are most often adopted by the wealthy because they're the only ones who can afford it. Take for instance the first Android device or the initial Google Glass head-mounted display; both had high price tags that were well beyond the reach of the mass-market consumer. As economies of scale improve, Google can then create affordable, self-driving cars for the middle class.

INTERVIEWER: Okay. What about the price?

CANDIDATE: Let's set aside the mass-market car and just focus on the initial luxury car. Our offering's price should be competitive with other luxury self-driving cars. Tesla's Model S goes for a base price of $70,000. We should identify a price point that's similar to Tesla's $70K number.

INTERVIEWER: Why not higher or lower than Tesla's $70K number?

CANDIDATE: If the price is more expensive than the Tesla, we would have to justify with features that are 100 to 200% better than Tesla's. Is that the case?

INTERVIEWER: No. Why does it have to be 100 to 200% better?

CANDIDATE: If it's only 10 to 40% percent better, the consumer is unlikely to stray away from the market leader, Tesla, to purchase the unproven challenger. Besides, many Tesla owners will assume that whatever new features are on the market will likely show up in the next Tesla upgrade.

INTERVIEWER: Why not a lower price?

CANDIDATE: Pricing significantly lower than Tesla could open it up to a new middle-class market, but we mentioned earlier that we're focusing on the luxury market. We could price is slightly lower than Tesla. However, given a wealthy clientele, saving a few thousand dollars is not likely to sway their purchase decision.

INTERVIEWER: Thank you for the explanation.

Pricing UberX

How would you go about pricing UberX?

Things to Consider

- Consider customer value, competitive pricing, and cost of goods sold.
- Acknowledge that in real life that you may do a pricing survey to gauge the appropriate price.
- In addition to a qualitative discussion, the interviewer may ask you to estimate potential revenue for this newly priced service.

Common Mistakes

- Forgetting to consider substitutes, such as walking or riding the subway, as competition too.

Answer

CANDIDATE: In real life, I would run a pricing survey with prospects. However, I imagine you want a back-of-the-envelope pricing calculation, correct?

INTERVIEWER: That's correct. Nevertheless, your pricing survey suggestion is noted.

CANDIDATE. Great, there are multiple variables we need to think about to price UberX. My top 4 include:

- **Supplier Costs.** The main supplier is the Uber driver. We need to consider the driver's opportunity cost. The driver's opportunity cost includes both compensation from alternative work options and car maintenance costs such as gas and repairs.
- **Customer's Willingness to Pay.** Customers have different transportation choices including walking or driving their cars. They can also take cabs or public transit.
- **Uber's Commission.** Uber provides value by matching drivers with customers. Just imagine how hard it would be to complete a transaction if it weren't for Uber. I am thinking a 30% commission to start.
- **Bonus Rates.** There may not be enough cars, so Uber may need to increase fees to attract more drivers. This could double or even triple during holidays.

I am going to make some assumptions.

Gas is around $3 per gallon. A fuel-efficient car has about 30 miles per gallon (mpg). So fuel costs for each mile is $0.10. But gas prices can go up, there are car maintenance costs, and most importantly, there's the driver's time. So let's factor that in. I would say we should increase the price to $1.50 per mile as a lower bound.

Most trips probably take about 10 miles. If you combine that with the car coming in and the time it takes to communicate, it should be around 30 minutes per trip. Therefore, we are talking 20 miles and 2 trips per hour. Also, remember that you will not get a passenger every time you are done, so to be safe it should be about 1.5 trips per hour.

So imagine if we did $1.50 per mile and there are 1.5 trips per hour. Doing the math brings us to $45. If Uber takes a 30% cut, that's $31.50 for the driver and $13.50 for Uber. This is the bare minimum, which is more expensive than the Caltrain.

If it's rush hour or holidays, it could go up to $40 per trip or even $60. This number seems good.

Finally, we need to add in a price for starting an Uber ride; otherwise people will try to do really short trips, which is bad for profit. On the other hand, that seems unfair to users who take long trips. A compromise would be to have a minimum ride cost, of say $5. This way, a driver in a more urban setting who ends up doing many short rides will maximize their earnings, but we can still offer great value to our passengers on long rides.

To conclude, I would price it as $1.50 per mile with $5 as a minimum charge for every ride.

Google and Teleportation

Let's say Google created a teleporting device: which market segments would you go after? How would you price it?

Things to Consider

- For market segments, develop your criteria first. Potential criteria can include customer need, willingness and ability to pay, and market size.
- For pricing, consider customer value, competitive pricing, and cost of goods sold.
- Do not forget to include substitutes, such as airplane flights, as a potential competitor for your pricing analysis.

Common Mistakes

- Not considering substitute products.
- Having poor rationale for target segments.

Answer

CANDIDATE: Can I ask some clarifying questions?

INTERVIEWER: Go ahead.

CANDIDATE: Is there a delay when traveling through time?

INTERVIEWER: It's instant.

CANDIDATE: Is there a cost attached to this? Does it cost more based on distance? Does it cost more based on the weight or size of objects?

INTERVIEWER: Nope, each trip costs $200K.

CANDIDATE: Is there a limit to the size or weight?

INTERVIEWER: Yes, you can't teleport anything bigger than an average person.

CANDIDATE: Can it teleport anything? Even life forms?

INTERVIEWER: It cannot teleport life forms.

CANDIDATE: How does it teleport? Like can it just teleport any object anywhere, or do you need another one on the other side?

INTERVIEWER: You need another one on the other side.

CANDIDATE: How many of these devices do we have? Does it have a cooldown? I want to understand our supply.

INTERVIEWER: We only have one, and we will not be getting any other any time soon. It has a cooldown of five minutes.

CANDIDATE: All right, can I get some time to brainstorm?

Candidate takes one minute.

CANDIDATE: Summarizing everything I've heard, we need to find a market where small, high-value, non-living goods can gain from being transported instantaneously to predictable places. Here are a few lucrative markets I came up with that could benefit from our product.

1. **Military.** Send supplies between military bases. Teleportation is faster and seemingly more secure than other transportation alternatives.
2. **Disaster Relief.** Send critical supplies between two teleportation locations. This would be particularly helpful with locations with poor transportation infrastructure.
3. **Government-to-Government Transfer**. There could be top-secret items that must be transferred in a secure way
4. **Luxury Uses.** A wealthy individual may want to impress others with teleportation activity.

I would price this at around $1MM, giving it an 80% profit margin. This reflects the rarity of our device and the unique value it brings (instantaneous transportation, security).

This price point would limit the luxury gifts market; it seems frivolous to waste money for fun, even for the ultra-wealthy. However, governments and militaries have trillion-dollar budgets. The value in sending critical objects instantaneously and safely would certainly grab their attention.

Chapter 9 Analytics: Pricing Existing Products

Kindle Pricing at Target

Target asked Amazon to give a 20% price discount on the Kindle. Should Amazon grant this pricing request?

Things to Consider

- The interviewer may want a qualitative or quantitative discussion. Clarify if it is not clear.
- For a quantitative discussion, approach it as a price elasticity question.
- For a qualitative discussion, a pro and con analysis would suffice.

Common Mistakes

- Not acknowledging or inquiring about whether the savings will be passed onto customers.
- Not acknowledging that granting a price discount for Target may require granting a similar discount to all retailers.

Answer

CANDIDATE: Do you mind if I ask a few clarifying questions?

INTERVIEWER: Of course.

CANDIDATE: First off, did you want me to talk about the decision from a qualitative or quantitative perspective?

INTERVIEWER: Quantitative. That is, let's see you crunch some numbers.

CANDIDATE: Quant it is.

CANDIDATE: Thanks. What is Kindle's average retail price at Target? And what is Target's wholesale price?

INTERVIEWER: The average price for a Kindle is $80. Target buys the Kindles for $54.

CANDIDATE: So instead of $54, Target wants to purchase the Kindles for $43.20?

INTERVIEWER: Correct.

CANDIDATE: How many Kindles did Target sell last year?

INTERVIEWER: Assume 1M Kindles.

CANDIDATE: What is the unit cost of the Kindle?

INTERVIEWER: Assume it is 30% of the retail price.

CANDIDATE: Next, I'd like to build a price elasticity table to determine what our breakeven volume would be for a 20 percent discount.

Candidate writes the following:

Profitability, Target Retail Channel

	Old	New	Change
Unit Revenue	$54	$43.20	-$10.80
Unit Cost	$24	$24	$0
Unit Profit	$30	$19.20	-$10.80
Volume	1M	?	?
Gross Profit	30M	30M	

INTERVIEWER: Can you walk me through what this all means?

CANDIDATE: Breakeven tells us what the new volume needs to be for the discount to be profit neutral. Any incremental units, beyond the breakeven point, would be additional profit.

INTERVIEWER: Okay.

CANDIDATE: So doing some quick math:

- Gross Profit = Unit Profit * Unit Volume
- Unit Volume = Gross Profit / Unit Profit
- Unit Volume = $30MM / $19.20
- Unit Volume = 1.562MM

Target would have to sell an additional 562K units.

INTERVIEWER: I follow the math. So what's your recommendation?

CANDIDATE: Based on the math, there are a number of reasons why we shouldn't offer the discount.

1. **Hitting breakeven volume seems unlikely**. A 56 percent increase in Target sales volume feels very aggressive. The $10.80 discount, if Target chooses to pass it along to customers, may not be sufficient to hit the new volume goal. However, even if Target could achieve that goal, there are other considerations in play…
2. **Channel parity**. It wouldn't be fair for one retailer to get Kindle units at a lower price than others.
3. **Domino effect**. Other retailers may catch wind of Target's negotiation prowess and demand similar discounts.
4. **Brand impact**. If Target decides to discount Kindle units in its stores, a reduced price could give consumers the perception that it's a low-quality, low-prestige device.

INTERVIEWER: Okay, I follow your logic and accept your recommendation. If you're to play devil's advocate, what are some potential benefits of providing the discount?

CANDIDATE: There are two benefits to granting the discount.

- **Further benefit from word-of-mouth marketing**. The bigger the customer base, the more likely existing users can influence potential users to buy Kindles.
- **Drive sales of complementary products.** The lower price point could get Kindles in the hands of more consumers. Amazon wants to establish Kindles as a media consumption device. Since they can generate profit from future media purchases such as books and movies, it's more important to sacrifice short-term profits to gain device market share. This is called the razor-and-razorblade model.
- **Reinforce the showroom benefit**. Trying out the Kindle is an important part of the purchase process. Prospects can now try Amazon devices in Target's showrooms. This is a significant advantage, as Amazon doesn't have much of a retail footprint today. One more thing, by providing a bigger discount, Target customers may pester Target employees to demo the Kindle more often.

INTERVIEWER: Thank you.

AWS Price Reduction

AWS has a Fortune 500 Company that is asking for a price reduction. What factors would you consider in the price reduction request?

Things to Consider

- Treat this as a negotiation request and utilize a negotiation checklist. Here's a sample:
    - Value to Fortune 500 Company (aka maximum price)
    - AWS Cost (aka minimum price)
    - Market alternatives (aka competitor's price)
    - Switching costs
    - Intangible value (aka using the Fortune 500 company as a customer reference)

Common Mistakes

- Not accurately assessing the customer's negotiation advantage. For example, any threats to leave must factor in the enormous switching cost.
- Over propensity to please the customer.
- Over propensity to stick with hardball negotiation tactics.

Answer

CANDIDATE: Here is how I would approach the problem:

1. Assess impact on our company
2. Evaluate the customer's negotiation leverage
3. Make a final recommendation

Assessing impact to our company

I would begin by asking about the revenues and profits we are generating from this customer. I would like to benchmark this against our average customer. I also want to know what this customer's revenue and profit percentage is relative to our entire revenue and profit pie.

Let's say this particular customer represents a significant portion of AWS's revenues or profits like 30%. If we decide to not grant the price reduction and lose this customer, we'll have to manage that fallout including impact to stock price and operational overhead. We'll also have to come up with a reasonable plan to fix the issue.

CANDIDATE: First, I would start by asking how much money we are making from this company. Once I have this number, I would want to know if this is average for a Fortune 500 Company. After that, I would want to know how many Fortune 500 companies AWS is working with as well as how much percentage this profit accounts for annually for AWS.

The reason is I am trying to gauge how important this customer is. Let us assume that this customer is very important. We then need to think about why they are asking for a price reduction. Are they not doing well financially? If that is not the case, are they asking because they are considering a competitor like Microsoft Azure or IBM's SoftLayer?

I would also consider their growth. Is this account already a customer on all AWS products or are they only using us for a couple of services? There might be potential to increase their long-term spend with us.

Obviously, if the discount they are asking for eliminates our profit, then I would not want to consider it.

INTERVIEWER: Okay, is that it?

CANDIDATE: I would also think about setting an unnecessary precedent. If we grant the price reduction and others find out, those companies may ask for a price reduction too. I understand non-disclosure agreements (NDAs) should protect us from this occurrence, but leaks have occurred in the past, even with NDAs in place.

I have to consider the ethical implications too. When granting price reductions, whose request do I accept? And whose do I reject? Will internal and external stakeholders perceive that I'm playing favorites?

Finally, I would consider this client itself. Besides its financial standing, does the client have influence? Could this client refer other customers? If so, I would have to consider the potential profit from these referrals.

CANDIDATE: To summarize all of this, I would first look at how much the company is spending with us and if there are opportunities for them to grow their account with AWS. Then, I would make sure the deal is still profitable for us, that I have the necessary authority within the company to give this discount and that this helps us get on the client's good side, and hopefully land referrals. Under these conditions, I would provide the discount.

Now that I am thinking about it, I forgot to consider the client's leverage accurately. You mentioned they are a Fortune 500 company, so we can assume that their cost of moving their infrastructure off AWS will not be trivial: not only will they have to manage the transition, but they will also have to re-train their staff. This fact might help us negotiate a smaller discount.

INTERVIEWER: Good catch.

Chapter 10 Analytics: ROI

Kindle Pricing Error

Assume an Amazon's Kindle normally retails for $199. However, a pricing error occurred and Amazon's website states that the retail price was $19. Before Amazon corrected the error, Amazon sold 300,000 units. The price was fixed on the website to the originally $199. Amazon has not shipped any of the $19 units. What would you recommend we do?

Things to Consider

- What is the financial cost of fulfilling the mispriced Kindles?
- What is the PR impact?
- What is the company's philosophy when it comes to handling customer-related issues?

Common Mistakes

- Not factoring in shipping costs.
- Not factoring in benefit from subsequent Kindle-related purchases such as books, movies, and music.

Answer

CANDIDATE: How much does the Kindle cost?

INTERVIEWER: Around $170.

CANDIDATE: Has something similar like this happened on Amazon before? What is our usual policy?

INTERVIEWER: Let us assume none of this has happened before. And even though we do have a policy for handling this in real life, let's assume for this question we don't.

CANDIDATE: In addition to losing money on the product sale, we'll also lose money on shipping.

INTERVIEWER: Why is that?

CANDIDATE: Prime customers normally would not have bought the Kindle had it not been for the pricing error. Since they bought it, there's an incremental shipping charge.

INTERVIEWER: Got it. How about the non-Prime customers?

CANDIDATE: I'm assuming at $19, this item would not qualify for super saver shipping.

INTERVIEWER: Correct.

CANDIDATE: So the non-Prime customers would have to pay out of pocket to get this product shipped or lump it in with other purchases. We'll assume the shipping costs on non-Prime customers are revenue-neutral, either because the customer paid for the shipping fees or the margins from incremental product sales offset the super saver shipping costs.

INTERVIEWER: Okay, that's a reasonable assumption.

CANDIDATE: It feels like 50% of Amazon customers are Prime customers, so let's assume that 50% of the $19 purchases are made by non-Prime customers.

INTERVIEWER: That works.

CANDIDATE: According to SEC filings, Amazon's shipping costs are 5 percent of net sales. I will assume the net sale is about $100, so my back-of-the-envelope calculation tells me that it takes about $5 to ship each order. Are you okay with that?

INTERVIEWER: Okay that works.

Let's calculate the loss on the sale first:

$$Sale\ Loss = Units\ Sold * (Actual\ Cost - Error\ Price)$$

$$Sale\ Loss = 300,000 * (\$170 - \$19)$$

$$Sale\ Loss = {\sim}\$45M$$

Then calculate the shipping loss:

$$Shipping\ Loss = Units\ Sold * \%\ Prime * Shipping\ Cost\ per\ Prime\ Order$$

$$Shipping\ Loss = 300,000 * 0.5 * \$5$$

$$Shipping\ Loss = \$750K$$

Finally, adding them together:

$$Total\ Loss = Sale\ Loss + Shipping\ Loss$$

$$Total\ Loss = \$45M + \$750K$$

$$Total\ Loss = \$45.75M$$

Therefore,

it will cost us around $45.75M if we let this order go through. That is a lot. Now let's think about what happens if we cancel this order.

1. **Customer Satisfaction**. It would make 300,000 customers very unhappy.
2. **PR & Brand Impact**. This will definitely blow up on the Internet, and many people will complain.
3. **Support**. Customer service is going to be very busy getting complaints from these users. In addition, fulfillment will have to cancel all 300,000 orders.

What are some positives to this?

1. Kindle uses the razor-and-razorblade model, so it's not as if we make a lot of profit from Kindle sales anyway. Profits come from digital purchases after the Kindle sale.

2. More Kindle users increase word-of-mouth marketing and engagement between users.

3. Kindles probably trended on the Internet as a result. The extra PR buzz may have led to increased awareness and interest in Kindle devices.

I remember reading that Amazon generates a few hundred million dollars in sales of items each day. If we assume that this means a few million dollars per day in profit, then letting this order go through is at worst one month's worth of profit for the retail part of Amazon alone. On the other hand, if we cancel these orders, we might lose a fraction of these customers forever. Given that this will not severely affect the company in the end, I believe that treating these customers right and acknowledging our mistake would be the right thing to do. After all, Amazon's core values include "Customer Obsession," "Ownership," and "Insisting on the Highest Standards."

Apple iPhone LTV

Calculate the lifetime value of an Apple iPhone customer.

Things to Consider

Use the following lifetime value equation:

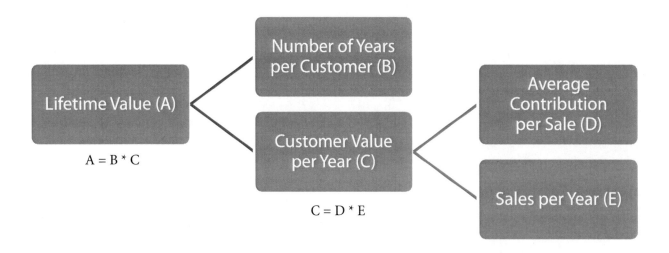

Common Mistakes

- Not knowing the customer lifetime value equation.
- Not factoring in both one-time and recurring revenue.
- Messy, hard-to-follow calculations.

Answer

Assumptions

- iPhone is replaced once every 3 years.
- The average iPhone costs $687.
- iPhone's gross margin is 69%.
- 75% of new users stay with the iPhone for their next purchase (aka customer retention rate).

- Average iPhone customer loyalty is 12 years.
- Typical iPhone user buys $5 of digital goods a month. Most of this is spent on apps, but can also include books, music, and movies.
- Apple's revenue share is 30% for digital goods.

Calculations

LTV from phone sales

LTV = Contribution per Sale * Transactions per Year * Number of Years Customer

LTV = ($687 * 69%) * (Once every Three Years) * (12 Years)

LTV = $474.03 * 1/3 * 12 = $1,896.12

LTV from digital goods

LTV = Contribution per Sale * Transactions per Year * Number of Years Customer

LTV = ($5 * 30%) * (12 Transactions per Year) * (12 Years)

LTV = $1.50 * 12 * 12 = $216

Total LTV

Total LTV = Phone LTV + Digital Goods LTV = $1,896.12 + $216 = $2,112.12

Chapter 11 Product Design: Customer Journey Map Exercises

Expedia Journey

Develop Expedia's customer journey map when buying airplane tickets.

Things to Consider

5Es Framework: entice, enter, engage, exit, and extend.

Common Mistakes

- Not adapting frameworks to a specific situation.
- Using a framework in a way that feels generic and forced.
- Not checking whether one has reviewed each step of the customer experience.

Answer

Research and Planning	Shopping	Book	Pre-Travel	Travel	Post-Travel
• Talk to friends • Search the Internet • Browse destination photos	• Lookup flight schedules • Lookup flight prices • Try alternative air routings • Compare prices	• Buy online • Check if flight can be purchased with loyalty points	• Print ticket or load ticket onto mobile device	• Contact customer service for assistance • Post travel content on social media	• Share travel experience with friends • Complain about experience on social media

Airbnb Journey

Develop the customer journey map for Airbnb's traveler and host funnels.

Things to Consider

- Do most consumers book flights first or book hotels first?
- Do travelers book instantly or not?

Common Mistakes

- Overlooking traditional alternatives like hotels.
- Forgetting that Airbnb is a marketplace and customers interact with hosts.
- Not acknowledging that new users may not feel 100% confident with Airbnb's concept.

Answer: Traveler

Entice	Enter	Engage	Exit	Extend
• Encourage traveler to go on a trip • Browse potential destinations • Plan trip • Purchase airplane tickets • Encourage traveler to consider Airbnb	• Browse Airbnb choices	• Compare Airbnb with alternatives • Ask Airbnb host questions • Purchase Airbnb travel • Depart for trip • Check-in at Airbnb room • Enjoy trip	• Post-trip feedback survey • Post-trip host rating	• Receive notifications to book future trips • Create lists of Airbnb's for potential future trips • Become an Airbnb host

Answer: Host

Entice	Enter	Engage	Exit	Extend
• Hear about Airbnb hosting via friends or Airbnb ad • Read about services offered to Airbnb hosts • Calculate how much you could earn by renting your property	• Sign up as an Airbnb host • Create listing for property to rent	• Add pictures and neighborhood information to listing • Set different prices for peak and non-peak periods • Get first request to book • Prepare property for guests	• Get feedback from guests about their stay • Post feedback for guests • Clean property	• Open more dates on the rental calendar • Tell friends about hosting experience • Act on guest feedback to improve experience

Job Search Journey

Draw the journey map for an Indeed.com job seeker who just graduated from college.

Things to Consider

Use the 5Es framework

Common Mistakes

- Accidentally drawing the employer journey map when the interviewer is asking for the candidate journey map.
- Not taking into account the career level of the job seeker.
- Not considering that a job seeker may eventually leave his or her job.

Answer

Entice	Enter	Engage	Exit	Extend
• Graduated from school • Prepare resumes & cover letters	• Search for specific jobs on Indeed.com • Browse job postings on Indeed.com	• Fill out applications on Indeed.com • (Optional) Link social media profiles to applications • (Optional) Share job postings with friends who are also graduating	• Wait for interview invites • Do interview • Wait for results of the interview • Get job offer • Accept or decline	• Resign from current job • (Optional) Take a vacation • (Optional) Prepare for relocation • (Optional) Get ready for new job

Home Improvement Journey

Develop the customer journey map for contracting a home improvement project.

Answer

Entice	Enter	Engage	Exit	Extend
• Figure out what needs to be worked on • Research project on Google by reading articles or watching YouTube videos • Evaluate whether it's better to do-it-yourself or to contract to a 3rd-party	• Identify a list of potential contractors using Google • Ask neighbors for suggestions • Post a request for contractors on a neighborhood-based social network	• Get estimates and vet contractors • Narrow down to a shortlist of potential contractors considering quality, cost, availability and completion date • Select a contractor and make necessary deposits • Kickoff project • Monitor project • Make milestone payments • Do a final walkthrough as project is completed • Request necessary changes	• End project by completing final payment • Recommend to others	• Receive a coupon for future work • Receive a request for a client testimonial • Contact company for subsequent projects

Customer Service Journey

Develop the customer journey map for a customer service encounter for a billing issue.

Answer

Case 1: customer receives poor customer service

Entice	Enter	Engage	Exit	Extend
• Receive billing statement	• Open and read billing statement • See a charge that's not familiar	• Call customer service • Talk to customer service agent • Agent not helpful • Get angry	• End call • Grumble on Facebook and Twitter • Complain to the CEO • Look for another provider	• Customer receives automated email asking to rate their service experience, give a poor rating or marks the email as spam

Case 2: customer receives good customer service

Entice	Enter	Engage	Exit	Extend
• Receive billing statement	• Open & read billing statement • See a charge that's not familiar	• Call customer service • Talk to customer service agent • Agent listens to complaint • Agent explains reason for charge • Agent readjusts the charge	• End call • Rate the vendor positively on Yelp or Facebook • Share great customer service experience with friends and coworkers	• Customer receives automated email asking to rate their service experience, give a good rating • Order from same vendor again

Online Course Journey

Develop the customer journey map for a free, online university course.

Answer

Entice	Enter	Engage	Exit	Extend
• Hear about the course via marketing material, friends or coworkers • Analyse course content to evaluate fit with one's needs • Make decision to attend	• Find sesssion dates that work • Book class • Share enrollment news	• Introduce yourself to others • Listen to lectures • Do homework • Take quizzes and tests • Ask mentors or other students' questions	• Post class survey • Earn proof of completion • Share class or proof of completion	• Save and archive class slides, notes and materials • Keep in touch with classmates and teachers • Consider taking next course in the sequence

UX Participant Journey

Develop the journey map for recruiting UX participants.

Answer

Entice	Enter	Engage	Exit	Extend
• User thinks about participating in a UX study	• User volunteers for a specific UX study	• Researcher reviews participant's request • Researcher accepts or declines requests • Researcher reaches out to user to make an appointment • User confirms appointment time • User completes UX task	• User selects a participation reward • User answers post-study satisfaction survey	• Researcher logs study and notes about participant • Researcher notes whether participant should be considered for future UX studies

Chapter 12 Product Design: Pain Point Exercises

Child's 1ˢᵗ Birthday Party

Rant about organizing a child's 1st birthday party.

Answer

CANDIDATE:

Rants-related to party planning

1. Putting together the invite list is a hassle.
    a. Have to invite both parents and kids.
    b. Don't know how many to invite.
        i. Too few gives others the impression that we don't have friends.
        ii. Too many will make the party complicated.
    c. People who don't get invited will feel offended.
2. Coordinating food and drinks for the party is not easy.
    a. Certain people will have food allergies.
    b. Some people will want alcoholic beverages. Those who don't want alcohol will judge people who do.
    c. Food that kids like to eat is often not popular with adults.
3. Finding a party location is difficult.
    a. Is the venue children-friendly?
    b. Is the venue baby-friendly? Does it have adequate diaper-changing facilities? Private nursing rooms?
    c. Adequate parking?
4. Determining the optimal party date feels like herding cats.
5. Identify party activities or entertainment for the party is not easy. There's pressure to come up with something new and interesting.

Rants-related to the day of the party

1. Critical dependencies, such as food, birthday cake, and entertainment, may not arrive on-time.
2. Children will probably cry at the party.
3. Kids will create a mess.
4. Kids get bored easily.
5. Can't think of what kind of gift to get the birthday child.
6. Parents will fuss about how boring the party is.

Other rants

1. It is pointless to hold a party when the child is too young to remember it.
2. Many attendees might not show up.
3. The weather might be bad.

4.   It's annoying to beg attendees to share event photos.

Best Handyman

Rant about finding the best home repair person.

Answer

CANDIDATE:

1.   Hard to find well-written reviews for home repair people.
2.   Other reviewers have different tastes or judging criteria from mine.
3.   They live in a different type of home. Is their review relevant to my situation?
4.   Have to provide directions to my house, and they will have trouble finding it.
5.   They probably cannot find parking here.
6.   Have to set up a time when I am home, and they are never available when I am out of work.
7.   Can't do anything or feel comfortable while they are working. Will take a few hours.
8.   Don't trust them in my house alone.
9.   Don't trust them in another room even though I am in the house.
10. They walk around with shoes on. Sure, they clean my carpet after, but I don't want them to walk around with shoes on in the first place.
11. Have to offer a tip even if they do a bad job.
12. Will probably have to pay in cash. I don't have cash on me.
13. They might ask for a deposit. I don't like working with companies that require a deposit.
14. They may charge me more because I don't know how much time it takes to complete tasks.
15. Have to clean my house a bit since they might judge me.
16. Maybe they think I am crazy with some of the stuff I have, and I have to hide them.
17. I don't like it when other people come in my house or my personal room.
18. Have to offer them water, which means I need to go buy plastic cups.
19. They are using my bathrooms. I don't like it when other people use my bathrooms.
20. They are doing work while I am away, and they don't pick up the phone or return my texts when I need to reach them.
21. They might waste time on-site, which will annoy me because I have urgent deadlines.
22. They might smoke or swear. Neither is allowed in my home.
23. They might do a bad job, and because I'm not an expert, I can't tell.
24. They might leave with my money never to be seen again.
25. They might accidentally break something in my home.
26. They might injure themselves or severely damage my house.
27. They might show up late, which means I cannot give them the keys and go on with my day.
28. They might take longer than anticipated to finish the job, leaving me with a half-repaired item for some time.
29. They might be inexperienced and get in over their heads.
30. They don't do everything as promised in the contract.

Job Search Pain Points

Rant about searching for a job.

Answer

CANDIDATE:

1. Don't know the exact job I want.
2. Don't know how to make my resume better.
3. Don't have time to make my resume better.
4. Don't have time to make a custom resume and cover letter for each application.
5. Don't know if I should write a cover letter or not.
6. Don't know which social media profiles to link.
7. Don't know the right layout to make my resume more effective.
8. Don't know how to write a resume to get past applicant tracking systems.
9. Don't know if the company accepts immigrant workers.
10. Don't know how many jobs I should apply for to get something that will suit me.
11. Don't know if I should apply to a job where I don't meet 100% of requirements.
12. Can't seem to network effectively with hiring managers to get a job interview.
13. Don't know anyone who works at the company I want to work for.
14. Don't know who to network with.
15. Don't know if I should wait until I get a referral to apply.
16. Don't know if I will fit with the company's culture.
17. Can't seem to interview well.
18. Get tongue-twisted when given an interview question.
19. Don't know what to practice for the interview.
20. Don't know how to dress for the interview.
21. Don't know if my interview went well or poorly.
22. Don't know the status of my application.
23. Don't know if I should email the recruiter back.
24. Don't know the salary of the job I'm applying for.
25. Don't know the schedule of the job I'm applying for.
26. Don't know the benefits of the job I'm applying for.
27. Can't stand all the waiting and uncertainty of the job search process.
28. Don't know why I was rejected.
29. Don't know how I can improve for future interviews.
30. Discovering new jobs and applying is time-consuming.

Finding Someone to Do Taxes

Rant about finding someone to help you prepare your taxes.

Answer

CANDIDATE:

1. Have to do taxes early; otherwise, I might not get it done in time.
2. Have to sit there and answer questions about "what is this?" and "what is that?"
3. Knows all of my financial transactions. I like to keep my finances private.
4. Do not remember every income or expense that is tax-deductible or needs to be reported.

5. Do not trust them with my financial information.
6. Will try to sell me other services.
7. I will have a lot of questions. They will be impatient about answering them.
8. Making me do all the work even though I am paying them to do this.
9. Don't know if they can find tax credits better than I can.
10. Will remember me and remind me to come again around the same time next year.
11. What if I think they didn't do a good job? I'll have to think of some excuse to refuse them.
12. It costs a lot to get tax preparation help.
13. Might not be knowledgeable about the type of work I do or business I run.
14. May make manual errors, leading to higher taxes or re-filing.
15. Might try to get me to do what's best or easiest for them and not for me.
16. Might charge me extras for things they didn't mention upfront.
17. Might make things seem overly complicated to increase my dependence on them.

Chapter 13 Product Design: Brainstorm Exercises

Validating the Newsfeed

Imagine you are the Facebook newsfeed PM. In your research, you have found that users crave validation. That is, when Facebook users write a new post or perhaps share a photo or video, they want someone to click Facebook's "like" button. They feel empty when their friends do not "like" it.

Brainstorm at least 10 solutions that solve this problem.

Answer

CANDIDATE: Here are my ideas:

1. Put new posts at the top of friends' news feeds, increasing the likelihood the Facebook user will get likes.
2. Create a marketplace where users can purchase likes.
3. Feature that user's posts in a "content just like this" recommendation widget, increasing the likelihood the Facebook user will get likes.
4. Similar to the previous idea, create a "users who like that content, also like this" feature that will increase potential likes.
5. Provide feedback on the user's posts, predicting the likelihood the post will get likes and offer concrete suggestions on how to improve their posts such as:
   a. Use a more positive or negative tone
   b. Use vivid language
   c. Tap into the reader's emotions
   d. Minimize typos and grammatical mistakes
6. Create simulated Facebook users (aka bots) that like user content when the content is worthy of a Facebook like.
7. Using a facial recognition feature, have a Facebook bot user apply a like when there's a smile in the photo.
8. Start a liking contest with friends. All contest participants can see posts and like the content. This will artificially create events to like Facebook content.
9. Create a search box that allows you to search for posts based on criteria.
10. Design a "show me a random post" feature. This self-explanatory feature increases the chance that someone will like a user's post.
11. Create a chart that tracks the most liked content for the entire system or subset. By highlighting posts, it increases the chance that others will like that user's posts.
12. Post stickers or badges on the user's content based on some criteria. For example, a post could get a flame icon if the post has a lot of views. This will generate extra attention, which will increase the likelihood of getting likes.
13. Automatically tag groups of people in photos. This will lead to more likes because the auto-tagged users will receive a notification, which increases the likelihood they will like the photo.
14. Create a 'Super Like' option for users, sending their friends an even bigger signal of validation.
15. Keep a count of all the likes a user has ever received and make it visible only to them.

Internet Car

Google is thinking of creating an Internet-enabled car.

Brainstorm at least 10 interesting use cases.

Answer

CANDIDATE: Here are a couple of ideas:

1. Automatic payment for tolls based on your Google Wallet.
2. Google Maps GPS built-in. GPS and tracking.
3. Roam as a mobile Wi-Fi hotspot.
4. Lock and unlock the car with a password, eliminating the need to carry keys.
5. Pay users to install a camera that automatically uploads recent Google Street View photos.
6. Communicate with other Internet-enabled cars to avoid collisions.
7. Panic button to ask for help and send messages to selected contacts via email and Hangouts.
8. Live stream your journey on YouTube.
9. Built-in calling or video calling via Google Voice.
10. Compare gas prices via Google Shopping.
11. Stream music through Google Music and YouTube Music.
12. Stream audiobooks through Google and YouTube.
13. Surf the Internet using the user's voice.
14. Allow the car to sell itself when it gets obsolete.
15. Allow the car to rent itself out to other drivers when it is not in use.
16. If the car is self-driving, it could deliver food and packages on its own.
17. Google search anything.
18. Voice your calendar updates via Google Calendar.
19. Voice your thoughts via Google Docs.
20. Monitor the environment as a CCTV solution, similar to the 1.85 million CCTV cameras monitoring the UK.

Voice-User Interface for Job Search

Apple's Siri and Amazon's Echo have made voice-user interfaces incredibly popular.

Brainstorm 10 solutions that solve the job search problem using voice-user interfaces.

Answer

CANDIDATE: I have a couple of ideas for each candidate and employer-side:

Candidate-side

1. Fill out job applications by voice.
2. Ask Siri or Alexa for improvements on your resume and cover letter.
3. Schedule interview appointments using voice.
4. Browse new job openings by voice.
5. Indicate job preferences using voice.

6. Eliminate paper resumes and replace them with a voice-based resume.
7. Ask questions about the job.
8. Answer screening interview questions by voice.
9. Using your voice to get colleagues to submit referrals for you.

Employer-side

10. Search applicants, using specific criteria, by voice.
11. Accept and reject resumes by voice.
12. Ask Siri or Alexa questions about the applicant.
13. Delete already reviewed resumes by voice.
14. Request candidates by voice.
15. Read a resume to the employer.
16. Playback a recorded interview by voice.

Mood API

Brainstorm some app ideas using a mood API.

A mood API is an API that has sensors that can learn about your mood.

Answer

CANDIDATE: I can think of a few app ideas and features:

1. Posts everyone's mood via a social network's news feed. Users can compare moods. Users can also receive alerts about others' moods.
2. Reveals the audience's mood at a conference or a meeting.
3. Shows happy pictures when your mood is sad or calming pictures when your mood is angry.
4. Plays music based on your mood.
5. Plays TV shows or movies based on your mood.
6. Shows you games that are appropriate for your mood.
7. Shows you things you can buy to counteract or enhance your mood.
8. Shows you places to go to counteract or enhance your mood.
9. Calls a therapist when you are feeling depressed.
10. Calls 911 when you are feeling scared or threatened.
11. Suppress or alert when you are attempting to a social media post when you are in an angry or otherwise negative mood
12. Highlight everyone's mood around you.
13. Calls a designated friend, depending on your mood.
14. Tells you who you should call, depending on your mood or theirs.
15. Monitor your current mood for self-awareness.
16. Track your moods over time to identify correlations such as waking up, going to bed, or interacting with certain people.
17. Let the API track your conversations with others, inform you of their mood is, and suggest how to best respond.

Relatable Review

Imagine you are the PM of TripAdvisor's reviews. Some users are unsure of whether they should believe reviews they read because they are concerned an author has different hotel preferences than they do. For example, one author may like luxury hotels, but the reader may like hostels.

Brainstorm 10 solutions that solve this problem.

Answer

CANDIDATE: I have a few ideas:

1. Provide a score that represents how similar you and other users are, according to past behaviors.
2. Show trip detail, such as trip length and budget, during a review.
3. Display a summary page of all the hotels this reviewer has ever stayed in.
4. Similar to the last idea, except you are showing it based on the hotel. Show the summary of all reviewers into one nice, simple summary page. You can then tell what kind of hotels people who reviewed this hotel typically like.
5. A filter where you can see reviews by people who stay at the same or similar hotels you do.
6. Show reviews from users who tend to stay in hotels you've liked before.
7. Filter a reviewer's helpful votes based on voters' preference of hotels.
8. Show alternative and outstanding hotels in the area and compare them with this hotel. You can filter them by type of hotels. You can see how your preferred type of hotel is doing compared to this one.
9. Allow a filter where they only see reviews with pictures. This way it provides more information on a review, and the user can then visually judge the hotel.
10. Compare all nearby hotels in the area and then show an aesthetically pleasing summary of average rating and top reviews based on hotel types, making it faster and easier for the user to choose.

Image Search for Recruiting

Smartphone cameras and image recognition improvements have made it easier to search by image.

Brainstorm at least 10 solutions that use image search for recruiting.

Answer

CANDIDATE: Here are my ideas:

1. Select a photo of a star engineer and suggest candidates with similar skills, experience, or accomplishments.
2. Identify similar candidates by selecting 10-second video snippets of candidates a recruiter likes.
3. Identify candidates by selecting logos of desired skills.
4. Identify candidates by selecting logos of desired former companies.
5. Identify candidates by selecting logos of desired universities where candidates graduated.
6. Use logos of desired former companies and universities to find similar companies and universities to recruit from.

7. Shortlist candidates based on candidates that show good body language during a video interview.
8. Take a picture of a meeting in a conference room, provide data on which candidates are desirable, similar to Yelp's augmented reality feature, Yelp Monocle.
9. Take a picture of a conference; provide data on which attendees are desirable recruiting targets.
10. Take a picture of employees in a competitor's parking lot and identify desirable candidates.
11. Take a picture of someone's portfolio such as a developer's GitHub account or a designer's Dribbble account and recommend other candidates who have similar work quality.
12. Take a picture of a piece of work that is interesting and get contact information for the team who made it.
13. Use a picture of a candidate to scan the web and return their different social accounts.

Restaurant Hours

We want to get the hours restaurants are open and closed.

Brainstorm 10 creative ways to make this happen.

Answer

CANDIDATE: Of the top of my mind, the two most straightforward ways to do this are:

1. Have the users fill it in.
2. Have the restaurant owners fill it in.

But you asked for creativity, so here are 11 unique ways:

1. Infer closing hours based on satellite images to see if there are lights still on in the restaurant.
2. Deduce closing hours based on satellite images to see if there are any cars left in the restaurant parking lot.
3. Dispatch Google Street View cars to check for opening and closing hours.
4. Crawl Yelp for opening and closing hour data.
5. Crawl restaurant websites to find opening and closing hour data.
6. Check third-party websites like Eat24 for opening and closing times.
7. Create a software program that automatically dials the business and requests the data.
8. Determine hours based on check-in data from FourSquare or Facebook.
9. Determine hours based on Android or iOS GPS data near the restaurant.
10. Hire people to take photos of hours open and closed signs at the restaurant and upload.
11. Scan publicly available photos such as Google Street View and Instagram for open hours.

Better Phone Batteries

Pretend that a group of scientists claimed that phone batteries could not get better.

As a contrarian, what would you recommend that we do to build a better phone battery?

Answer

CANDIDATE: When you say, "better phone battery," do you mean longer-lasting, faster-charging, or something else?

INTERVIEWER: That's a good clarifying question. I'm just testing your creativity. So you're free to suggest ideas that will make phone batteries charge faster, last longer, etc.

CANDIDATE: Got it. Give me a few moments to brainstorm some ideas.

Candidate takes one minute.

CANDIDATE: I came up with several ideas. I'll start with my favorite ones:

1. Charge the battery wirelessly.
2. Charge the battery based on warmth.
3. Charge the battery based on kinetic movement.
4. Invent technology to make batteries easily swappable.

I also have some ideas related to using existing phone battery technology more effectively:

1. Invent software to manage power consumption more effectively. For example, the phone could go into low-power mode during times the user is or should not be using the phone such as sleeping or driving a car.
2. Create a product that allows a user to charge disposable phone batteries. An example of a disposable battery is your traditional AA battery.
3. A software service that allows you to clone another phone so that when one phone's battery runs out you can pick up where you left off with the backup phone, thanks to the cloning service.
4. Allow the user to put the phone in low-resolution rendering mode. Rendering less precisely reduces computing cycles, which conserves battery power.
5. Create phone chargers that charge batteries faster.

We can also look at improving processes and operations that drain a battery's energy:

1. Automatically install app updates that improve battery performance. The auto-install policy will encourage developers to improve their app's battery performance.
2. In the app store, indicate which apps are known as energy hogs. This will prod developers to create future versions that remove the "energy hog" icon.
3. Phone manufacturers could financially reward development teams that improve a phone's energy consumption. Conversely, apps that are energy hogs could be penalized with a carbon tax.

Next, I have a few conventional ideas that increase the battery's capacity:

1. Use bigger batteries on the phone.
2. To allow for a bigger battery space, development teams can reduce the size of other phone components.

Finally, I have a few oddball ideas that may not seem practical, but might be worth exploring:

1. Use other types of batteries, like nuclear, assuming that real and perceived health risks are addressed.
2. Add solar charging panels to the phone, assuming that the user remembers to take the phone out of their pocket or purse.

Traffic Cones

What is a traffic cone good for other than regular traffic control?

Answer

CANDIDATE: I have a few ideas:

1. A hat.
2. A pyramid.
3. A fountain.
4. A container.
5. Bowling pins.
6. A decoration.
7. A sound amplifier.
8. A funnel for pouring liquid.
9. Use as a goal for throwing tennis balls.
10. Use them to make a course for bikes or cars.
11. Tear them apart and use them as floor mats.
12. Stack enough of them and you can use them as support columns.

Chapter 14 Product Design: Putting it Together

People You May Know

What is the best decision tree for Facebook's "People You May Know" feature?

Things to Consider

- What are real-life signals for identifying friends?
- What data does Facebook have available?
- Did you come up with clever ways to suggest friends to Facebook users?

Common Mistakes

- Answering too casually.
- Not drawing the solution on a whiteboard.
- Using all seven steps of the CIRCLES Method™ especially when it is clear that this is strictly about implementation.

Answer

CANDIDATE: Hmm, I cannot think of a decision tree off the top of my head. I would like to brainstorm first to think of all the things we can do to find a new friend for a user.

INTERVIEWER: Go ahead.

CANDIDATE: So let me assume A is the user. B is the possible new friend.

- Does A and B have a mutual friend C?
- Does B have the same interests as A? We want to prioritize this based on how well-liked these interests are by A and B. We can rank these based on related pages or posts.
- Does B attend the same events as A?
- Does B like the same pages as A?
- Does B attend the same school as A?
- Does B work in the same place as A?
- Does B already know A via email or other contacts?
- Does B have the same major as A?
- Does B live close to A?
- Has B ever lived anywhere that A has?

INTERVIEWER: Could you draw this on the whiteboard, organizing it into a decision tree?

CANDIDATE: Sure.

Candidate takes a moment to draw.

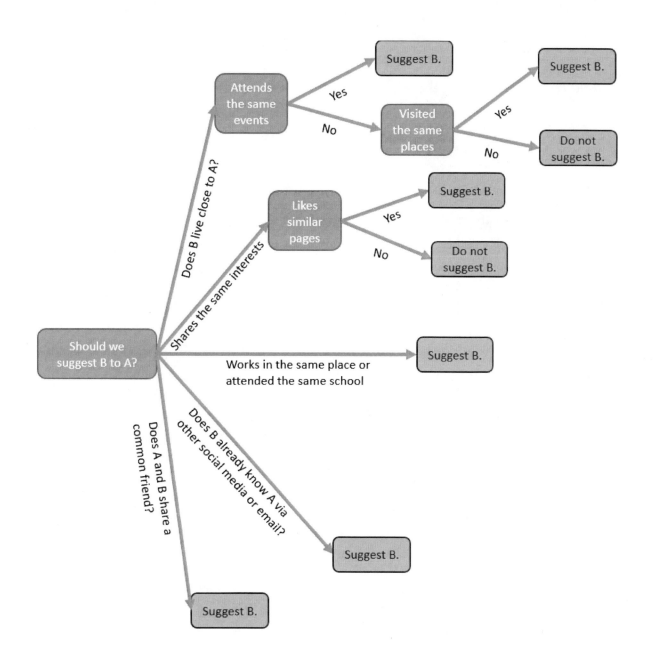

INTERVIEWER: I feel like there is some stuff missing from your tree. What if A and B went to the same school but don't know each other? I mean, there are many people who attended the same school. How would you know which one to suggest first?

CANDIDATE: You bring up a good point. Maybe a point value system would be an alternative. That is, we would have a list of criteria such as "does A and B attend the same school?" If they do, they will be awarded a certain number of points. We will add the points together for a final value. We'll suggest pairs of people that meet a certain point threshold. And of course, we'll show pairs who have the most points first.

INTERVIEWER: So which criteria do you think are worth the most points?

CANDIDATE: Here are my top three criteria:

1. Share a mutual friend
2. Know one another through other social media or email

3. Attended the same university or worked at the same place during the same time period

INTERVIEWER: Can you think of a better algorithm for suggesting people you may know, focused on the college student market?

CANDIDATE: Give a moment to reconsider.

Candidate takes 10 seconds.

CANDIDATE: I think one of the flaws of the points approach is that it does not capture the dependencies between variables. For example, on the one hand, age x school can indicate a strong friend relationship. On the other hand, age x work may indicate a weak relationship, especially as professionals hit mid-career.

A simpler and more representative algorithm would be as follows:

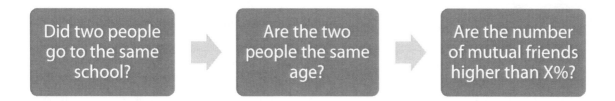

If a pair meet all three criteria, then our algorithm should suggest those two social network strangers.

INTERVIEWER: Thank you. This decision tree seems reasonable and simplifies it substantially. I'm glad you factored in age. I was going to tell you that just because someone graduated from Stanford in 2015 doesn't necessarily mean they're likely to be friends with someone who graduated in 2003.

Design In-Game Store Menus

Pitch designs for an in-game store menu.

Things to Consider

- This question tests a candidate's UI wireframing skills.
- It is better to have multiple recommendations to increase a candidate's chances of having a winning design. It also protects the respondent from being defensive about their only solution.

Common Mistakes

- Fear of wireframing.
- Missing commentary that explains critical design choices, despite detailed and visually stunning designs.
- Drawing out unconventional UI interfaces. For instance, a photo-capture mobile UI with the capture button on the top, not bottom, especially if there is no reason to do so.

Answer

CANDIDATE: Can I get some time to brainstorm?

INTERVIEWER: Of course.

Candidate takes one minute.

CANDIDATE: I have three ideas in mind:

Candidate draws the following on the whiteboard.

←	💎 123,456,789	G 1,234,567

Gems	**Gold**	**Items**	**VIP**

💎	100,000	+ 100%	= 200,000	$99.99
💎	50,000	+ 50%	= 75,000	$49.99
💎	20,000	+ 30%	= 26,000	$19.99
💎	10,000	+ 20%	= 12,000	$9.99
💎	5,000	+ 10%	= 5,500	$4.99
💎	1,000	+ 0%	= 1,000	$0.99

CANDIDATE: This idea puts all purchases on one screen. The focus is on the bonus percentage and the final currency. Then we organize into four tabs:

1. **Buy Gems**. It gets the first position because spending money to buy hard currency is the most important.
2. **Buy Gold**. It gets the second position for similar reasons.
3. **Buy Items**. This tab has additional items a player can purchase.
4. **VIP**. This is a critical factor in most games. Hence, it will appear in the fourth tab.

The purchases rank from highest to lowest to encourage players to buy the highest amount. Then show the player's currency totals at the top. When the user purchases more gems or gold, the user gets the satisfaction of seeing their totals go up.

In the upper left, there is a back button. I intentionally omitted a close 'X' button on the right; the reasoning is that I wanted to avoid unintended clicks, especially on a critical monetization page.

CANDIDATE: The second design option is vertical instead of horizontal. The design is familiar, but there are two differences.

First, I cannot fit all six purchases here, so the screen will be scrollable. I also added space for scrolling, animated ads. While ads can be annoying, monetization is critical, even with free users. If a user purchases a product, we could perhaps disable ads while they have paid gems remaining in their account, giving people a bigger incentive to purchase gems.

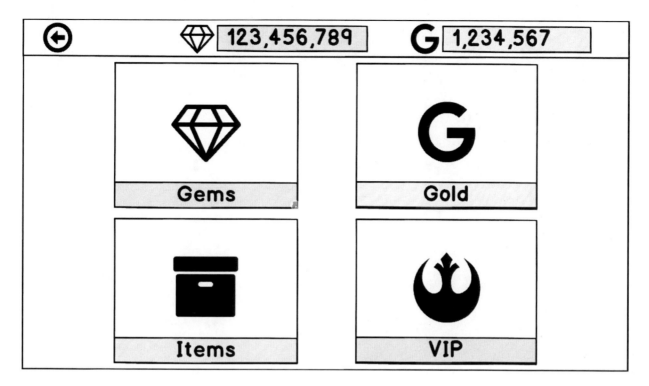

CANDIDATE: The Metro design style inspired the third and final design option. We start with four big buttons: gems, gold, items, and VIP; they correspond to the same categories as the two previous designs. After pressing an option, you will see the items listed in this manner:

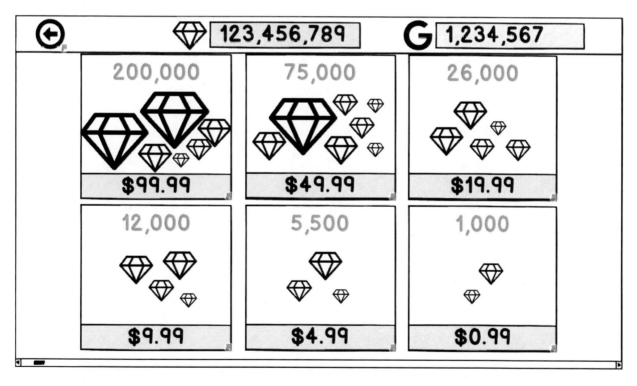

This design is simpler than the previous designs, which can be less intimidating. However, the drawback is that this requires additional clicks, which can be annoying.

One more thing I wanted to call out with this design: the button background color is consistent with the currency: green for gems (shown) and yellow for gold. This will help players more quickly recognize the purchase they are considering. We should incorporate that insight, regardless of which design we choose.

Amazon Home & Lighting

Assume you are on the Home and Lighting team for the USA market, how would you go about improving our category page?

Things to Consider

- Use the CIRCLES Method™
- Give memorable names to your feature and product ideas.
- If you are not familiar with Amazon's Home and Lighting category page, either ask the interviewer or share your best guess before proceeding. It puts you and the interviewer on the same page. It also gives the interviewer a chance to correct any misunderstandings.

Common Mistakes

- Not thinking creatively or big enough.
- Answering too casually. The interviewer is looking for a detailed and thoughtful response.
- Spending too much time asking for context. It comes across as not wanting to answer the question.

Answer

CANDIDATE: Could I ask some clarifying questions?

INTERVIEWER: Sure.

CANDIDATE: What is our goal with this change? Are there specific metrics we are targeting? Engagement? Retention? Revenue?

INTERVIEWER: What would you recommend?

CANDIDATE: I would target revenue.

INTERVIEWER: Okay. What's next?

CANDIDATE: I would evaluate which customer segments have the most revenue potential.

Here are three different types of users I can think of:

- **Busy Young Professionals.** These users are time-sensitive and used to shopping online. If we create a good enough experience for them, they would love to skip the store and order online. They are likely to live in a smaller home such as an apartment. They might not have a strong design sense; due to their youth, they haven't had much experience curating their own design sense. They are also likely to live in urban environments; making several trips to the store is not something they want to do given how hard it is to get out of the city. They are likely to be impatient and demanding.

- **Adult Homeowners.** These users are the bulk of the consumer market today. It's everyone who shops for lights at a hardware or department store. They are middle-aged and mostly middle-class; they accustomed to purchasing offline. Unlike young professionals, they are less likely to be tech-savvy. However, they are more likely to have a strong design sense. They are also more likely to live in the suburbs and have a car; thus, they do not feel inconvenienced when making trips to the store.
- **Small and Medium Businesses.** On the one hand, most large companies have large purchasing departments that handle office equipment and lighting purchases, resulting in volume discounts. On the other hand, a single person handles purchases for small and medium-sized businesses. This means that we need to capture a single customer who is buying for an entire business. Saving time is the biggest attraction of buying online.

All three are potentially valuable markets. I'd recommend that we choose one for the sake of time.

INTERVIEWER: Sure, that sounds reasonable.

CANDIDATE: By way of deduction, I'd cross off small and medium businesses from the list. It's not to say it's not a lucrative opportunity. However, it would discussion toward business-centric features such as invoicing and financing options like net 30. I don't think it'll be exciting or sexy.

INTERVIEWER: That's fair.

CANDIDATE: So that leaves us with busy young professionals and adult homeowners. There are pros and cons to both. The biggest tiebreaker is the fact that young professionals are comfortable buying online, and we are an online company. It's also promising that they are likely to be Amazon customers already. Young professionals are a promising market that is likely to grow. It is also important to build brand preferences early.

Are you okay if we focus on young professionals?

INTERVIEWER: Yes, I agree with your rationale. Why do you think young professionals buy on Amazon today?

CANDIDATE: There are a couple reasons why young professionals buy on Amazon:

1. **Convenience.** One-click shopping. Amazon Prime delivery to your door. Need I say more?
2. **Assortment.** World's largest selection.
3. **Competitive prices.** Cheaper than most competitors.
4. **Trusted brand & customer service.** If problems arise with my purchase, Amazon is a company I can trust to resolve my problem.

INTERVIEWER: Good list. What do you think are their pain points when shopping for furniture?

CANDIDATE: Young professionals are concerned that the furniture:

1. Will not look good
2. Will not fit
3. Will be difficult to assemble

What makes these pain points more acute is that online furniture purchases:

1. Are not easy to return
2. Furniture's resale value is terrible

INTERVIEWER: So which pain point would you focus on?

CANDIDATE: I would like to focus on the fit and aesthetic pain points. Not only are they the two biggest pain points, but also they are related. Do you mind if I take some time to brainstorm some ideas on how I would solve it?

INTERVIEWER: Of course not. Go ahead.

Candidate takes some time.

CANDIDATE: I have a few solutions in mind.

Candidate writes the following ideas on the whiteboard.

- *Recommendations*
- *Try at Home*
- *Panorama Augmented Reality (AR)*

Recommendations

The Recommendations feature suggests lighting options that are ideal for your home. For example, if you were considering a particular light, the page would display complementary light fixtures. It is similar to Amazon's "Other people also purchased this" except this would be more geared toward visual matching. We could even push this further by asking you for your address and window locations. By knowing where you live and where your windows are located, we can predict and make recommendations based on how the sun lights your home throughout the day.

Try at Home

Try at Home is a unique feature just for this category. Customers can buy these lights and try them on for a few days. If they don't like it, they can ship back the products to us and purchase something else for free. People want to know if the lights look good in their home. If we can give them a guarantee that they can return and choose something else if it doesn't fit, it would most likely make the purchase easier. Also, people tend to keep the same lights in their homes, so investing in the "test" light bulbs until the consumer finds one they love might make them a lifetime customer of their chosen lights. Zappos and Warby Parker are two companies with successful Try at Home programs.

The Panorama AR feature allows you to visualize what lights would look like in your home or office. Here's how it would work:

1. User takes a panorama of their room
2. User can drag and drop different light options into the room

3. The software will allow the user to see how the rooms look with lights on vs. off, including lighting warmth and shadows
4. User can select different times of the day to see how the lighting options feel during dawn, day, dusk, and night
5. As an optional feature, we might allow users to adjust the windows in the room, the color of the wall and furniture

I'm excited about this feature because people want to see how lighting pairs with their current home; compared to buying, trying, and returning a product, this saves the user time and hassle while saving us the cost of processing returns.

Notice how I am focusing on helping users decide and pick based on aesthetics. Amazon has a disadvantage compared to stores like Home Depot. I can go to Home Depot and look at what my light actually looks like. As an Internet retailer, Amazon has a harder time depicting this. If we can overcome this main challenge, then we can count on Amazon's strength in delighting customers to turn busy yet demanding professionals into profitable lifelong customers. And since we already have their home data, it makes even more likely they'll return to us first because of the setup time required when going with a different retailer.

INTERVIEWER: I appreciate your insights. Which one would you recommend, if you could only pick one?

CANDIDATE: If we are optimizing for long-term revenue, Try at Home and Panorama AR have the advantage of bringing home a larger share of wallets because it makes sense to pick features that will not only result in a customer's initial purchase, but also all of their lighting purchases.

For me, Try at Home and Panorama AR not only fits best, but also it's a dramatically different feature from Recommendations

Between these two, Try at Home is definitely the easiest to implement. It's not as much of a product feature as a business policy that we need to make clear to the customer: "Try all the lights you want with us until you find the perfect one." As I mentioned, this feature might be costly, as customers likely will return used lights, which we can't sell. The one-time setup investment is relatively small, but the marginal cost, accumulated over the long-term, could be large.

Panorama AR has the opposite cost structure: it's a large investment, in the near-term, that might pay large dividends, in the long-term. PAR increases lighting purchases while decreasing returns. This feature might be more engineering heavy, but I feel like it's better off for Amazon to invest in building great features rather than paying for lights that customers don't want.

To summarize, I'd go with Panorama AR, because it provides the opportunity to increase our revenue by allowing users to more easily test lights in their homes, has some of the characteristics of our improved Recommendations and its cost structure is better long-term than Try at Home.

INTERVIEWER: Okay, now that we've figured out what to do, how do you convince engineering managers to support your idea? Keep in mind engineers are a limited resource.

CANDIDATE: I would first put together my argument using data that shows how this feature will increase revenue. One data point would be, "How many users return purchased lights because they did not look right?" I would cross-reference this data with "How many lights on average do customers consider before making a purchase?" This would reveal choosy customers that frequently return lights because the lights do not work well in their homes. I would also check whether these customers purchase lights even after a return. If they do not, then they may have lost faith in Amazon's purchasing experience.

I hope the data would convince engineers that this is a worthwhile product to build, but I'd also want them to be enthusiastic about it. To build enthusiasm, I'll discuss why Panorama AR would be challenging and frame this as an opportunity to create world-class, cutting-edge work.

Adding to Amazon Prime

We are considering adding a new feature to Amazon Prime, while continuing to price it at $99/year. What should the additional feature be?

Include a light analysis of the feature you have chosen. For instance, estimate the revenues from additional subscriptions and costs that would come along with the additional feature; give justification for your assumptions.

Things to Consider

- Start by exploring needs for existing and/or prospective Amazon Prime customers.
- Brainstorm several ideas, not just one.
- The cost of the membership must remain constant, so minimize the marginal cost of the new feature.

Common Mistakes

- Believing that Amazon Prime is perfect, as-is.
- Not wanting to suggest new ideas, fearing criticism.
- Afraid of doing the calculations and talking about benefits from a qualitative, not quantitative, perspective.

Answer

CANDIDATE: Can I get some time to brainstorm?

Candidate takes a minute.

CANDIDATE: First, I would like to understand why users purchase Amazon Prime. Here are a few reasons I can think of:

Candidate writes the following on whiteboard.

1. *They enjoy getting items quickly. Paying an attractively priced flat-fee for two-day shipping on all products feels like a good value.*
2. *They appreciate the included Amazon Prime videos, music and books.*

From here, we can design our new features. The point of adding new features is to acquire new Amazon Prime members and generate more revenue.

I propose these three ideas:

- **Better Selection of Kindle Books for Amazon Prime customers.** Amazon Prime offers its user the Kindle Owners' Lending Library. However, reviews indicate that the selection is dismal. I would recommend that Amazon expand its selection. Amazon started as a bookstore; many of its loyal customers are avid readers. A better selection may attract new Prime users. Exclusive books or magazines would be a big plus.
- **Loyalty Program.** Any Prime user that purchases enough items in the current quarter would get next quarter's Prime membership free. The idea is to keep Prime users spending. If the spend requirements drove sufficient incremental revenue, this benefit could pay for itself. From here, we could extend the program by replicating loyalty program innovations from adjacent industries such as airlines and credit cards.
- **Exclusives.** I like how Amazon allows Prime customers to pre-order games, a benefit non-Prime customers do not have. I recommend that we expand these benefits further, which I will call Exclusives. Sometimes, Exclusives will allow Prime members to purchase new products early. Other times, Prime members will get exclusive discounts instead. We might be able to get vendors to subsidize the cost, who may consider this an opportunity to get more awareness for their products. Who wouldn't want to be on the front of the Prime Exclusives page?

INTERVIEWER: Hmm, interesting. Which feature would you recommend?

CANDIDATE: I recommend Exclusives. This does not require a lot of technical effort on our part. However, it will require work from our business team. Creating the Exclusives program and Prime Exclusives pages is something we can do internally; I would recommend leveraging knowledge from the Amazon App Store team. And as I mentioned earlier, vendor partnerships might lead to unique exclusives as well as discount subsidies.

INTERVIEWER: How much additional revenue do you think this will make? And what will it cost?

CANDIDATE: Are we talking about annually?

INTERVIEWER: Yes, annually.

CANDIDATE: Okay, can you give me some time to organize my thoughts?

Candidate takes a minute.

CANDIDATE: For revenue, I believe there are two parts:

- **Incremental signups**. How many more people will sign up for Amazon Prime?
- **Incremental revenue**. How many more sales would we get from featuring products?

For cost, there is just one part:

- **Discount subsidies**. How much does it cost? This number could change if we can get companies to subsidize.

Let's calculate incremental signups and the corresponding revenue first:

I feel 3 percent of Amazon customers would be compelled to sign up for the program. My reasoning is 2 percent of my friends are coupon clippers, but my friends have higher income than the average person does. So let's adjust the 2 percent upward to 3 percent.

From there, let's assume that the Amazon Prime annual membership is $100 to make the math easy. Last time I checked, Amazon Prime had about 50 million users. Jumping into the calculations:

$$New\ Prime\ Membership\ Revenue = Current\ Members * Incremental\ Signups * Prime\ Price$$

$$New\ Prime\ Membership\ Revenue = 50\ million * 3\% * \$100$$

$$New\ Prime\ Membership\ Revenue = 50\ million * \$3$$

$$New\ Prime\ Membership\ Revenue = \$150\ million$$

CANDIDATE: Next, let's calculate incremental revenue:

I have read that Amazon Prime users purchase about $1,100 worth of products each year. I'm guessing that Prime users purchase often to maximize their shipping benefits, so if I were to guess, they make roughly two purchase transactions per month as a Prime user. If I do some quick math:

$$Amazon\ Prime\ Customer\ Annual\ Spend = \$1,100$$

$$Purchases\ per\ year = 12\ months\ per\ year * 2\ purchases\ per\ month = 24$$

$$Prime\ Customer\ Monthly\ Spend = \frac{\$1,100\ annual\ spend}{24\ transactions\ per\ year} = \$45.83 \cong \$50$$

Therefore, the average transaction would be around $50.

Next, "What are the incremental sales from featuring products?" As a proxy, I'm thinking of the featured app feature on Google Play or Apple's App Store. Let's assume these two app stores a similar DAU as Prime every day. I know from anecdotal experience that getting something to feature on the App Store would get you about 50K organic installs a day; Google Play would be around 100K installs, so the total number of new installs each day would be 150K. The conversion would be a lot less in Amazon Prime since it's a purchase, not a free install. So let's call the conversion 70% of what we'd expect across those two platforms. So let's say the new purchases are 150K * 70% = 105K.

Let's say the average Amazon item costs $50, and we're going to do a 20% discount on the featured products, making it $40. Jumping into the calculations:

$$New\ Purchasing\ Revenue = New\ Purchases * Item\ Price * Days\ in\ a\ Year$$

$$New\ Purchasing\ Revenue = 105,000 * \$40 * 365$$

New Purchasing Revenue ~ 1.5 billion

CANDIDATE: Finally, we want to calculate the initial cost of subsidizing the items. We can use the numbers we used in the previous formula. I would say this would probably only last 3 months before we can get manufacturers and vendors on board and have them subsidize their own products. We can calculate this with the following formula:

$$Subsidy\ Cost = New\ Buyers * Item\ Price * Days\ in\ 3\ Months$$

$$Subsidy\ Cost = 105,000 * \$40 * 90$$

$$Subsidy\ Cost = \$378\ million$$

CANDIDATE: Please keep in mind that this is the potential cost. Meaning we are making less profit when people buy things. I know Amazon has a low-profit margin, but it should definitely be higher than 20%, which is the price cut we made, so I don't think there is actually any cost.

Now we can talk about the cost of shipping the items. We can also use numbers from the earlier formula. First, let's think about the average shipping cost. Two-day shipping should be around $12.

$$Additional\ Shipping\ Cost = New\ Buyers * Shipping\ Cost * Days\ in\ a\ Year$$

$$Additional\ Shipping\ Cost = 105,000 * \$12 * 365$$

$$Additional\ Shipping\ Cost = \$459.9\ million$$

CANDIDATE: To conclude, the additional revenue would be 1.5 billion, and the cost will be around 837.9 million.

Recommendation Algorithm for Amazon Video

Jeff Bezos would like you to improve Amazon Video's recommendation algorithm.

1. What are the considerations and data points that go into it?
2. Broadly, how would you go about implementing it?
3. What data points would you use to evaluate success?

Things to Consider

- Part 1 is asking for the features or variables that would predict whether a recommended video would be suitable.
- Part 2 is about execution. Do you know how to launch the feature?
- Part 3 is about identifying relevant success metrics.

Common Mistakes

- Incorrectly focusing on the UX, not algorithm, design.
- Proposing a rule-based, not artificial intelligence-based (aka neural network) system.

- Not brainstorming enough features (aka prediction variables) for the AI-based system.

Answer

CANDIDATE: Can I take some time to brainstorm?

Candidate takes one minute.

CANDIDATE: I think the best approach for such a system is to leverage machine learning. From what I have read, it's what most big companies do, and it produces results that are better than other approaches. Machine learning systems are powerful because they can take a wide range of inputs and reduce them down to a small number of outputs, which in our case would be the recommendations. Given this fact, I believe we should try to incorporate as much potentially relevant data in our model as possible. Here are some inputs I thought of:

- **Similar Genre**. If someone is really into *Game of Thrones*, we want to show videos that are fantasy and/or intended for the more mature audience. It makes sense they would like something similar.
- **Similar Length.** If someone loves watching TV series with 30-minute episodes, they probably want to see more of the same. Showing recommendations for 2-hour movies may not do as well.
- **What Others Are Watching.** Similar to "People who purchased this also purchased" feature on Amazon. If you watched *Game of Thrones*, you probably would like similar shows that other *Game of Thrones* fans watch.
- **Demography.** If someone is a parent, we want to recommend videos that parents often watch. This is especially important when you throw kids into the mix.
- **Geography.** What people watch may (or may not) change according to our geography, but we would want to feed this data to our model to detect any trends.
- **Device.** Maybe people watch shorter videos on mobile than on desktop.
- **Time of Day.** Maybe what people watch varies depending on when they watch it. For example, perhaps they tend to watch cooking shows in the afternoon, but feature-length films in the evening.

INTERVIEWER: How would you go about implementing this?

CANDIDATE: Well, to start, I would validate my theory first by pulling up some data. We would want to see if any of the variables I've mentioned above influence what people watch. Once that is verified, I would work on specific user segments first.

To start, we can start with movies. I would begin with a genre that has numerous films, say, comedy. I would slowly add other genres and video types once this has shown success and continue to tweak my algorithm based on user data.

INTERVIEWER: What data points would you use to evaluate its success?

CANDIDATE: Here are some metrics I'd consider:

- Clicks on recommended videos
- Times that a recommended video was watched
- Satisfaction with the recommended videos

We should also see greater convergence in the videos that our users watch. That is, if our recommendation engine has improved, we should see our user base spending more time watching more relevant and satisfactory videos than not.

INTERVIEWER: Thank you.

Changing Amazon Prime

What factors would you consider in making changes to Amazon Prime?

Things to Consider

- Think broadly about Amazon Prime's definition. It is not just free two-day shipping or videos. It is a membership club, with the purpose of driving customer loyalty.
- Consider other membership clubs such as Costco or credit cards with high annual fees.
- Assume we are making these changes with the goal of increasing the number of Prime subscribers.

Common Mistakes

- Erroneously focusing on a secondary metric such as increasing share of wallet of existing customers when Amazon's true goal is to increase Prime signups.
- Thinking small by suggesting underwhelming adjacent features. For example, triggered by Amazon's video offering, many candidates suggest that Prime should offer free Audible books.

Answer

CANDIDATE: This is an interesting question. Here are the factors I would be considering:

- Free super saver shipping's cost to Amazon.
- Prime two-day shipping's cost to Amazon.
- Number of users using Prime.
- Number of users not using Prime.
- Numbers of packages Prime users buy vs. non-Prime users. This impacts our shipping costs.
- Average spend per package for Prime users vs. non-Prime users.
- Prime vs. non-Prime users purchase frequency per month. This helps us calculate yearly revenue.
- Average profit margin per purchase for Prime users vs. non-Prime users.
- Average digital purchases for Prime users vs. non-Prime users. These represent additional sales revenue without any shipping cost for Amazon.
- Current annual fee for Amazon Prime.
- Typical purchases for Prime vs. non-Prime users.
- Other Prime perks.

With this information, I can understand our business model and compute our profit. I'll also know the breakdown of non-Prime vs. Prime users and what they buy. Here are a few things I would do:

- **Increase revenue**. We may be able to increase membership fees without a material change in membership.

- **Manage costs**. If users are abusing free two-day shipping, we can impose requirements. For instance, members can't just buy a pack of gum and get free two-day shipping.
- **Target new audiences with new benefits**. Add game rentals as a new perk, in an effort to target new audiences.

INTERVIEWER: I like your list of factors. What other benefits does Prime provide Amazon, aside from membership revenue?

CANDIDATE: Of course, there are a few:

- People tend to buy more because they think they will lose money if they don't. This has retention and engagement benefits as well.
- People feel a sense of exclusivity with Prime.
- People talk to other people about Prime, increasing our word-of-mouth marketing.

Improving Facebook Login

What would you do to improve the Facebook login?

Things to Consider

- What are some of the flaws of the Facebook login?
- What is the purpose of the Facebook login feature?
- This is the login button into Facebook, not the "Login with Facebook" button.

Common Mistakes

- Assuming there is no room for improvement for Facebook login.
- Suggesting half-hearted ideas like making the button more visible or colorful.

Answer

CANDIDATE: Do you mean in terms of user experience?

INTERVIEWER: It's up to you.

CANDIDATE: Do you mean mobile or browser? Also, you mean logging onto Facebook and not using the Facebook account to log onto a third-party website or app, right?

INTERVIEWER: Yes, I do mean the Facebook website and app. Why don't we try mobile?

CANDIDATE: Okay. I would say there is really only one thing we are trying to improve here: activation. Once a user has already downloaded the app, we already got the acquisition. Now there are two scenarios:

1. **User does not have a Facebook account**. We need to work on the signup process.
2. **User already has a Facebook account**. Perhaps that user was just too lazy to login on their phone.

I am going to work on both of these separately.

User already has a Facebook Account

Let's start on the use case where they already have a Facebook account. This one is pretty well thought out already, but it's missing an essential function. In most cases, a user's browser on their phone will synchronize with their browser on the computer. Assuming this is the case, why don't we let the user login through the computer's browser the first time for authentication purposes? This way they don't even need to input a password. They can just log in with just one click. Obviously, there is a security risk associated with this, but I think we can mitigate if a user has already confirmed their phone number on their desktop account, and then use the same phone to log in.

User does not have a Facebook account

Now, for the new user, I have a few ideas:

- **Sign Up Using Apple or Google ID**. Here's how this would work. First, the user would sign in with their Apple or Google ID. Second, the user would authorize Apple or Google to share their profile data including their name and email address with Facebook. From there, Facebook could ask for their remaining sign-up information including a unique Facebook password. This process will save users from typing in their personal information, increasing the likelihood of getting a signup. Please note that I am not saying we are tying your Facebook account to these accounts.
- **AutoFill Information**, including your real name, birthday, and gender. This information is probably tied to your phone. Getting permission will be a challenge; I'm not sure if Apple and Google would be comfortable with apps getting this info. If they do, it would make the process faster and easier.
- **Existing Account**. I noticed Facebook doesn't check if your account already exists until the last step. This is inefficient and frustrating. It should check as soon as the user enters an email. Also, given the sheer number of Facebook users, if someone has Internet access, odds are they have a Facebook account already.

INTERVIEWER: Which one would you recommend?

CANDIDATE: All of them can work, but the existing account one is the "lowest hanging fruit" so to speak. It's easy to do technically. The other two may have many problems just figuring out if they are doable.

INTERVIEWER: It's interesting you specifically mentioned not tying the Facebook account to Apple ID or Google ID. Why are you so adamantly against it? Plenty of websites allow Facebook or Google login. Wouldn't offering the same service make it more convenient for the user?

CANDIDATE: The strength of Facebook is the user base, among other things. We have more users than any other social media service. Apps and websites want to use Facebook login to make it easier for other people. We don't need to do that because we have enough incentives for new users to join. In addition, Google and Apple are competitors. If we allow this, we are giving up our advantage. Moreover, even if we agree to this, there's no guarantee that they'll let Facebook be a way to login on their website. So no, I don't think we should offer the same service. Also, if we think about those that still don't have Facebook accounts, most of them are likely not going to have an Apple or Google account. Both Facebook and Google are currently trying to get more people on the Internet, in part to gain more users. I am not saying that there isn't anyone who would fit that profile, but that for the potential risks, there does not seem to be enough users to add by integrating Google or Apple sign-in.

Instagram UX

Instagram currently supports 3 to 15-second videos. We are considering supporting videos of unlimited length. How would you modify the UX to accommodate this?

Things to Consider

- Ponder how user behavior changes when interacting with a three-second vs. a 15-second video. 12 seconds does not feel like much, but user needs can change dramatically.
- Which use case are we focusing on? The person viewing a video? Or the person posting a video?

Common Mistakes

- Freezing up
- Unstructured, stream-of-consciousness discussion.
- Assuming user engagement is identical for 3 and 15 second videos.

Answer

CANDIDATE: Are we considering the web or mobile interface?

INTERVIEWER: Our web experience lags our mobile experience, so help me fix that.

CANDIDATE: And did you want me to discuss both the viewing and uploading use cases? It seems like for the sake of time we should just focus on one.

INTERVIEWER: You are right. Please focus on the viewing use case.

CANDIDATE: Okay. My understanding is that Instagram videos do not currently have video controls. You can only play or pause with a tap of the finger like this:

Candidate draws on the whiteboard.

Screenshot / @kimkardashian, processed by pho.to

INTERVIEWER: That's correct.

CANDIDATE: When I think of user needs, here's some new information and controls that the user would need:

Information

- Popularity, including likes and comments, as before
- Length
- Time remaining

Controls

- Play and pause, as before
- Fast forward and rewind

As far as I know, Instagram doesn't give viewers the option to choose different video playing resolutions, like YouTube. Therefore, that's a control we don't have to worry about. I believe simplicity is the best UX.

INTERVIEWER: Agreed. Your recommendations seem reasonable. Can you draw what the UX looks like on the whiteboard?

CANDIDATE: You mean now?

INTERVIEWER: Yes.

CANDIDATE: Okay, I will give it a shot.

Candidate draws on the whiteboard.

CANDIDATE: The bottom left shows what happens the mouse cursor hovers over the image. A play control appears in the dominant center position, making it clear that is the desired call-to-action.

The bottom right screenshot depicts the neutral state. It gives the user an indication of how long the clip is, along with its popularity.

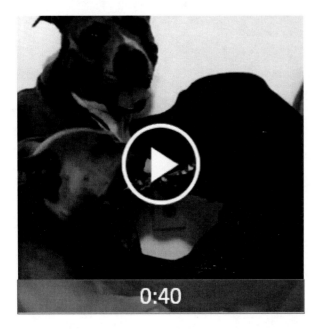
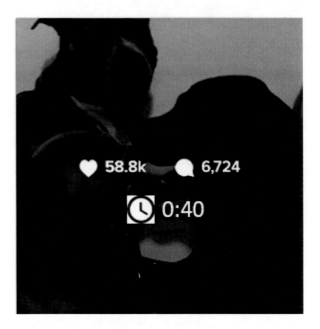

Screenshot / *The Product Manager Interview* and Instagram

The following rendering shows what the UX looks like when it is playing but paused.

Screenshot / *The Product Manager Interview* and Instagram

Finally, this last diagram shows what the UX looks like when the video is playing.

Screenshot / *The Product Manager Interview* and Instagram

You can see I wanted to keep the control familiar without adding excessive functionality. By reducing barriers, I feel we will maximize engagement.

INTERVIEWER: That's a good tradeoff. Thanks for the drawings.

Bing's Salesperson Use Case

A Bing.com salesperson has a 30-minute sales meeting with a prospective advertiser. Build a feature that will help this salesperson prepare for the meeting.

Things to Consider

- Use the CIRCLES Method™.
- Empathize deeply with the salesperson's pain points.

Common Mistakes

- Not factoring in the 30-minute constraint.
- Automatically assuming that this is about improving Bing.com. The prompt is really about helping the salesperson in general.

Answer

CANDIDATE: Just to clarify, we are developing a feature for a Bing salesperson that will prepare her for an advertising pitch with a general manager (GM) in 30 minutes. Is that correct?

INTERVIEWER: Yes.

CANDIDATE: Okay. Do we have any restrictions?

INTERVIEWER: No.

CANDIDATE: Okay, when I think of the typical salesperson, here are the biggest pain points:

1. Don't know much about the product they are selling.
2. Has knowledge of the product, but feels uncomfortable selling the product because their product isn't the market leader.
3. Don't know who the influencers are in the organization.
4. Don't know how the product aligns with a person's goals.
5. Don't know how to tailor the pitch. This includes customizing the sales script and presentation.

All of these are reasonable pain points to me, but the one that caught my attention is #3. In college, I majored in organizational behavior. I would like to focus on that one if that's okay with you.

INTERVIEWER: Sure.

CANDIDATE: Here's why influencers are important:

1. GMs are busy; they rely on their influencers to vet enterprise purchases.
2. GMs can be unsure; they want influencers to help them decide.
3. GMs want to protect themselves; having influencers involved in the decision can help them deflect blame.
4. Most companies do not allow a single authority to make unilateral decisions. GMs' influencers may be mandatory decision-makers.

INTERVIEWER: Okay, I see where you are going. Influencers are important. And I'm guessing there's no tool that points out who the key influencers are in an organization?

CANDIDATE: That is correct. This is what we call the "hidden network." And LinkedIn doesn't have this information either. So given how important this is, revealing the hidden network is the feature I'd like to build.

INTERVIEWER: So how would you build it?

CANDIDATE: Give me some time to brainstorm.

Candidate brainstorms silently for a minute and writes the following ideas on the whiteboard:

1. ***Anonymous survey**. Ask employees for the information via an emailed survey.*
2. ***1:1 interviews**. Ask employees for the information in a 1:1 interview.*

153

3. **Computer vision**. *See how often and how much time people spend with each other.*

4. **Email analysis**. *Analyze the frequency of emails between pairs of people.*

5. **Chat analysis**. *Same as email analysis, but for chat messages.*

6. **Assumed inheritance**. *Assume that those that influence a particular executive must also influence those that are around him.*

I came up with six ideas. I'm going to strike out 3, 4, and 5. All of these require access to internal data such as emails and chat. I can't imagine a company giving access to that data to an external company. 6 is intriguing, but we have to get influence data on a particular executive first.

So that brings us to options 1 and 2. Both of them entail reaching out to employees for information on who influences who.

INTERVIEWER: Why would an internal employee provide influence information to an external vendor?

CANDIDATE: It would be a quid pro quo model. If they share the information, we'll provide the compiled report to the respondents.

INTERVIEWER: I'm not convinced.

CANDIDATE: First, the respondent will find value. They're curious to find out themselves who influences who. They can use that information for themselves.

Second, the anonymous quid pro quo model is quite prevalent, and something many folks are familiar with. For instance, Glassdoor requires users to provide at least one salary, company, or interview review to access their entire database. And third-party salary surveys do the same thing too.

INTERVIEWER: Let us say you get this data. How does it help our salesperson?

CANDIDATE: With this influence information, the salesperson can:

1. Suggest people meet either during the meeting or in separate meetings
2. Try to build alliances with influencers before the big meeting
3. Use these influencers to get information on how to best influence the GM

INTERVIEWER: And this information isn't available on LinkedIn?

CANDIDATE: No, it's not available on LinkedIn. An individual's influencer network is what organizational behavior experts would call the "hidden network." As the name implies, it's hard to get. And valuable too.

INTERVIEWER: I concur the information is valuable. But I imagine it's going to be a lot of work to collect it.

CANDIDATE: Whoever collects that data is going to make a lot of money.

INTERVIEWER: Agreed.

Improve Facebook for the Web

Redesign the Facebook Newsfeed for the Web.

Things to Consider

- Use the CIRCLES design framework.
- Do not confuse Facebook's Newsfeed and Timeline feature.

Common Mistakes

- Suggesting unoriginal improvements.
- Considering only superficial problems such as removing ads.
- Considering only superficial needs such as "User needs the ability to share photos."

Answer

CANDIDATE: Which version of the newsfeed are we looking to redesign: desktop, mobile, or both?

INTERVIEWER: Let us focus on desktop.

CANDIDATE: Why are we redesigning the Newsfeed? This is Facebook's core, so I assume we have a reason for making a design change: either something we want to optimize or a problem we are looking to fix.

INTERVIEWER: Indeed, we do. We are looking to improve engagement on the desktop web version.

CANDIDATE: All right, can I get some time to brainstorm?

Candidate takes one minute.

CANDIDATE: Many different people use Facebook. I think we should first start by thinking about the users. Here are some users I am thinking of:

- **Always-Ons**. These people love updating their friends about their lives. It could be through shares, status updates, pictures, or videos. They both create and consume a lot of content.
- **Regulars**. These people are not hardcore Facebook users. They go on Facebook between once per day and once per week to catch up on what is going on. They consume much more content than they share.
- **Influencers**. These people post a lot for a purpose. They are looking to promote something.

Now, I would like to think about situations where each of these users may have problems engaging with their Newsfeed. I can think of a few:

- **Always-Ons:**
  - Sometimes want to post things in a more real-time manner. There are innumerable Newsfeed items, which makes it difficult to do that, as new posts would pop up on the feed.
  - Sometimes feel like they have gone through all the interesting content in their Newsfeed.
- **Regulars:**
  - The collapsed Newsfeed comments are not so user-friendly. It is hard to find where a thread starts, especially since there are so many threads.

- o If you have numerous friends or subscribe to many pages, you could get a torrent of updates, especially if you do not check Facebook that often. Sometimes I am only interested in a certain page, and I cannot filter. I have to click on that page to see all their news.
  - o There is no way to save something that you found interesting in your Newsfeed and look at it later. When you come back, the new information overtakes the old information you are trying to retrieve.
- **Influencers:**
  - o Popular influencers do not have time to engage with all the incoming responses.
  - o Other than that, Influencers behave similarly to other users and have similar problems.

Given what we know about our users, I feel like our best shot at increasing engagement is to focus on the Regulars. The Always-On users actively engage with everything. The only point where they stop is when they have no more content to read, and Facebook already deals with this by suggesting friends and pages to like. As we mentioned before, Influencers consume the content on their Newsfeed just like any other user. Solving their problem of interacting with fans leads us away from our goal. For these reasons, I suggest we focus on the Regulars.

INTERVIEWER: Go ahead.

CANDIDATE: All right. I can think of a few solutions to the problems we stated that could increase engagement:

- **Filtering**. We could add tags on the side. For example, we can filter by closest friends, pages only, and other options. This way, when they log on, the most relevant content shows up first. The desktop interface gives us the "real estate" to do this, but the trick is getting the filters right. If we have too many it will repeat the problem since the user can't decide. If we have too few, it's somewhat pointless to have this feature in the first place. Ideally, the user can pick, say, "closest friends," and see updates for their closest friends. We will have to define what a close friend is in the algorithm.
- **Showcase Main Comment Thread (SMCT).** Users can flood popular posts with comments. For users who weren't at the beginning of the conversation, it can be hard to follow or chime in. When I look at my feed, I often see that many comments are people tagging their friends. These comments aren't meant to start a conversation. While they generate some engagement, it is restricted to the user who tags someone and the tagged person. We could probably use AI to track the main "conversation thread" in a comment section and show this to a user while hiding all the comments that aren't relevant to it. We could perhaps even push it further and analyze what the conversation or post is about to create a custom prompt for the user in the comment box.
- **Save For Later.** When Regulars use Facebook, we mentioned that they often come back to their Newsfeed to a deluge of new content. This means it can be hard to find something you wanted to engage with but didn't have the time to on your last login. For example, an article that was too long to read on the fly, or a family member's post that requires a thoughtful response. Yet, there is no way for users to put these items aside and come back later to engage with them. A "Save for Later" feature would help with that, and let users who aren't always available engage thoughtfully at a later time, which will likely happen when they are at a desktop.

INTERVIEWER: Those are all good suggestions. Unfortunately, we can't implement them all. If you had to go with one, which would you choose and why?

CANDIDATE: Well, let's refocus on our goal. We said that we wanted to increase Newsfeed engagement on desktop. Our first suggestion, Filtering, seems like it would help do this because users will see posts they care about. On the other hand, this feature requires a lot of work from users, who need to manually set their filters. Also, the end result is similar to what the Newsfeed already does algorithmically, which means the engagement boost might not be that strong.

Our second feature, SMCT, feels like it has the potential to significantly increase engagement on posts. It might be hard to implement because we need to be right about which thread is the main one, but if we get it right, the combination of a curated comments section and the custom prompt is likely to increase how many users contribute to the discussion. The downside is that it only increases engagement in a single dimension: comments.

Our last feature, Save for Later, feels like it would solve the problem we just mentioned. If we let people save anything in their Newsfeed, not only are we increasing the odds that they engage with it later, but we are also creating a new engagement action: Save. The caveat here is that most of the saving will likely happen on mobile because that's when users lack the time to properly engage with posts, but our goal was to improve desktop engagement. Desktop engagement is also likely to improve if people use desktop to engage with previously saved posts, but there's no guarantee that that will be most of the engagement created by this feature.

To summarize, I think if we want to stay focused on our goal of only improving the desktop newsfeed engagement, then we should go with SMCT. If we want to be bolder and think about the Newsfeed holistically, then we should build Save for Later. This feature might be more challenging to build, but if we do it right, it will increase engagement on both the desktop and mobile versions of Newsfeed.

Improve Facebook Mobile

Redesign the Facebook Newsfeed for Mobile.

Things to Consider

- Use the CIRCLES design framework.
- Ask the interviewer if you can refresh your memory and look at Facebook on your phone. It'll trigger your brainstorm: both for pain points and new solutions. It will also preserve your credibility by not recalling, incorrectly, how a feature works.

Common Mistakes

- Mumbling and/or speaking too quickly
- Spending too much time with the CIRCLES design framework such as too much time spent talking about goals or personas.
- Coming with unimpressive solutions because the candidate forgot to ask for time to think.

Answer

CANDIDATE: Let me look through Facebook and see if I can spot any problems.

Candidate looks through Facebook on her phone.

CANDIDATE: I notice a few problems I would like to tackle:

- **Annoying mobile ads**. Users get annoyed when Facebook's mobile app is cluttered with ads. It's even more acute on a small smartphone device.
- **Reading messages requires a separate application**. Facebook decided to separate the timeline and messaging experience across two apps: Facebook and Messenger. While there are some strategic reasons for doing so, users get annoyed that checking messages requires a separate download. And the Messenger app loads very slowly.
- **Seeing fake news**. Users get upset when fake news and political propaganda misinform them.

Is there any specific one you want me to tackle?

INTERVIEWER: Let's see how you solve the ad problem.

CANDIDATE: Okay, I'm sure you're eager to hear solutions, but I do want to take a moment to consider, in more detail, why candidates are annoyed by mobile ads.

1. **Ads are obstacles**. It's an annoying speed bump to the content that they do want to read.
2. **Ads are irrelevant**. This one is self-explanatory.
3. **Ads are creepy.** Facebook's behaviorally targeted ads will show ads for products I see elsewhere on the Internet. For example, I was considering a book purchase on Amazon on my laptop; two minutes later I see an ad for that exact book *on my smartphone*. Even if it was relevant, it triggers an unfavorable reminder that Facebook seems to follow me wherever I go on the web.
4. **Ads are embarrassing.** I don't know if Facebook has these kinds of ads, but I hate it when an ad unit plays an unmuted video ad. Sound, from a video ad, is very embarrassing, especially if it's at work.
5. **Ads slow down the user experience.** Ad units are often filled with rich media that slow down the user experience. I'm not sure if Facebook mobile is guilty of this, but I get very annoyed on other properties when a news article has clearly loaded, but I can't scroll down the page because the page is waiting for an ad unit to close or load.

INTERVIEWER: That's a long list. So which one would you focus on?

CANDIDATE: All of them are problems, and I believe all of them need to be addressed. However, if we need to prioritize, our biggest opportunity is to convince our users that ads can be relevant.

INTERVIEWER: How would you define relevant?

CANDIDATE: I would think of relevant as the ability to:

- *Entertain*, especially for users who are bored or lonely
- *Feel smart*, especially for those who are educationally inclined
- *Provide utility*, especially for those who are stressed and are looking for solutions

INTERVIEWER: Sounds reasonable to me. So what solutions do you have for more relevant ads?

CANDIDATE: All right, sure. Can I get some time to brainstorm?

Candidate takes one minute.

CANDIDATE: I can think of a few solutions:

1. **Location-based stickers and emoticon packs.** For example, we can capitalize on the Pokémon Go phenomenon. For instance, let's say they see a boxing gym and post a photo with a boxing glove sticker. They'll get rewarded with a special UFC sticker pack.
2. **Ads relevant ads to a user's post.** Say you posted something about going to a burger joint, a small ad inside the post shows the viewer's local burger restaurant. It's tiny and unobtrusive. It's also nice because it's relevant to the topic at hand. Again, it can upset and confuse some people.
3. **Coupons based on your location.** Trigger discounts based on businesses around you. For example, get a $1 off a Starbucks Frappuccino or one quid off McDonald's.
4. ***Did you know?* coupons.** Perhaps the user is driving past San Bernardino, California on their way to Coachella. On the drive there, a Facebook newsfeed item or notification would say:
   - *Did you know that San Bernardino, California is where McDonald's was founded? Allegedly the McDonald brothers lost out on millions of dollars royalties by not having a written contract. Visit the museum to learn more, and get $5 off your admission.*
5. **Articles you'll read.** Suggest articles based on Facebook's knowledge of one's problems. For example, maybe the user has been researching back pain treatment. Facebook can suggest articles that the user can read. They can go even further to only suggest articles that are certified to be trustworthy. Facebook will be paid for traffic they send to the publisher.

INTERVIEWER: Interesting. Which one would you recommend?

CANDIDATE: *Articles you'll read* is interesting, but I'm not convinced about the monetization potential for non-eCommerce traffic. *Coupons based on your location* and *Did you know? coupons* are clever, but we'd have to do user testing to see if location-based coupons are ideal. It may be more appropriate for an app that users associate with location discovery like TripAdvisor.

That leaves us with *Ads relevant to a user's post* and *Location-based stickers and emoticon packs*. The former is not bad, but it may not always be relevant. For example, just because I posted a complaint about a burger restaurant doesn't mean I'm ready to try another burger place.

So I'd vote for *location-based stickers and emoticons*. It's entertaining, clever, and consistent with Facebook's mission, which is to connect with one another.

INTERVIEWER: I like your powers of deduction. That was going to be my choice too.

Improving Pinterest

How would you improve Pinterest?

Things to Consider

- Use the CIRCLES design method.

- Do not forget to clarify the purpose of the product improvement.
- Do not get defensive if you get push back from the interviewer.

Common Mistakes

- Damage credibility by proposing a seemingly innovative solution, only to have the interviewer explain that Pinterest does that already.
- Proposing unimpressive features such as faster load times or a cleaner UX.
- Incorrectly assuming a complete and accurate understanding of how Pinterest works.

Answer

CANDIDATE: So why are we improving Pinterest? We could target several metrics including:

- Revenue
- Retention
- Engagement
- Customer satisfaction

INTERVIEWER: How is engagement different from customer satisfaction?

CANDIDATE: Just because someone is engaged, in terms of daily active usage or time on site, does not necessarily mean they are happy and satisfied. For instance, Toyota's procurement managers may use Toyota's supply chain software every day, but that doesn't mean that they're happy using it.

INTERVIEWER: Ah, I see.

CANDIDATE: I personally would focus on customer satisfaction as our goal, if that is okay with you.

INTERVIEWER: Sure, go ahead.

CANDIDATE: Next, I would want to consider potential personas we could optimize for. As an outsider looking in, here is what I believe to be the different Pinterest user segments:

Candidate writes the following on whiteboard.

- **Social butterflies**. *Use Pinterest as a form of socializing. They comment about pictures they find with fellow Pinterest users.*
- **Designers**. *They use Pinterest for inspiration.*
- **Curators**. *They are obsessed with collecting and organizing photos.*
- **Marketers**. *Small business owners use Pinterest to attract attention. For instance, it could be a dessert shop owner or a wedding photographer who is looking to drive sales.*

For the sake of time, I would like to focus on the designer persona, if that is okay with you.

INTERVIEWER: Please go ahead.

CANDIDATE: When it comes to inspiration, designers are:

- Searching for inspiration
- Saving inspiration

Starting with searching here are some problems designers have:

- **Irrelevant search results**. Pinterest's search interface isn't optimized for all searches. For example, let's say an artist is trying to find a digital painting of a casino dealer and tries the following tags: "digital," "painting," "casino," and "dealer." The user is left with results that aren't relevant. This yields a bad user experience and lower customer satisfaction.
- **Insufficient search results**. While Pinterest does have an extensive library of curated images, for long-tail searches, a user can get the sense that they are looking at the same five to eight images.
- **Cannot search by picture type**. Designers can look for certain types of images such as concept drawing, pencil drawing, cell shading, or 3-D modeling. Pinterest does not currently support this.
- **Inspiration is not tactile**. Images have no texture or depth to it.

When it comes to saving inspiration, here are some problems:

- **The pinning board is fixed**. There is no way to rotate images or change the layout.
- **Inspiration is a flat image**. Let us say a designer is collecting lamps. It would be more impactful to get the actual lamps themselves than a simple image.

INTERVIEWER: That is a good list. Which one would you fix?

CANDIDATE: The one that resonates most is insufficient search results. Pinterest's mission is to "help people discover the things they love, and inspire them to go do those things in their daily lives." If the inspiration is incomplete, then Pinterest disappoints its customers. Give me a moment on how Pinterest can provide better search results:

1. **Saved searches**. Search results can differ based on the query. As a result, allow users to save and share search queries for one another. For instance, a search query might be labeled as, "Search query for the perfect shade of red for a cartoon car drawing." It's like creating a recipe on IFTTT.com.
2. **Natural language searches**. It is difficult to put intent into a search query language. So instead, allow a user to express their search in natural language and then use AI algorithms to deduce which images to show.
3. **Hire a librarian**. Pinterest users can describe the inspiration they are looking for. They can pay a fellow Pinterest user (aka "a librarian") to search for inspiration and create pinboards for our designer.
4. **Elsewhere on the web**. Suggest images that aren't stored on Pinterest's site but may still be relevant to the user. Perhaps these are images found on Behance or on the Google search engine. It does create a potentially negative impression that Pinterest isn't a one-stop inspiration shop. However, I'd argue that a more mature company would be comfortable sending its companies off its site. Take Amazon for instance. Amazon features third-party sellers on their site; Amazon could be embarrassed by not being able to sell all products to consumers directly. However, by allowing third-party sellers, they are helping customers get the product they want (i.e. increase satisfaction). Amazon found a lucrative new revenue stream too because they receive a 15 percent commission for any third-party sales.

INTERVIEWER: So which one would you recommend?

CANDIDATE: I would go with saved searches for the following reasons:

1. **Scale**. One user's saved search can potentially help thousands of other Pinterest users.
2. **Strategic**. The labeled data from the saved searches ("Search query for the perfect shade of red for a cartoon car drawing") can enable our future forays into natural language searches.
3. **Builds community**. With the option to saved searches, the community may help each other out in finding inspiration, building stronger ties, and growing engagement.

INTERVIEWER: Thank you.

Improving Amazon

How would you improve Amazon?

Things to Consider

- Use the CIRCLES Method™.
- Amazon has a lot of products and features. Clarify with the interviewer which product he or she would like you to focus on.

Common Mistakes

- Not clearly describing suggested ideas.
- Suggesting an idea that already exists.
- Assuming revenue is the only goal and being perceived as very business-focused rather than product (or customer) focused.

Answer

CANDIDATE: What do you mean when you say, "Improve Amazon?" Are you referring to the core Amazon.com product experience?

INTERVIEWER: Yes.

CANDIDATE: We can improve the core Amazon shopping experience by focusing on engagement, retention, revenue, and acquisition. Which one do you want me to concentrate on?

INTERVIEWER: Which one do you recommend?

CANDIDATE: I would like to focus on retention. Right now, there is no reason for people to come back unless they intend to sell something, which is why the only way Amazon is boosting this is through sales. I feel like by getting people back on Amazon more often, it would indirectly lead to more revenue.

INTERVIEWER: Sounds good.

CANDIDATE: Can I brainstorm for a bit?

Candidate takes one minute.

CANDIDATE: I have a few ideas in mind:

- **Items Just for You**. Amazon will recommend to the user a list of eight to ten items, every few days. Amazon suggests items that the user is likely to buy. This feature will give users a reason to come back or at the very least, just keep Amazon top-of-mind. We can provide discounts as well to entice customers further.
- **Daily Ratings**. Every day a user can log on Amazon to look at some pre-selected products. These are products that are not selling well for some reason, and we want user feedback. The user will take a look at the entire product page and write down what they think needs to be improved. Is the price too high? Are the product images poor? Users will then get a stackable 3% off coupon. These coupons can be stacked up to 10 times. This not only boosts retention; it would also give us feedback.
- **Retention Coupon**. If a user has not recently visited or purchased, that user will receive a special 10 to 15 percent off coupon. This can apply to any item. This will encourage users to come back to Amazon and buy.

INTERVIEWER: Out of all of these ideas, which one would you recommend?

CANDIDATE: I would recommend "Items Just for You." I believe we already have most of the data, so we can offer a sale based on the profit margin (e.g., Item X has a profit margin of 20 percent, so give a 10 percent off coupon). It would be easy to implement. Obviously, we should start by testing this on a small subset of users.

INTERVIEWER: Why offer a discount on products we predict users will buy anyway?

CANDIDATE: That is a valid concern. Here are a few reasons why the discount would work well:

- When users buy something, they usually buy other things too. In some cases, they may buy unnecessary items to qualify for the $25 free shipping threshold. It's likely we won't be offering sales on expensive items through this anyway since most people don't buy expensive items on a whim.
- This will most likely increase sales. More sales, at a lower profit margin, mean more profit. Isn't this the motto Amazon heralds?
- We can offer items that do not sell as well but still might be relevant to a user's purchase history. That is, we can offer bigger discounts to items that do not sell well and smaller discounts to items that do. Obviously we would not markdown popular items.

Improving Dropbox

How would you improve Dropbox? Which feature is still missing?

Things to Consider

- Use the CIRCLES design framework.
- Think of adjacent areas beyond file sharing such as:
    - A more robust UI for specialized file types. Think photo, music and video sharing.
- Use the SCAMPER brainstorm framework. For example, what happens when you combine Dropbox and:
    - Airbnb?

- o Facebook?
- o Microsoft Outlook?

Common Mistakes

- Not showing enthusiasm, making the answer boring.
- Choosing a persona that the candidate does not know well.
- Not using the whiteboard to help the listener visualize a proposed improvement.

Answer

CANDIDATE: Are there any constraints to this problem?

INTERVIEWER: No constraints.

CANDIDATE: Okay, and what about goals? Are we improving Dropbox for a specific type of user? Is there a metric we want to optimize?

INTERVIEWER: We have nothing particular in mind. We are looking to build the best possible product and that is what you should consider in your answer.

CANDIDATE: Thank you. Can I get some time to brainstorm?

Candidate takes one minute.

CANDIDATE: Before we jump into how to improve Dropbox, I'd like to define my user segments, with the goal of tightening up my scope. I see Dropbox users in three main categories:

- **Casual Consumer.** They have a Dropbox folder on their desktop and perhaps their phone. They use Dropbox either to share things with others or synchronize files across their devices.
- **Only When Necessary (OWN).** These people don't use Dropbox until it's absolutely necessary. They use Dropbox when they receive a file. Or when they need to send a large file that exceeds email attachment limits.
- **Business User.** They use Dropbox because their company uses it to synchronize internal files. I've read once that Dropbox's B2B acquisition strategy is to target only companies where a large portion of employees are consumer users of Dropbox; this means that most Business Users are very familiar with Dropbox.

For clarity, I'd like to focus on only one of these users and build the perfect product for them. Does that work with you?

INTERVIEWER: Yes, but please justify your choice. Who do you think you can build the best feature for and why?

CANDIDATE: Of course. First, the Casual Consumer is an interesting choice, because they are our most numerous type of user. The Casual Consumer use Dropbox for its simplicity, so we want to be careful about adding features. The OWN persona is also interesting because they are the group that is currently least informed about Dropbox features and can grow the most. For these, I feel like a more appropriate approach might be to improve feature discovery since they don't use all of Dropbox's features. Last, we have the Business User. These users are already more likely to be power users and paying. For these two reasons, I think we should focus on them: they'll be eager to try new features to improve their Dropbox use and will feel like they are getting their money's worth.

INTERVIEWER: That's logical. What would you build for our business users?

CANDIDATE: Before we go ahead and build, I think it's useful to put myself in the shoes of our business users and analyze what their needs are. Here are some I can think of:

- **Real-time collaboration.** You might want to have multiple people editing the same file at the same time. Currently, this is possible with a small subset of Dropbox files, but perhaps we could extend to all files.
- **"Git blame" for Dropbox (GBD).** Developers use Git for version control of their code. Sometimes, there might be old code for which you want to find the author, and using the command "git blame" will show who wrote each line of code. I can imagine this being useful in a Dropbox enterprise setting for reports, spreadsheets, and so on.
- **Reminders.** If you have a deadline, it could be helpful to have reminders.

Of these, it feels to me like Reminders is the most incremental of the three, so I wouldn't focus on it. It might be a quick feature we ship, but it's not a game-changing experience for users. The two other use cases both revolve around communication, and I think we can develop features that try and improve how business users communicate using Dropbox. Does this make sense to you?

INTERVIEWER: Yes, it does. What are some features you think would accomplish that?

CANDIDATE: I can think of two interesting features:

- **Chat**. Dropbox currently does not support chat. Having chat would be nice. When users are collaborating on the same projects, they can instantly chat with each other to solve problems and easily link to specific files.
- **More Information**. Currently, if I am working on some files with a few people. There is no way for me to know who changed which file. Thanks to the Dropbox and Microsoft Office integration, I can preview the file and even work synchronously with someone else on it. However, it would be even better if I can always see who is working on a file, even if it isn't a MS Office one. It will minimize change conflicts. This way, I can collaborate in real-time if Dropbox allows it. Or if that isn't possible, I can alternatively be notified to stay away. This feature would be a mix of the "git blame" use case mentioned above and real-time collaboration.

INTERVIEWER: Interesting. Of these two, which one would you implement and why?

CANDIDATE: I feel like Dropbox's core value proposition is around storing and syncing files. Chat can be useful, but we already support commenting, which is similar. On the other hand, I feel like the GBD feature, which provides real-time information about who is working on what file, what they edited and whether you can work on it too is something that makes Dropbox stronger at file collaboration, which is what Dropbox does best. Because of this, I would lean towards GBD.

Improving Google Play Store

What would you change in the Google Play Store?

Things to Consider

- In addition to user needs, consider how Google Play is different or similar to other marketplaces.
- Scope the question appropriately: Google Play can refer to Apps, Music, Movies, or Books.
- In addition to the user experience, consider the developer experience as well.

Common Mistakes

- Incorrectly thinking that a structured thinking process is sufficient. The answers matters.
- Raising common or superficial improvements such as improving the recommendation algorithm.
- Claiming one can improve the UX, without showing how. Draw the proposed UX on the whiteboard, if relevant.

Answer

CANDIDATE: Interesting question. Why do we want to change the Google Play Store? Is there something we want to fix? A metric we want to improve? If so, which one?

Alternatively, is there something in the broader ecosystem? Perhaps Apple has made some recent improvements to its App store, and it somehow caught the attention of a Google executive?

Interviewer laughs.

INTERVIEWER: We are getting bigger at Google, but there is no executive mandate to overreact due to a competitive move.

You can assume that there is nothing specific to fix. Nor is there a particular metric to optimize. Imagine you are a PM on the Google Play Store and tasked with making it better. What do you do?

CANDIDATE: I see. Well, I believe metrics are a good way for a team to work together towards a specific goal, so I would focus on one to improve. Given that this is Google Play, I imagine that what we want is for people to download items repeatedly. This is a combination of engagement and retention.

INTERVIEWER: Okay, sounds good.

CANDIDATE: Can I get some time to brainstorm?

Candidate takes one minute.

CANDIDATE: I can think of a few things:

- **Screenshots**. This is a mobile issue. Screenshots may come in as portrait or landscape. Most users browse through a portrait view, so when they see a landscape screenshot the first thing they do is tilt their phone. What Google Play Store doesn't do is that it doesn't lock the screen. It should, so the screenshot doesn't change the display. This might seem trivial, but UX issues might make the difference between a user leaving the Google Play store and staying to download an app.
- **Referral Credits**. Many apps give referral credits when users invite friends, but they always have to be spent in-app. Perhaps we could give developers the option to spend referral credits in the entire Google Play Store. This might make it more attractive for users and end up generating more referrals, across more apps, which means more downloads.
- **Dead Simple UX**. Google's homepage is famous for having a minimalist design. However, when you visit Google Play, the store shows users download suggestions for everything. I understand that this might lead to impulse buying, but this is overwhelming. This is a risky change, but I think if we had a minimalist UI, we might make it easier for people to get to what they want and increase overall engagement.

INTERVIEWER: It is interesting you mention changing the UX. Impulse downloads, through recommendations, represent a significant part of Google Play's total downloads. Do you still stand by this idea?

CANDIDATE: Thank you for sharing this. Before I answer, I have a clarifying question. Do you know if the impulse purchases happen primarily from the main page or a page that a user navigated to?

INTERVIEWER: I do not. Why do you want to know this?

CANDIDATE: Well, I believe this signals download intent. Consider option one, where impulse downloads originate from the main page. Then I would be more skeptical of my idea because it seems that showing many options to the user as they come to Google Play is working well.

Then let us consider option two, where most impulse downloads originate from pages the user has navigated to themselves. Then I would still be quite confident in my solution. The latter scenario suggests that once a user is on a page they wanted to access, they are open to recommendations. This might imply that we should focus on getting users to where they want to go as fast as possible and that their "shopping" experience only starts there. A parallel to this would be the suggestions on Amazon.com's homepage versus the recommendations on a product page. I might not be the typical user. However, I have found that I'm much more likely to buy things that are shown on the product page, rather than the home page. Maybe this applies to Google Play too.

INTERVIEWER. Interesting. Going back to your referral credits idea, don't you think some developers would be frustrated that we are sending their referral credits to other apps?

CANDIDATE: Of course, that's a great point. Not everyone will want to take part in this feature. I think it's fair to give everyone the right to opt-out. However, I still think it can be valuable for developers to include in their app for the following reasons:

- **Improved Visibility.** Within the Apps section of the Google Play store, we can highlight applications that include our referral feature. We could also tweak our algorithm so that apps with this feature enabled show up in higher in search results or in their category.

- **Increase in Referrals.** If users get credits for the entire Google Play Store when referring someone on an app, they might be more likely to refer people to stack up credits. This may result in a net increase in referrals for apps that enable Google Play Store referral credits.
- **Easy to Implement.** Referral systems can be cumbersome to build, and many developers are time-constrained. If we build a great API, similar to how Google Analytics works, it might be simpler for developers to integrate this referral system into their app than build their own from scratch.

With all of this, I believe our product would deliver a lot of value to developers. It will not be perfect for everyone, no product ever is, but I think it has a chance at increasing engagement and retention on Google Play.

INTERVIEWER: Thank you.

Improving Google Hangouts

How would you improve Google Hangouts?

Things to Consider

- Brainstorm several ideas, not just one.
- Give your ideas memorable names.
- Be clear on how your suggested solutions work and why they are important.

Common Mistakes

- Not being thoughtful in the recommendation.
- Insisting on walking through the full CIRCLES framework when the interviewer is simply looking for a subset.

Answer

CANDIDATE: When improving Google Hangouts, here's how I would approach the question:

1. Understand the goal
2. Dig into the customer personas and corresponding pain points
3. Prioritize the pain points
4. Brainstorm solutions
5. Analyze tradeoffs for each one
6. Make a recommendation

Is this process okay with you?

INTERVIEWER: It sounds like a good process in real-life, when we have more time. However, there are other questions I want to get to as well. Can you just clarify the goal and walk through some of your suggested improvements?

CANDIDATE: Okay. For the goal, I could suggest improvements that grow Hangouts' revenue or market share. However, I think the most important goal is to improve product engagement. It aligns with Google's motto: "Focus on the user and all else will follow."

INTERVIEWER: Okay, go ahead.

CANDIDATE: Excellent. I'll take a moment to brainstorm some solutions.

Candidate takes one minute.

CANDIDATE: I can think of several things:

- **Find New Friends**. One of Google Hangouts' strengths is that it uses your Gmail contacts. However, there is no way to search a friend directory. So that's my first idea: a feature where Hangouts can help you find friends based on your criteria such as age, gender, and proximity. Also, introduce friends your friends know, kind of like a social network. This will increase engagement.
- **Status during Image and Video Sending**. Whenever you send large images or videos, Hangouts never tells you the status. All it shows is, "Sending…" If it fails, it simply says the upload fails. What it should do is tell you the upload percentage. This makes for a better user experience because otherwise, this is a bad user experience.
- **Personal Status**. Google+ is not doing well as a social network, partially because nothing happens on there. This idea draws on Tencent's QQ and WeChat, which started as messaging applications for the PC and mobile, respectively. By offering a simple personal status feature, it'll offer personal expression and create intimacy. This could be the first step toward turning Hangouts into a social network. A simple status is a great opener for any conversation that will increase engagement.

INTERVIEWER: Interesting. Which idea do you recommend?

CANDIDATE: I would say personal status. It should be the second easiest to implement out of the three ideas and aligns with the goal of improving engagement. Lastly, it sets the stage for a more robust social network.

INTERVIEWER: Thank you.

Monetizing Google Maps

How would you monetize Google Maps?

Things to Consider

- Use the CIRCLES Method™.
- Although the question prompt revolves around Google Maps, reflecting upon competitors' strengths and weaknesses can help.

Common Mistakes

- Having trouble suggesting monetization ideas aside from ads.
- Afraid of suggesting dumb ideas. Most companies, especially Google, would strongly prefer to hear one audacious, moonshot idea than ten good ideas.

Answer

CANDIDATE: I'm going to tackle this question in three steps.

1. Explore pain points with Google Maps, especially ones with monetization potential.
2. Brainstorm solutions.
3. Make a recommendation.

INTERVIEWER: Sounds good.

CANDIDATE: Let's start with pain points. Here's what comes to mind:

- Not sure which mapping application has the best directions, whether it's Google Maps, Waze, or Apple Maps.
- Drives can be boring, especially long road trips.
- When driving, I see interesting things like lakes, castles, and mountains. I wish I could search Wikipedia for more information, but my hands are busy. Or if my hands aren't busy, it will take too much time to complete the search.
- When driving, I see places I would like to visit someday, such as restaurants, museums, or stores. But I cannot recall them later.
- When I travel to a place with no cellular data connection, I can't pull up directions.
- To get offline maps, I need to download it in advance. However, I never know when I need to download offline maps in advance.
- I'm looking for the best-priced gas station along my route.
- I'm worried about getting a speeding ticket.
- I don't know why a person has bad driving behavior. The person is tailgating me, cut me off, or won't let me into his or her lane. Is there a way I could communicate and tell him or her to stop it?
- I hate it when ads show up while I'm driving on mapping apps, especially on Waze. To clear the ad, I have to close it. I have to look down and take my eyes off the road. In addition, the close button is very, very tiny.
- I sometimes see interesting billboards, but can never remember them afterward.
- I am always trying to find the best place to put gas: I do not want it to be too expensive, but I do not want to run out either.
- When driving somewhere new, I would like to learn more about the place I am in.

CANDIDATE: Can I get some time to brainstorm solutions?

INTERVIEWER: Go ahead.

Candidate takes one minute.

CANDIDATE: I can think of a few ideas:

- **Advertising.** I believe Google already does this, but I might be wrong: let's say a user is looking for something like, "Nearby Italian restaurants," Google Maps would show this information. The first two or three could be sponsored restaurants. Another use would be highlighting sponsored shops, companies, and even billboards on the GPS as the user is driving past.

- **Sightseeing.** Tourism is a multi-billion dollar industry, and this Google Maps can tap into it. Travel sites can build companion travel guide apps that will lead tourists around the city built on top of Google Maps. It will feel like a personal tour guide, powered by software.
- **Prepaying for gas services.** Give an option to prepay, perhaps with Google Wallet, for gas. The user can choose to use the prepaid gas credit at any affiliated gas station, minimizing worry and effort for the consumer.

INTERVIEWER: Which one would you recommend?

CANDIDATE: I'm not a fan of advertising because of the negative consequences, especially when driving. Prepaying for gas services is interesting, but I don't think that opportunity is as big as the sightseeing idea. Sightseeing is a largely untapped and completely new market. I believe it complements the Google Maps experience, creates a new monetization opportunity, and furthers Maps' engagement goals.

The cons for this opportunity include the effort, the opportunity costs, and the creation of a new outreach team for travel developers. Lastly, some may think this is a small opportunity. However, more people are traveling than ever, especially millennials. Millennials value (travel) experiences over possessions. That's why Airbnb has grown to be a multi-billion dollar company that's served tens of millions of guests.

INTERVIEWER: That's a good point.

CANDIDATE: Given that this is a monetization question, did you want me to do a back-of-the-envelope calculation of the market opportunity?

INTERVIEWER: There's no need. I got a good sense of your analytical abilities on an earlier question, and I'd like to move on to the next.

CANDIDATE: Sounds good.

Disney Experience with Your Phone

Create an experience around Disney theme parks using your phone.

Things to Consider

- You are not compelled to use Google products.
- To help you get started, here are some pain points to consider:
    - What to do?
    - Where is my kid?
    - Where can I find good bargains?
    - How do I minimize my wait times?

Common Mistakes

- Suggesting a Disney theme park map that provides the optimal route to maximize rides or any other idea that feels unoriginal and overused.
- Suggesting an auto-recommender feature and being vague about the implementation by stating "machine learning" is the solution, without going into details.
- Trying to force the CIRCLES Method™ into the discussion, when the interviewer simply wants a list of ideas.

Answer

CANDIDATE: I would begin by understanding goals and objectives. Then I'd jump into customer personas, evaluate their needs, brainstorm solutions, talk about tradeoffs, and then make a recommendation.

INTERVIEWER: That sounds like a reasonable plan, and I think you would want to do that if this were your full-time job. Unfortunately, we only have a few minutes left. Can you just brainstorm some creative ideas for me?

CANDIDATE: Okay.

Candidate takes one minute.

CANDIDATE: Here are my ideas:

- **Smart photos.** Whenever you take a picture, the app will suggest photo edits. The app will indicate characters and objects related to the place you are capturing (e.g., Aladdin and his flying carpet appear next to his palace). The app will also recognize individuals wearing costumes based on Disney characters.
- **Snapchat & Instagram-like filters**. When taking selfies, superimpose Disney characters on you or your friends' heads.
- **Enhanced Info.** As you review your Disneyland photos, you can turn on the enhanced information feature. It will point out key Disney characters and locations to your photos with a summary caption. There is also an on-screen link where you can get more Wikipedia-like information.
- **Mickey is Calling.** Whenever you walk to a place, you will get a phone call from the major characters related to the place. For example, if you walk near Aladdin's palace, Aladdin or the Genie to call and talk to you.
- **Social upgrades.** You can gain points to skip the line or get free souvenirs if you share your photos to Instagram or Snapchat.

INTERVIEWER: Which ideas do you think will offer the best experience?

CANDIDATE: I believe the smart photo idea is the best. People naturally take photos during a trip to Disneyland, especially selfies. Many tourists do not go to Disneyland every day, and they do not want to miss major sights and sounds. Smart photos will minimize regret by pointing out every single photo opportunity they should exploit during their vacation. Finally, there is high potential to share those photos, helping Disneyland generate social proof and word-of-mouth marketing.

Mobile App Design for Nest

Design the next product that Nest should offer.

Things to Consider

- To increase your chances of getting one impressive idea, brainstorm at least three solutions.
- Explain why you suggested certain ideas.

Common Mistakes

- Answering casually.
- Giving a stream-of-consciousness answer that is hard to answer.

Answer

CANDIDATE: Hmm, can I get some time to brainstorm?

Candidate takes one minute.

CANDIDATE: I have a few ideas in mind.

- **Smart Garage Door.** I am thinking of a smartphone app that reports your position to the garage door opener. It would then check traffic based on Google Maps and estimate how far you will be from home. It will then have the door open by the time you enter your driveway. The inverse happens when you leave: it would automatically close the door when your car leaves the driveway. The garage door would close based on your iPhone's location. Your garage door can also infer your location when your phone loses connection with your home's Wi-Fi network.
- **Smart Water Heater.** There are devices that heat your home's water based on time of day or water level. It would be more impressive if a user's devices share water heating scenarios where there is a high likelihood of hot water usage, such as when a person finishes a sports activity. With fitness trackers becoming ubiquitous, this type of information sharing is becoming more likely.
- **Smart Pet Feeder.** You can set a pet feeding schedule. You can also receive a notification when your pet is hungry and starts banging on the machine. With a phone swipe, you can dispense food remotely.

There are some common themes for all of these product ideas: monitor and control your home while you're away. It gives homeowners peace of mind. I'd be surprised if this isn't Nest's mission statement.

INTERVIEWER: Which idea do you recommend?

CANDIDATE: Based on market potential?

INTERVIEWER: Yes.

CANDIDATE: If I had time, I would build a profit forecast to understand the business impact to the company. Did you want me to do a back of the envelope calculation now?

INTERVIEWER: That's not necessary. Just go ahead and tell me which one your gut says has the most market potential.

CANDIDATE: Based on my gut, the smart garage door has the most potential. There are many homeowners in the United States. They are worried about home safety. Having a device that monitors whether a garage door is open or closed gives them peace of mind. The smart water heater provides conservation but not safety benefits. Lastly, the smart pet feeder, while it is cruel to have a loved pet go hungry, it is unlikely to drive as much peace of mind as a smart garage door.

Local Service Recommendation Engine

How would you design a better local service recommendation engine? We want it to be better than Yelp. The recommendation engine will cover everyone from pediatricians to plumbers. Answer this from a consumer, not a small business perspective.

Things to Consider

- Use the CIRCLES design framework.
- Build a customer journey map to help uncover pain points.
- Push yourself to come up with big, innovative ideas.

Common Mistakes

- Oversimplifying the solution.
- Proposing a magical solution without going into the implementation details. For instance, "Yelp will magically find the best local service for our customers. It will be so easy. Just press the 'I'm Feeling Lucky' button and voila – Yelp will suggest the perfect service."
- Not picking a specific scenario and/or customer problem, leading to generic solutions.

Answer

CANDIDATE: Can I get one minute to brainstorm?

Candidate takes one minute.

CANDIDATE: I am a Yelp user; I usually use it for restaurants, so maybe my perspective is a bit different. Since we are going for all types of stores, it's hard to break down our users into segments. Therefore, I think it's easier to talk about users in general.

I can think of several problems when I use Yelp:

1. Not enough information about store environment and cost.
2. Not enough information about parking and directions.
3. No "what others who like this service also likes _____" recommendation service.

For the first one, Yelp doesn't actually tell you what the environment is like. For example, how should I dress for a particular restaurant: casual, business casual, or jacket and tie? You don't know. You end up having to flip through pictures just to spot how other people are dressed. Cost is likewise ambiguous. Yelp indicates price on a one to five scale, indicated by dollar signs. A restaurant marked as $$ could range from $11 to $30 per person. That is a big range.

For the second one, there is not a lot of information on the optimal way to park at a restaurant. You have to scour through the customer comments in order to find it, assuming someone commented on this. A picture of where the parking is would also be great. Sometimes stores have parking away from the premise. Another thing is directions. A map is not enough. I want a street view of what it looks like so I don't miss it.

For the third one, if you are looking at a store and you don't like it, I have to go back to the search results and click on the next one. Why doesn't Yelp suggest "stores like this"? It would save a lot of time.

All of my problems relate to customer convenience, which would increase user engagement and retention. There are also opportunities, especially in the third case, to increase monetization.

INTERVIEWER: How would you improve it if you were making a similar product?

CANDIDATE: I would address the problems above. Let me provide solutions for them all.

For the first one, I would have more information. I would ask the store to fill this information first. For the environment that's easy to do. For the price, a manual upload of the menu and averaging the cost would work. Customers could also verify this. The problem would be getting stores and customers to engage and fill in, but that's an existing problem on Yelp anyway. I think by providing a field for it, people would be more likely to fill it in.

For the second one, I would see if I could grab Google Map's Street View. That would solve both problems. If you don't see parking in front of the store, then that's when you need more information. I would ask customers or stores to fill in. As long as we have a field for it people would be more likely to fill it in.

For the last one, we just need an algorithm to do this. We can track based on what others like. We can rank based on how many users like restaurant B who also like A. We rank every restaurant that is related to A this way, then present the best. We can also display restaurants that are advertising through us on this which will increase our revenue. Obviously, these need to be within the proximity too. I know Yelp currently has something similar, but it's more weighted toward proximity as far as I know.

INTERVIEWER: Your suggestions are geared toward restaurants but not other types of services.

CANDIDATE: I can't deny that, but I feel like many services would benefit from this as well. Numerous services require parking and could benefit more from clear, precise price information. They could definitely also benefit from Street View-like images. I can't tell how many times I've gotten lost because a store or a clinic is hidden behind several buildings.

INTERVIEWER: Which one would you recommend?

CANDIDATE: I would recommend the third one: the service recommendation engine. It directly boosts our revenue and customer satisfaction. It would be the hardest technically, but it requires no user adoption which means it just depends on how fast we can do it.

INTERVIEWER: How would you track its success?

CANDIDATE: I would see how many users are actually clicking on recommendations. We could also survey users on whether they found the recommendations helpful, either in the interface or through an email survey three days later.

Another way would be to see if our ad revenue is going up. If sponsored restaurants saw a business increase, then they would decide this is cost-effective and spend more marketing dollars with us.

Lego

If you were the CEO of LEGO, what new product line would you come up with to increase revenues? Why? Who is the target customer? How do you reach them? How does the product function and what does it look like (UX/UI)? What is the potential market size?

Things to Consider

- Even though this prompt has many sub-questions, tackle it in two parts. Part 1 is a product design question. Part 2 is a market estimation question.

Common Mistakes

- Not wanting to make calculations because the candidate is insecure about calculating numbers.
- Feeling overwhelmed with the multi-question answer and reacting with a hard-to-follow, poorly thought-out response.
- Not being clear to the interviewer about which sub-question you are tackling and what your overall approach will be.

Answer

CANDIDATE: Can I get some time to brainstorm?

Candidate takes one minute.

CANDIDATE: I am thinking of targeting adults who have played with Legos in the past. In other words, let's capitalize on nostalgia. Nostalgia drives sales in many consumer-oriented industries including video games, movies, and books. You often hear people talking fondly of playing with Legos. Another data point: the popularity of *The Lego Movie*, especially with adults, shows that nostalgia can be profitable.

- **Pre-built sets.** Sell nostalgic pre-built sets for adults. Nostalgic sets have built-in familiarity and hence demand. Adults can buy them and place them around home. I recommended pre-built because adults have no time to play with Lego either building them from scratch or tinkering with them.
- **Lego-fy.** This lets you buy pieces that you can use to Lego-fy your home. Examples would be cup-holders or utensil holders in your kitchen. This has become a trend lately and would work well in nostalgic adults.
- **Adult Sets.** Try to sell it to adults who have more time and want to reminiscence. These Adult Sets would be more complicated than your standard Lego set. I know Lego tried this in the past, but it did not work because it was too different from the standard Lego set. We would learn from past mistakes by

including detailed instruction booklets (think Ikea) and online videos. It's up to the adult if they want to follow the instructions or attempt to build the set on their own.

INTERVIEWER: Which one do you recommend?

CANDIDATE: As a kid, I found it most rewarding building Legos and feeling a sense of accomplishment afterward. I strongly believe that pre-built sets would take the fun away. Lego-fy is an interesting trend, but I am not sure how big that market is. Therefore, I would recommend the adult sets. Grown-ups would love adult-themed Legos.

INTERVIEWER: How would you market to these people?

CANDIDATE: I would focus on efficient advertising vehicles where the Lego enthusiasts would hang out. I have found that engineers are more likely to be Lego fans. Therefore, I would target websites and social media networks where engineers hang out including:

- Reddit
- Stack Overflow
- Hacker News
- TechCrunch
- Wired
- Gizmodo
- Mashable
- TheVerge

Social media, such as Instagram, Facebook, and Snapchat would make a lot of sense, especially if we have exciting teaser videos. I would also take advantage of our retail presence. I believe Lego operates approximately 100 retail stores around the world.

INTERVIEWER: Can you identify the potential market size?

CANDIDATE: Okay, for the sake of time, can I do a back-of-the-envelope calculation for the US only?

INTERVIEWER: Sure.

CANDIDATE: I will also assume that nostalgic adults, from 35 to 50 years old, are the most likely customers for the Adult Sets.

INTERVIEWER: Works for me.

Assumptions

- US Population is around 320 million.
- US Life Expectancy is around 80 years. For the sake of simplicity, let us assume a uniform age distribution.
- The age range from 35 to 50 years old spans a total of 15 years.

- Lego's adoption rate is probably around 30%.

Calculating Potential Market Size

$$Market\ Size = US\ Population * Target\ Market * Adoption\ Rate$$

$$Market\ Size = 320\ million * \left(\frac{15}{80}\right) * 30\%$$

$$Market\ Size = 18\ million$$

INTERVIEW: Thank you.

Better Starbucks

Design a better Starbucks.

Things to Consider

- Use the CIRCLES design framework.
- Rant for hard-hitting pain points.
- Brainstorm many ideas to increase your chances of having a memorable and impactful idea.

Common Mistakes

- Blurting "Just make the coffee better" and other similarly hasty responses.
- Not empathizing with the customer deeply enough, limiting your ability to come up with innovative ideas.
- Copying competitor's innovations, like Blue Bottle's cold-drip coffee makers below, is a sign of an unoriginal and uncreative candidate.

Answer

CANDIDATE: Is there a goal or focus for the improvement? That is, do we want to generate more revenue, get more customers, or improve customer satisfaction?

INTERVIEWER: What would you recommend?

CANDIDATE: I would focus on customer satisfaction. It starts a virtuous cycle that leads to repeat purchases and word-of-mouth marketing, all of which are positive for long-term revenue.

INTERVIEWER: I like that. Okay, go ahead.

CANDIDATE: Can you give me some time to brainstorm?

Candidate takes one minute.

CANDIDATE: Let us consider first Starbucks' problems, analyze them, and then propose solutions.

INTERVIEWER: All right, sounds fair.

CANDIDATE: I can think of a few problems.

Candidate writes the following on whiteboard.

- **Long Lines**. *The stores have long lines, which could lead to lost sales.*
- **Crowded**. *Sometimes it is hard to find seating when there are so many people.*
- **Limited Electrical Outlets**. *Customers often bring their laptops. There are not enough outlets.*
- **Poor furniture**. *Chairs are uncomfortable, especially for those who are spending hours studying or working. The tables are too small, making it awkward to have anything more than a laptop or a single book on the table.*
- **Small food portions**. *I understand eating smaller portions is healthier, but I would never consider Starbucks food for anything more than a light snack.*
- **Expensive prices**. *Some Starbucks beverages are so expensive. Instead of a Starbucks' Grande Frappuccino, I can buy a complete meal, beverage included, at McDonald's.*

INTERVIEWER: Which problem do you think is the most severe?

CANDIDATE: I would choose long lines. Starbucks' mobile order pay feature has helped, but I believe there is room for improvement.

INTERVIEWER: What is your solution for it?

CANDIDATE: I can think of a few solutions.

- **Waiting Area.** Have a special area where customers can wait for their orders. Comfortable sofas with a TV and some magazines would be a start. Customers can relax while waiting for their drinks.
- **Store Status.** Check your local store's status on Starbucks' mobile app and website. Get information like an estimated wait time. This way you can decide if you want to go or not. You can also add additional features like checking food and beverage inventory.
- **Reservation.** Allow customers to reserve tables. The store can then gauge how many users are coming in over the next hour and give you a warning if you are reserving for an hour that is already flooded with people. It can show an estimated wait time so you can decide if you want to reserve it for a particular hour.

INTERVIEWER: Which idea would you implement?

CANDIDATE: By the process of elimination, I would eliminate the Waiting Area first. Having a Waiting Area would take space away from sitting customers. Reservation is interesting, but it could annoy walk-ins if they see an empty table they cannot use.

That leaves us with Store Status. I'm a big fan of this idea. Expectation setting is important for a good customer service experience. Leading transportation companies, such as UPS and FedEx, have done a fantastic job setting expectations on when customers can expect to receive their deliveries, down to the minute.

One of the biggest challenges with implementing Store Status is how to give reliable estimates. Before the advent of smartphone technology, wait time information would be a manual and error-prone process. However, with smartphones and high adoption of the Starbucks app, we can estimate wait times based on how many Starbucks app users are at a given store. We can calibrate and re-calibrate the estimates based on the smartphone app data and empirical observation. In other words, we would apply machine-learning algorithms for the Store Status feature.

INTERVIEWER: Let us say you launch the Store Status feature. How would you know if it is working as intended?

CANDIDATE: For Store Status, here are the metrics I would track, in priority order:

1. Decrease in wait times
2. Increase in daily store revenue
3. Increase in daily store visits
4. Increase in net promoter score
5. Decrease in queue length

INTERVIEWER: Thank you.

Favorite Product

Tell me about your favorite product. How would you improve it?

Things to Consider

- Get on the same page on what constitutes a favorite product by sharing your criteria.
- Compare with alternate products to help the interviewer appreciate why your chosen product is special.
- If necessary, explain what the product is, in case the interviewer is not familiar with it.

Common Mistakes

- Not providing a scorecard upfront.
- Choosing a product that the interviewer is unfamiliar with, causing the interviewer to get bored.
- Picking a trite example such as the iPhone.

Answer

CANDIDATE: Can you give me some time to brainstorm?

Candidate takes one minute.

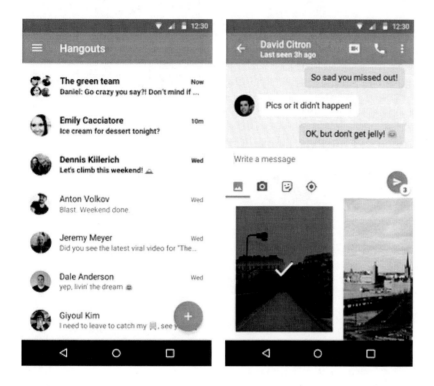

Screenshot / Google Hangouts

CANDIDATE: My favorite product is Google Hangouts. It's my favorite because it satisfies my three requirements for a good product. That is:

- Is it useful?
- Is it innovative?
- Is it easy to understand and use?

Let me go into more detail.

First, Google Hangouts is extremely useful. I use it every day to talk to all of my Gmail contacts. Since Gmail is the primary email most people use, it's useful to have all of your contacts in a single chat program.

Second, Google Hangouts is innovative. Sure, the concept of an instant messenger isn't exactly new, but who built on top of email? Google did. One of the biggest requirements for an instant messenger is the user base. A large pre-existing user base gives users more utility; it's less useful if a user's friends aren't on it.

It's also useful for the company because they don't have to spend as much time or money trying to acquire new customers. Google is lucky that they can use Gmail to bootstrap a new product like Hangouts.

Third, Google Hangouts is easy to use and understand. The UI is intuitive. And there's a crawl, walk, run adoption path. If users aren't comfortable downloading a mobile app, they can get started by using the Hangouts-like chat function inside Gmail. That Gmail chat function is so simple that there's no need for a tutorial, especially for savvy tech users.

To summarize, I like Google Hangouts because it's useful, innovative, and easy to understand and use.

INTERVIEWER: How would you improve it?

CANDIDATE: Can I get some time to brainstorm?

Candidate takes one minute.

CANDIDATE: I would argue that engagement is the most important metric for Google Hangouts. Hangouts serves as a valuable strategic asset: it competes with WhatsApp, Skype, WeChat, and Facebook's Messenger application. Users spend a lot of time on messaging applications; Google could monetize that time spent on messaging applications with its Google ad network. I'd argue that Google should delay monetizing Hangouts. Placing ads on Google Hangout now could lead to short-term revenue. However, short-term engagement could decline which could affect long-term profits.

INTERVIEWER: Why should Google only choose between showing and not showing ads on Hangouts? Why not be messaging platform-agnostic and show ads on all messaging platforms: Facebook Messenger, Instagram, Snapchat, and WeChat. That way Google can make money regardless of who is winning the messenger race.

CANDIDATE: It sounds good in theory, but there are a few problems:

1. **Competitors have their own ad networks**. For instance, Facebook has the second-largest ad network. It's unlikely that Facebook would show Google ads on WhatsApp and Facebook Messenger.
2. **Platform control**. Skype could choose to show ads from Google one day and a competitor the next. That is a risk we do not want to take.
3. **Traffic acquisition costs**. We would have to split ad revenue with the property owner, which can be costly.
4. **International restrictions**. Western companies cannot easily access international markets like China, due to government restrictions.

INTERVIEWER: Good assessment. So how would you improve engagement on Google Hangouts?

I would like to improve customer satisfaction by making it more convenient. I can think of a few ideas.

1. **Status when sending videos and images.** Whenever you send an image or video right now, it just says "sending…" on Google Hangouts. I can't tell how much longer I should wait or if the system is stuck. Sometimes it fails for no reason, which is frustrating. I would like to know the current upload status to minimize my anxiety.
2. **Friend finder.** Google Hangouts is built on Gmail contacts. Some people would like to find new friends, beyond their Gmail contacts. A way to find people by location would be good. For example, let's say I meet someone new at lunch. I'd like to add that person, who happens to be sitting one meter away from me. Google also needs a way to find your business contacts. Perhaps a user directory feature that allows you to search or add a user by phone number or name.
3. **Status.** Google+ isn't working out, and Google, I am sure, would love to get in social networks. Google can attempt to build a social network on top of Google Hangouts or Gmail. They can start small by adding a status message. It would be similar to the status feature on the now-defunct AOL Instant Messenger. The benefit of the status field is that it allows you to share a little bit about you and what's

going on. If people really like this feature, we can add more and grow it one step at a time to a social network.

INTERVIEWER: Which idea would you recommend?

CANDIDATE: I think the sending image and video status would be the easiest to do, but besides making the experience a bit better, it's not as impactful as the other two. Friend finder is nice, but I think I like Status a lot more. I think we have a real opportunity to grow Hangouts into a social network.

I currently use an app called WeChat that is made by Tencent. Tencent has QQ, originally a desktop instant messenger in China. WeChat is similar but more focused on the mobile experience. By having something a bit more complex but not too much more than status, WeChat is growing into a large social network. I think Google Hangouts with something small like a status feature has similar potential. Also, if you look at how users in the USA use Slack, the popular workplace chat app, a lot of them will include a small status in their name field to share with coworkers such as "Remote" or "Meetings All Day."

INTERVIEWER: Thank you.

Favorite Website

What's your favorite website and why?

Things to Consider

- First, establish your criteria for what would qualify as your favorite website.
- Then, explain what the website is.
- Lastly, explain why the website meets your criteria.

Common Mistakes

- Not explaining (or explaining poorly) what the website is because the candidate assumes the listener knows the product that they are talking about.
- Neglecting to draw what the current or proposed website looks like. Pictures are more effective than words. A low fidelity sketch, taking no more than a few minutes, will suffice.
- Not aligning with the interviewer on what constitutes the "favorite" website.

Answer

CANDIDATE: Can you give me a minute to brainstorm?

Candidate takes a minute.

CANDIDATE: When I think about my favorite website, it has to meet these three criteria:
- How useful is it?
- How innovative is it?
- Is it easy to use and understand?

The first website that comes to mind and meets these criteria is Splitwise. Splitwise is a website where friends and roommates can track bills and other shared expenses. It's useful because it's hard to remember who owes whom and for what reason. It's even synced with PayPal and allows friends to pay each other back. Therefore, it meets my usefulness criteria.

It also meets criteria number two: innovative. I haven't found another website that offers a similar solution. I admire Splitwise because it fixes one problem well and in the simplest way possible.

Lastly, Splitwise meets my last criteria: it is easy to understand and use. As soon as you enter the website, it shows your payment history in the main panel and a big red "Add a bill" button. You can click on any payment and see more details. It doesn't surprise me that there's no first-run tutorial because it is so intuitive to use.

To conclude, Splitwise is my favorite website because it satisfies my requirement for a good website: useful, innovative, and easy to use.

Screenshot / Splitwise

Car for the Blind

Enumerate and prioritize use cases for a self-driving car targeted for blind people. Justify everything with sound logic.

Things to Consider

Don't forget to clarify the interviewer's intent if it's unclear. Here, the interviewer only wants a subset of the CIRCLES Method™, articulating use cases and then prioritization, not the full framework.

Common Mistakes

Not mentioning safety issues

Answer

CANDIDATE: I have a quick clarifying question. When you say, "self-driving car for blind people" do you mean a self-driving taxi service (think: Uber) for the blind? Or selling a self-driving car, targeted to blind drivers (think: Tesla)?

INTERVIEWER: The latter.

CANDIDATE: Okay. I would think about constraints first. Are we limited by tech?

INTERVIEWER: What do you mean by tech?

CANDIDATE: Can we make these self-driving cars? I don't really see any other way blind people can drive around otherwise. Even with self-driving cars, we might have some legal issues.

INTERVIEWER: Let's say we can do self-driving cars, and we don't have legal problems.

CANDIDATE: Okay, then I would first think about our users. I'll then think about our use cases. I'll list out the gaps and address them through new features in our car. I'll then prioritize them.

INTERVIEWER: Okay, go ahead.

CANDIDATE: Blind drivers are our primary users, but we'll also have to consider their friends, relatives, and caretakers. I can see a couple of use cases:

- Drive
- Park
- Location information
- Additional information
- Safety

Use Cases

Drive

You can break this down to very specific use cases, like switching lanes and stopping at red lights. Either way, the car needs to do this without the driver's assistance. The good news is that self-driving car technology is capable of doing this already. The bad news is that California requires self-driving cars to have the driver put at least one hand on the steering wheel. They do take traffic laws seriously and according to traffic laws, blind people can't drive. However, I guess that is the question's challenge, "What if blind people can have a self-driving car?"

The other challenge is that since blind people cannot see what is going on, it makes it hard for the driver to assess whether the car should speed up or slow down. One potential way to alleviate this is with audio feedback. For instance, the car can alert the driver that it is turning left or stopping at a red light.

Park

The car needs to auto-park. Once again, cars are capable of doing that today. Our key requirement here is audio feedback; the car can inform the user of the nearest landmark. For example, "Your car is parked in front of the Starbucks on Third Avenue" or "Your car is on the third floor of the parking garage, in spot 312."

Location Information

The driver may also want to share this location data when meeting friends.

Additional Information

Outside of location information, there may be some additional information the driver or passengers might find helpful such as which direction the blind driver is facing or whether the blind driver should be careful when exiting the car, especially if he or she parked next to a curb or if there is oncoming traffic.

Safety

In instances where either the car or driver is unable to drive effectively, the car should have the appropriate safety features to prevent the drivers from harming themselves or others. Options to have the car pull over and stop or perhaps allow a remote person to control the vehicle, like a drone operator, would be helpful.

INTERVIEWER: Thank you.

Phone for the Deaf

Design a phone for the deaf.

Things to Consider

- The interviewer is testing your ability to empathize with the target persona, even if you may not be deaf yourself.
- While you may not be familiar with what it's like to be deaf, you will be surprised with what you uncover, if you take the time to contemplate their needs.

Common Mistakes

- Rather than answering the question, responding with a process that you'd use to approach this problem in real life.

Answer

CANDIDATE: Are we talking about a cellphone or a home phone?

INTERVIEWER: Cellphone.

CANDIDATE: A smartphone or flip phone?

INTERVIEWER: A smartphone.

CANDIDATE: Our primary users are going to be deaf people. I would also say their relatives and friends will be secondary users.

Let me think of some use cases and their flaws:

1. **Call someone.** A deaf person can't tell what the person on the other line is saying.
2. **Receive a call.** A deaf person cannot tell if the phone is ringing.
3. **Listening to someone.** A deaf person cannot tell what the person on the other line is saying.
4. **Alarm.** A deaf person can see visual alarms but cannot hear an audio one.
5. **Apps.** Apps that require hearing, such as music apps, will not be useful.

We can solve these problems with the following features:

1. **Vibrations.** We have to be thoughtful about how we vary vibrations so that different vibrations can represent different things, whether it is an incoming call or a wakeup alarm.
2. **Haptics.** Similar to vibrations, haptics provides tactile feedback that is more subtle than a vibration. The phone should allow developers to program or signal different haptic or vibration patterns.
3. **Lights.** We need to make sure the phone lights up more when a call is coming in or the alarm is sounding.
4. **Captioning.** We need call captioning. Therefore, when someone is talking with the deaf person on the phone, the computer converts spoken words into text.
5. **Text-to-voice.** On the other end, the other person may not want to read and want to hear voice instead. For this reason, there is an option to have the phone voice the text the deaf person typed during a call.
6. **Specialized app store.** We need a section in the app store for deaf-friendly apps.
7. **Request that the other party engage in a video call.** A video call can help those who are lip readers.

INTERVIEWER: That is a good list. Thank you.

ATM for the Elderly

How would you design an ATM for elderly people?

Things to Consider

- Use the CIRCLES Method™.
- Rant to get deeper and more insightful customer pain points.

Common Mistakes

188

- Needlessly defining the persona further, given that the interviewer the persona already.
- Going straight into solutions and not discussing pain points first.

Answer

CANDIDATE: Would non-elderly use this ATM?

INTERVIEWER: Yes.

CANDIDATE: Let me think about some of the pain points the elderly have with ATMs:

- Can't see the text.
- Get tired standing up.
- Need human assistance.
- Potential confusion on whether the ATM card should be swiped or inserted.
- Get startled when the machine beeps or takes a long time to complete an operation.
- Unclear why I can only deposit cash at some ATMs but not all of them.
- Concerned when there's a long line of customers waiting behind me.

CANDIDATE: All right. Let me think of some features that address the needs of the elderly while not taking out features that would make it harder to use for the non-elderly.

- We have to make sure it's placed inside. It might get windy and cold outside.
- The text on the screen needs to be big because elderly people might have difficulty seeing.
- The sound needs to be louder because elderly people might have trouble hearing.
- It should be an ATM that allows you to sit down.
- The ATM should allow wheelchair access.
- Chairs should be available. Waiting customers may want to sit.
- Hand supports might be an option, especially if they're having trouble maintaining balance.
- There should be a big, noticeable button to ask for help.
- Have a sign noting that the elderly or handicapped have priority for this ATM and that they should be encouraged to go before others in line for this ATM, similar to signs on reserved seats on busses.

Lastly, it goes without saying, ATMs for the elderly should have all the features of regular ATMs such as withdrawing and depositing money, inquiring about your account balance, and printing statements.

Physical Product

What is your favorite physical product? Why? Also, give me big ideas on how you would triple its revenue.

Things to Consider

- This is a combination question. Part 1 requires you to identify a favorite product and explain why. Part 2 asks you to brainstorm ideas.
- For part two, use the CIRCLES Method™.
- In your answer, don't forget to connect your ideas with the goal: increasing tripling revenue.

- Coming up with ideas that don't meet the 3X revenue objective.
- Answering part 1 and not part 2. Or vice versa.
- Failing to come up with a big, game-changing idea.

Answer

CANDIDATE: Hmm, my answer is somewhat weird, but I am going to stand by it. My favorite physical product is a water boiler I have. It fits my three great criteria for a good product:

1. As little design as possible
2. Easy-to-understand
3. Thorough down to the last detail

First, it is not complicated. There is only one button on the device. I press it, and it boils water.

Second, it's easy-to-understand. The power cord clearly goes into the electrical outlet. There is a lid to refill it with water. Once I've filled it, I set it onto the heating plate and then press the button to boil. A light turns on to indicate it's warming up. When it is finished boiling, it makes a sound and the light turns off. It doesn't get easier to understand than that.

Third, it is thorough down to the last detail. Here are some examples:

- **Auto shut off** eliminates my anxiety. It also frees me up to work on other tasks while boiling.
- **Pot handle** makes it easy to transport with one hand vs. two.
- **Heating plate** decouples the electrical cord from the pot. If the inventor attached the electrical cord to the pot, then the cord would flap around awkwardly when pouring.

To conclude, my water boiler is my favorite physical product. It is not complicated, it's easy-to-understand, and it is thorough down to the last detail.

INTERVIEWER: How would you improve it with some big ideas to increase its revenue by three times?

CANDIDATE: Hmm, give me some time to think.

Candidate takes one minute.

CANDIDATE: I can think of a few ideas.

- **Water quality inspector.** I often boil water to use in my coffee press. Using filtered water improves coffee quality. I often forget to use filtered water. If my pot could detect the water quality and remind me to use filtered water, I would enjoy my coffee more.
- **Water temperature keeper.** Some people like hot water whereas some people like warm water. In addition to indicating the temperature, the boiler should maintain a user-specified temperature.
- **SUDO Make me a hot beverage.** SUDO refers to UNIX's superuser command that feels like having the superpower do anything a user wants. This is my big, and yes crazy, idea because you challenged me to

triple revenue. Boiling water is often a means to an end. When using a water boiler, my end objective is to have a hot beverage. A hot beverage could be something simple like tea or hot water with lemon and honey. It could be something more complicated like coffee or a latte. Or it can be very sophisticated like soup. If we had a magical machine that would create multiple hot beverages, at a reasonable price and high quality, the convenience factor alone could expand revenue potential dramatically.

INTERVIEWER: I like the SUDO reference. And I'm with you. This does not seem as far-fetched as it sounds. Keurig and Nespresso machines do what you suggest. Let's say it's an instant soup machine. How would that work?

CANDIDATE: I would design it like a Nespresso machine: the machine will take canisters of food along with a water reservoir. The food canister includes the soup base and freeze-dried food ingredients. The machine would warm up the water, mix the food canister ingredients with water, and then serve the hot soup to the user. Anyone who's had instant soup or ramen knows this is within the realm of possibility.

INTERVIEWER: I am a huge fan of soup, especially during cold winter months. Sign me up for your soup-making water boiler.

Chapter 15 Metrics: Brainstorming Exercises

Metrics for eCommerce

What are the top metrics you would track for an eCommerce website?

Things to Consider

- Examples of top e-commerce websites include:
    - US: Amazon, Walmart, Apple
    - India: Amazon, Flipkart, Snapdeal.
    - China: Tmall, JD, Suning
    - Europe: Tesco, Zalando, Otto
- Consider sales, marketing, and website metrics
- Use AARM Method™: Acquisition, Activation, Retention, Monetization

Answer

Acquisition

- Daily sessions
- Cost per acquisition (CPA)
- Cost per click (CPC)
- Cost per impression (CPM)
- Top search engine terms leading to website
- Mailing list click-through rate
- Mailing list open rate
- Mailing list conversion rate
- Mobile app downloads

Activation

- New registered users
- Mobile app opens
- Number of searches on website or app
- New cart started
- User information given (address, credit card, etc.)
- New customers with a successful purchase

Retention

- Conversion rate
- Recommendation engine conversion rate
- Shopping cart abandonment
- Shopping cart size

- Visits from activated users per month

Monetization

- Revenue per customer
- Lapsed customers
- Purchases per year
- Revenue per click
- Cost of sale (ad spend / revenue)
- Customer lifetime value (CLV)
- Cost of shipping

Other

- Average listing position on the Google search results page for the most important keywords
- Cost of goods sold
- Shipping time
- Stockouts
- Returns
- Checkout errors
- Number of reviews left by customers
- Viral coefficient (Number of users that each customer refers)
- Market share
- Customer engagement on social media
- Net or gross margin

Metrics for Two-sided Marketplaces

What are top metrics you would track for a two-sided marketplace?

Things to Consider

- Examples of two-sided marketplaces include:
    - Ridesharing: Uber, Lyft, Kuaidadi
    - Lodging: Airbnb, Booking.com, Expedia
    - Peer-to-peer marketplaces: Craigslist, eBay, OfferUp
    - Talent: Indeed.com
- Keep in mind that the interviewer is likely referring to metrics that a marketplace owner, such as Airbnb, would track. Do not offer buyer or seller metrics, unless explicitly asked to do so.

Answer

Marketplace Metrics, Buy-Side

Acquisition

- Mobile app downloads

Activation

- Users with at least 1 search

Retention

- Searches
- Searches with 1+ Matches
- CTR for search result
- Percent satisfied transactions
- Net promoter score

Monetization

- Revenue
- Avg. transaction size
- Number of transactions

Marketplace Metrics, Sell Side

Acquisition

- Sellers
- Seller growth rate

Activation

- Sellers with at least 1 listing

Retention

- Listings per seller
- Net promoter score

Monetization

- Gross marketplace volume
- Percent of fraudulent transactions

Other

- Seller concentration, that is the percent of revenue generated by the top X percent of sellers
- Marketplace as a percent of overall channel sales

Metrics for SaaS

What are top metrics you would track for a Software as a Service (SaaS) application?

Things to Consider

Examples of SaaS applications:

- CRM: Salesforce
- Messaging: Slack
- Financial and human capital management: Workday

Answer

Acquisition

- Leads
- Virality

Activation

- New registered users

Retention

- Daily active usage
- Time onsite
- Interval between logins
- Churn

Monetization

- Conversions
- Deal size
- Renewal rate
- Monthly recurring revenue
- Revenue per user
- LTV

Other

- Uptime

Metrics for Mobile Apps

What are top metrics you would track for a mobile application?

Answer

Acquisition

- Number of mobile installs
- Cost per install

Activation

- Number of accounts created, after mobile download

Retention

- Daily and monthly active usage
- Time in app
- Star rating
- Session length
- Percent of users that rate the app

Monetization

- Percent that are paid users
- Lifetime value
- Average revenue per user
- Churn

Metrics for Publishers

What are top metrics you would track for a publisher's website?

Things to Consider

Examples of publishers:

- News: New York Times, India Times, Sina.com
- Sports: ESPN
- User-generated content: Reddit, Quora, Medium.com

Answer
Acquisition

- Unique visitors per month
- Sessions per month
- Monthly page views

Activation

- Number of registrations

Retention

- Pages per session
- Session duration
- Monthly minutes on site
- Daily, weekly, and monthly active usage (DAU, WAU, MAU)
- DAU/MAU ratio
- Churn
- Bounce rate
- Exit rate

Monetization

- Display ad rates (per thousand)
- Banners per page
- CPC (Cost per Click)
- CPC ads per page
- CTR (Click through rate)
- Total CPC ads shown
- Total Clicks
- CPA ads per page
- CPA (Cost per Acquisition)
- Total CPA ads
- CTR on CPA Ads
- Total Clicks on CPA Ads
- Conversion Rate on CPA Ads
- Total Conversions
- Average Sale
- Total Sales
- Value per Visit
- Traffic Acquisition Costs and other Affiliate Payments

Metrics for User-Generated Content Website

What are top metrics you would track for a user-generated content website?

Things to Consider

Examples of user-generated content websites include Reddit, Quora, and Medium.com.

Answer
Acquisition

- Visitors
- Returning visitors

Activation

- Registered users

Retention

- Voters or Flaggers
- Commenters
- Posters
- Moderators

Monetization

- See items from the answer, Metrics for Publishers

Metrics for Support Tickets

What metrics would you track for support tickets?

Things to Consider

- What are the business goals?
- Which metrics correlate with saving money?
- Which metrics correlate with increasing customer satisfaction?

Answer

- Number of customer tickets
- Number of customer tickets by type, including email, call or chat
- Average resolution time
- Concern classification
- Net promoter score
- First call resolution
- Average number of calls per resolution

Uber KPIs

Based upon what you know about Uber and its business model, what are some of the KPIs (key performance indicators) that you would want to focus on to judge how a market is doing overall?

Things to Consider

- From a business goal perspective, what is more important to Uber: revenue or market share?
- From a marketing perspective, what is most important: awareness, interest, trial or purchase?
- What are the most important recurring usage metrics?

Common Mistakes

- Not getting familiar with the topic beforehand, considering how widely Uber's business model and metrics are covered by mainstream business press.

Answer

Acquisition

- Total app downloads

Activation

- Total signups
- % of signups with payment information
- % of signups with at least one ride request
- % of smartphone users who have tried Uber at least once

Retention

- # of Uber customers that open the app and do not see Uber cars in the area (aka zeroes)
- # of requests for an Uber car
- # of completed trips
- Completed trips / Requested trips
- # of rides per month per customer
- DAU, WAU, and MAU
- Miles per ride
- % cancelled trips
- Average driver rating
- % rides with surge pricing
- Median arrival times

Monetization

- Total revenue, by market
- Average fare per trip
- Average fare per driver hour
- Active drivers
- Service hours
- Service hours per driver
- Service hours per driver per day
- Total trips
- Trips per driver
- Trips per driver per day
- Uber's service fee percentage

Chapter 16 Metrics: Prioritization Exercises

Most Important Metric: eCommerce

Pretend you are a venture capitalist. What is the most important metric for any investment you would consider?

Things to Consider

- Venture capital is a high-risk and high-reward business. In other words, they are looking for opportunities where they can recoup their investment multiple times over to cover the cost of risky, yet failed, ventures.
- For an eCommerce company to be worth billions of dollars, the company will have to be dominant in the industry, like Amazon. By dominating, they can enjoy the economies of scale benefits such as:
  - Brand power
  - Extensive logistics infrastructure
  - Negotiation power over suppliers
- Gross merchandising volume represents the total sales volume, in dollars, flowing through an eCommerce site.

Common Mistakes

- Giving a short, uninspiring response (e.g. "I'd go with profits.")

Answer

CANDIDATE: There are several eCommerce metrics to choose from including:

Conversion Rate	Customer acquisition cost	Site traffic by source
Average order size	Margins	Gross merchandising volume
Shopping cart abandonment	Site traffic	Newsletter subscribers

If I were to choose one metric, I would choose gross merchandising volume. Here is why:

- As a venture capitalist, I would like to know how big the business could be. Gross merchandising volume (GMV) can give me a sense of how large the business might be.
- From GMV, we can compute revenue, whether the eCommerce site is based on extracting a commission like eBay or deriving gross margins by selling goods like Amazon.
- GMV is also driven by important metrics such as traffic, conversion rate, and average order size.
- GMV is also a proxy for market position.

As much as I like the GMV metric, there are a few drawbacks:

- GMV does not factor in customer acquisition cost.
- GMV does not consider the cost of sales or other margin information.
- GMV may not be correlated with cash flow.

We could mitigate those drawbacks by tracking those metrics separately.

To summarize, for a prospective eCommerce investment, I would consider GMV as the most important metric.

Most Important Metric: Two-Sided Marketplace

What is the most important metric for a two-sided marketplace like Uber?

Answer

CANDIDATE: Supply-side capacity is the most important metric for two-sided marketplaces. For Uber, supply-side capacity is the number of drivers. For eBay, it's the number of seller listings. For Airbnb, it's the number of apartment rentals.

Take Uber for example. The more drivers there are, the more likely Uber can:

- *Cover a geographic location,* with low wait times.
- *Increase the likelihood of matches,* improving customer satisfaction. Uber calls this process minimizing zeroes. Zeroes are situations where a passenger fires up the app and cannot find a driver.
- *Minimize customer wait times.*
- *Minimize usage of surge pricing, improving the number of completed transactions.*
- *Increase word-of-mouth recruiting for drivers,* especially if current drivers tell potential drivers about the compensation possibilities.

While it may feel that addressing customer demand could be as important, consider the following:

- Uber riders need drivers more than the drivers need the riders.
  - Drivers can find reasonable alternatives to make money.
  - Riders have poor alternatives, especially if they do not own a vehicle. Taxis have spotty coverage and poor service. Public transportation can be inconvenient and unreliable, especially in smaller cities.
- If the riding experience is not of sufficient quality (largely controlled by the drivers), then riders are *unlikely* to adopt Uber's service.
- If the riding experience is of sufficient quality but unavailable (not enough drivers in a geographic area), then riders *cannot* adopt Uber's service.

Most Important Metric: Mobile App

What is the most important metric for a B2C mobile app?

Things to Consider

- For B2C mobile apps, common ways to generate revenue are app purchases, advertising, in-app purchases, and subscription fees.
- For the sake of practice and preventing duplication from the previous question, consider a B2C mobile app that is not Uber.

Answer

CANDIDATE: We should track metrics that tie to an overall goal. I imagine the most important goal is to make money, right?

INTERVIEWER: Yes.

CANDIDATE: There are a few revenue models for B2C mobile apps:

App purchase	$1.99 per download
Advertising	Charge per impression, click, or conversion
In-app purchase	Sell gold, gems, or other upgrades
Subscription model	Charge a recurring monthly fee

Did you want me to consider all of these, or just focus on one?

INTERVIEWER: Since we are short on time, just cover the advertising revenue model.

CANDIDATE: Okay. Let me brainstorm the drivers of B2C app advertising revenue. Give me a moment.

Candidate sketches an issue tree on the next page.

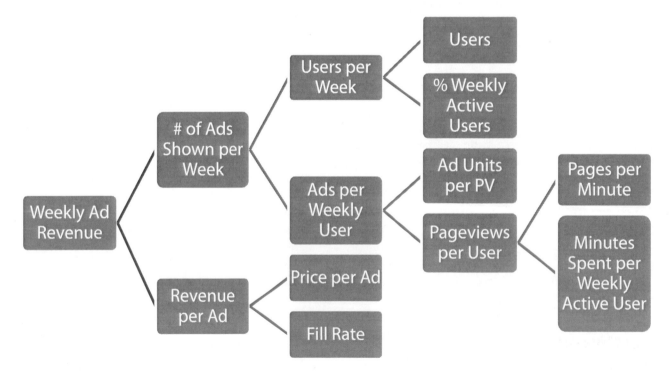

I sketched out the key drivers of mobile app revenue. Looking at the issue tree, the most critical drivers of ad revenue, in my opinion, are users per week and pageviews per user.

I would focus on the following metrics, depending on the company's growth stage:

App Maturity	Focus Metric
New apps	Number of users per week
Newer apps, with product-market fit	Pageviews per user
Mature apps	Ad revenue

INTERVIEWER: That makes sense. Thank you.

Chapter 17 Metrics: Diagnose Exercises

Shopping Cart Conversions

The number of shopping cart conversions is down. What things would you check to diagnose?

Answer

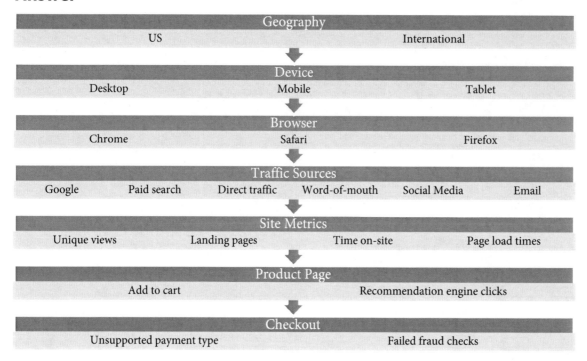

Mobile App Ratings

The number of mobile app ratings is down. What things would you check to diagnose?

Answer

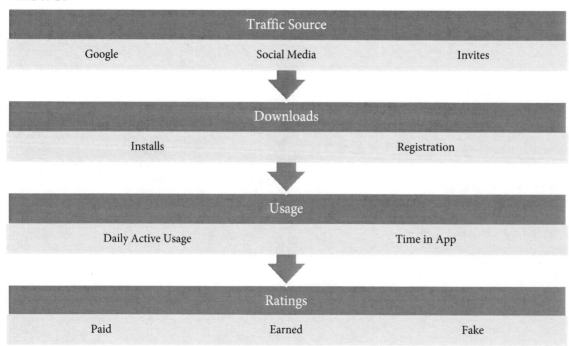

Home Loan Website

You're the product manager for a financial services website. The number of home loans booked through the website is down. What things would you check to diagnose?

Answer

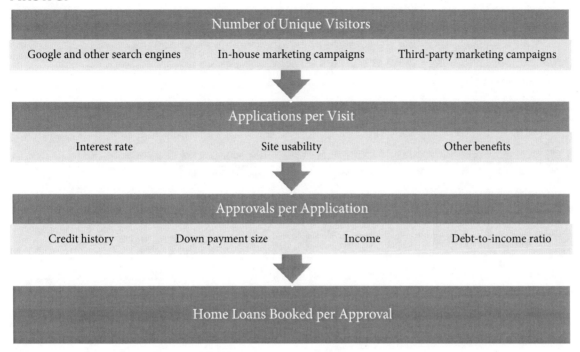

CRM Conversions

Pretend you are the product manager for a popular email marketing automation platform. Your dashboard tells you that aggregate conversions, from customer emails, are down 7% week over week. What happened?

Answer

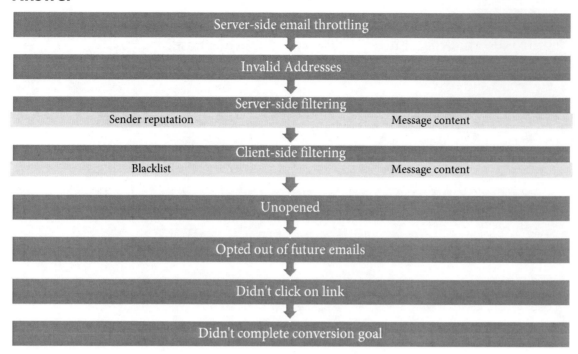

Reddit Posts

The growth in Reddit.com posts has slowed. To diagnose the problem, what would you check?

Answer

CANDIDATE: Many variables can affect post creation growth including new signups, posts by return visitors, and incoming traffic. To keep it organized, here is a checklist of things I would investigate, off the top of my head:

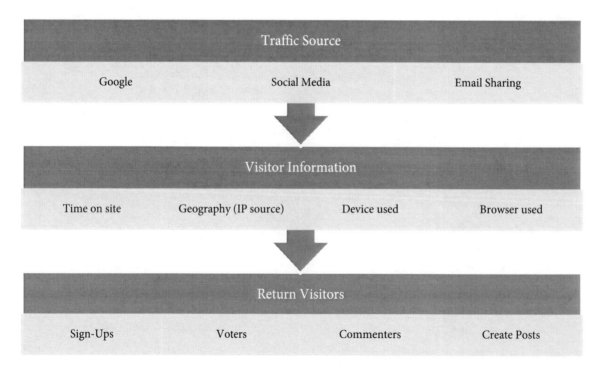

CANDIDATE: If everything above looks good, then I would focus on post creation itself. Here are some things I'd like to examine:

- Is there a technical glitch preventing the "create post" page from being accessed?
- Is there a technical glitch preventing posts from being submitted?
    - If so, are the users under the impression that their posts have been submitted?
- Is this happening across the entire website or only specific subreddits (i.e. communities)?
- Is this happening across all post types?
    - If not, which post types are affected?
        - Link posts?
        - Photo posts?
        - Text posts?
- Is this part of a larger technical problem that affects other operations or features? For instance, is Reddit.com down? Are there other falling metrics we can correlate with this problem?

Do you want me to elaborate on what I believe would be the most likely among these?

INTERVIEWER: No, it is not necessary. I was just looking for a checklist. I like your answer, and I am ready to move on to the next question.

Chapter 18 Metrics: Putting it Together

Your Favorite Google Product

What is a Google product you love? Imagine you are responsible for one of its features.

How would you monitor its use? And how would you measure its success or failure?

Things to Consider

- Use the AARM metrics as a starting point

Common Mistakes

- Not committing to a particular goal

Answer

CANDIDATE: My favorite Google product is Google Hangouts. It has the following features:

- **Voice Call**
- **Video Call**
- **Text Messaging**, including text, images, and videos
- **Group Chat**, including the ability to add or remove from a group
- **Voice Messaging**, leaving voicemails for your contacts

Which feature do you want me to focus on? I would pick text messaging.

INTERVIEWER: Sounds good.

CANDIDATE: All right. Here are a few metrics I would track:

- **Messages Sent.** How active are the users?
- **Messages Received.** A user may be sending many messages but not getting responses.
- **Session Frequency.** How often are users coming back throughout the day?
- **Session Length.** How long is each session? This could be an indicator of how engaging our app is or how captivating the conversation is. Keep in mind that a short session length might not be a bad thing, especially if a user returning to the feature several times during the day.
- **Retention.** I want to see whether a user actively uses the messaging feature as days go by. The number of daily active users is the number I would measure. We can also compare behaviors from different cohorts vs. cohorts that have lapsed.
- **Mobile Push Notifications.** Are users allowing push notifications? Push notifications are effective in driving engagement. However, users may choose not to opt-in because they do not want to be flooded with notifications. We will have to prove that turning notifications on is for their benefit if they turn it on.

Depending on what we find, I'll put together a plan to improve performance by improving or adding features. Ultimately, to go back to your final question, the feature's reason for being is to send and receive messages. If we benchmark against our competitors and find that we are less successful than they are in sending and receiving messages, on a per-user basis, then we've failed.

Drop in Hits

There was an 8% drop in hits to google.com. Larry Page walks into your office. He asks you to think and list what the reasons might be.

Things to Consider

- Seasonality, geography, and device
- Changes in referrers
- Changes in website layout or content
- Changes in website loading times
- Technical issues such as bugs and maintenance downtime

Common Mistakes

- Saying that you would "find out by looking at the data" and not providing specifics
- Having a short, unsatisfying list of metrics

Answer

CANDIDATE: I would first begin by examining if this is country or region-specific. Maybe there is censorship happening or a country has a problem with its network infrastructure, or maybe our servers for that area are down. If that's not the case, I would see if this is desktop vs. mobile. I would continue to check if it's platform-specific (e.g. iOS, Android, Amazon, Windows Phone) if it's mobile or browser-specific (e.g. Chrome, Edge, Safari, Opera) or even if it's OS-specific (Windows, Mac, and Linux).

I would also check with our tracking software. Sometimes there could be issues with tracking instrumentation or how the tracking logs were loaded into the dashboard.

I would analyze changes in user behavior. Perhaps a recent UI redesign is causing users to dislike our page. Or maybe our competition recently released a new feature or product that is siphoning our users' attention.

It's possible our distribution partnerships can affect large drops in traffic. Search engine preferences, either from the browser or the operating system, can influence the number of visits to google.com.

We can also look at other referral sources? Perhaps Gmail and YouTube, drivers of referral traffic, may have dropped their links to google.com recently.

INTERVIEWER: That's a good list of items to diagnose. Let's move on to the next question.

Amazon Web Services Metrics in Sydney

Imagine you are the AWS PM in Sydney. Which daily metrics would you look at?

Things to Consider

- For those who aren't familiar with AWS, it helps to first brainstorm a list of potential metrics to make sure nothing is missed.
- Be prepared to defend your positioning with clear rationale.

Common Mistakes

- Coming across as spineless by first blurting out three metrics and then changing them later.

Answer

CANDIDATE: Interesting question. Just to be sure I understand clearly, are you asking which metrics I would look at to evaluate the overall health of AWS Sydney? Or are you asking about metrics related to a specific product or feature?

INTERVIEWER: Assume this is about the overall health of AWS in Sydney. You are the lead PM there and are concerned with AWS's health as a business.

CANDIDATE: Thanks for the clarification. Could I brainstorm for a bit?

Candidate takes 30 seconds.

CANDIDATE: If this is okay with you, I'd like to first go over all of the relevant metrics that I'd want to be aware of, and then I'll highlight the three most important.

INTERVIEWER: Go ahead.

CANDIDATE: Okay, here are the AWS metrics that came to mind:

Acquisition

- Number of Australia- and New Zealand-based visitors to AWS page
- Number of new AWS users who have an Australia- or New Zealand-based address
- AWS market share, as a cloud provider in Australia- and New Zealand
- Percentage of new visits and users for all of AWS originating from Australia and New Zealand

Activation

- Percentage of users from the Sydney region with at least one running service
- Number of services requested by users in the Sydney region (ex: EC2 instances, S3 buckets, etc.)
- Percentage of total AWS requests that are made in the Sydney region

Retention

- DAU across all AWS services in the Sydney region
- Churn rates of users across all different AWS services in the Sydney region
- Comparison of above metrics for the Sydney versus all of AWS

Monetization

o   Customer Lifetime Value (CLV) of users with address in Australia or New Zealand

o   Percentage change in the Sydney region customer spending in last month and year

o   Percentage of revenue originating from the Sydney region for average AWS user worldwide

Now that we've got a good overview of the situation, here are the three metrics I would look at daily:

- **AWS Market Share as a Cloud Provider in Australia and New Zealand.** Although this isn't something that will fluctuate daily, I believe it's an important metric to keep at the top of one's mind and share with the team. AWS's goal is to be the leading cloud provider in the world and to accomplish that, we need to be sure to capture as much of the market as possible. Keeping track of our market share and comparing it with other regions' will help us assess how we are moving towards our long-term goal.

- **Percentage of Total AWS Requests Made in the Sydney Region.** While my first metric gives a good indication of how AWS is doing in Australia and New Zealand, this metric gives us a feel for how well Sydney compares to other AWS regions. If the percentage of requests that are being made in Sydney goes up, it means that customers find it valuable to host their services in this region. On the other hand, if the number goes down, it indicates that something makes Sydney a less attractive region for AWS customers, and we should fix it. For example, perhaps our uptime isn't as good as other regions or maybe our instances are too costly.

- **DAU Across All AWS Services in Sydney Region.** Both the metrics I mentioned help us keep track of how AWS Sydney is performing against its long-term goals, but these can be difficult to act on day-to-day. Monitoring DAU, we could see in a more granular way if we are progressing towards these goals. An increasing DAU number from Australia and New Zealand would make us more confident that we are gaining market share.

INTERVIEWER: Thank you for the thorough answer. While I agree these metrics will give you a good sense of your market share and importance as a region, there is nothing here regarding revenue. Why?

CANDIDATE: Fair point. The question asked for three metrics, and I felt these were the most important. In real life, I would keep an eye on monetization metrics as well. Given AWS' growth, I'd want to track the average customer spend over time. The metric that best represents this is the percentage change in the Sydney region each month or year.

The reasons I've left monetization out of my top three choices has to do with Amazon's philosophy as a company. Our goal isn't to generate the most revenue right now, but to put AWS in the position to generate more revenue later. Amazon is famous for going years without posting a profit because it was reinvesting in growth.

I believe it makes sense for AWS to pursue a similar strategy. That is, we should first focus on becoming a dominant cloud provider in terms of service quality and market share. Later, we can optimize for revenue.

Once our customers have their entire business running on AWS, they will likely be less price-sensitive, due to the switching costs involved with moving to another platform.

Amazon Operations' Employee Performance

Assume you work in Amazon operations. What metrics do you think we use to assess employee performance?

Things to Consider

- Attendance
- Complaints
- Productivity
- Peer satisfaction
- Safety and compliance
- Alignment with Amazon's values

Common Mistakes

- Choosing a vanity metric that's easy-to-collect but not actionable.

Answer

CANDIDATE: I would think of the following:

- **Cost.** How much does it cost us to keep them?
- **Revenue Generated.** How much revenue does the employee generate? We contrast this with cost to get effectiveness.
- **Work Done.** For certain employees that cannot have their work measured in monetary value, we can measure in terms of work done. This could be packages shipped, bugs fixed, etc.
- **Peer Review.** Based on a 1 to 5-star rating and a short description.
- **Manager Review.** Based on a 1 to 5-star rating and a short description.
- **Managed Employee Review.** Based on a 1 to 5-star rating and a short description.

INTERVIEWER: Why did you include peer review, manager review, and managed employee review?

CANDIDATE: This is an all-encompassing rating system. First, your peers work with you every day, so they know if you have been slacking off or have been efficient. Your manager also has an idea of this, but from a more top position point of view. You may be a manager yourself, and I think we would want to know how effective you are as a manager.

INTERVIEWER: What if a manager is rated low but he is efficient?

CANDIDATE: I assume you mean he is efficient at managing his employees. Maybe he's a slave driver and that's bad because the employees may be burnt out and disgruntled.

That isn't going to last in the long run. Results are not everything. Employee retention is important. Getting peak performance for a week means nothing if his team quits the company next month. Leaving and replacing someone wastes a lot of time and resources, so it's better if we prevent it as much as possible.

Declining Users

Facebook users have declined 20 percent week over week. Diagnose the problem. How would you fix the issue?

Things to Consider

For diagnosis, think about the root causes of a decline. Drawing out an issue tree can help.

Common Mistakes

Jumping to conclusions that a competitor's actions are the cause and hence the company should react by releasing identical features.

Answer

CANDIDATE: Hmm, interesting question. I would first start asking if this is mobile or desktop. If it's mobile, is it a specific platform (e.g. iOS, Android)? If it's desktop, is it a particular OS or browser (e.g., Chrome, Edge, Safari)?

INTERVIEWER: Let's say it's an even distribution.

CANDIDATE: I am going to assume it's not a hardware problem, like with our hosting servers. Because if it is, I think we would have discovered this a while back. Is there a particular page or feature that is having problems?

INTERVIEWER: It is not.

CANDIDATE: Okay, then I can say it's not a technical problem. Could there be a general downturn? Like the whole tech industry is seeing a 20% decline?

INTERVIEWER: It's just us.

CANDIDATE: Is this specific to a certain country or territory?

INTERVIEWER: It's across the globe.

CANDIDATE: Does this problem affect new or existing users? If it's existing, maybe it is our web design or content? Did a recent redesign cause existing users to leave? Or perhaps our content is having problems. Maybe the feed is acting up and not delivering as much content as before. Or maybe our chat is broken. We could also be having a problem with our internal search. Maybe users are not finding certain pages because our internal search is broken.

Is there anything wrong with our content or system? Or do we have a growing competitor on the rise?

INTERVIEWER: Nothing of that sort.

CANDIDATE: Then it must be a new user problem. What is the status of our marketing lately? Have we dropped our marketing budget lately? Or perhaps the user acquisition price has increased, but we are still using the same rates so we are not as competitive?

INTERVIEWER: Doesn't seem to be the case.

CANDIDATE: Or maybe it's our target audience. Are we targeting the right audience? If not, perhaps we are running out of first-rate audiences and we are targeting second-rate audiences so they are not as good in quality.

New users come from three sources: search, direct or referral. For search, are we indexed correctly on Google or other search engines? For direct, we already determined that our website is okay, but is there something up with the DNS lookup? For referral, is there something wrong with our ads on different sources?

INTERVIEWER: Seems to be our new user traffic. Specifically, it seems to be our referral ads. Before we exit this question, how would you fix this?

CANDIDATE: Give me a couple of seconds to brainstorm.

Candidate jots down the following.

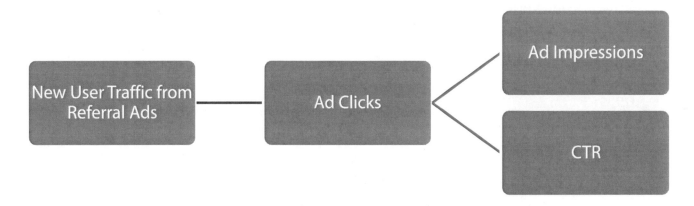

New user traffic from referral ads is really a function of the number of ad clicks we get. The two biggest drivers of ad clicks are ad impressions and the ad's click through rate (CTR).

Here is a checklist of things I would optimize to increase either CTR or ad impressions:

CTR

- Experiment with ad copy or call-to-action
- Experiment with an ad's images

Ad impressions

- Increase ad bids
- Increase budget, including daypart adjustments
- Increase keyword targets, if it's search engine marketing. This includes adjusting keyword match types such as switching from an exact match to either phrase or broad match.
- Expand audience, including more demographic segments

INTERVIEWER: That is an excellent list. Thank you.

Engagement on Dropbox

What metrics would you use to track Dropbox user engagement?

Things to Consider

- Active users
- Upload frequency
- Download frequency
- % of storage used
- Upgrades from free to paid
- Referrals

Common Mistakes

- Not factoring one of the biggest drivers of Dropbox engagement: whether or not a new user uploaded a file.

Answer

CANDIDATE: I can think of a few metrics:

Usage Metrics	Sharing Metrics
Average number of new uploaded files per day Indicates engagement by a single individual. It can also drive engagement by that individual's contacts.	**Average number of collaborators per file** Could indicate whether its consumer or business account.
Average number of new downloaded files per day More downloads per file indicate more valuable or engaging content.	*Average number of collaborators per folder* Could indicate whether its consumer or business account.
Average number of saves per day focused on existing files Another engagement indicator.	**Average number of edits per team member** An engagement metric that shows whether people are simply broadcasting or collaborating on Dropbox files.
Average number of devices This includes computers, tablets, and mobile devices.	**% of Total Employees using Dropbox at a single company** Not sure if this is easy to track, but it could be a good measure of company-wide adoption.
Logins via Dropbox's web site This could indicate an opportunity to encourage the installation of the desktop or mobile app.	**Number of invites to use Dropbox per user** This measures word-of-mouth new user acquisition.
% of Total Files are on Dropbox I am not sure if we could track it, but it'd be interesting to see how much space a user uses on Dropbox relative to the space that their Documents folder occupies on their computer hard drive.	

INTERVIEWER: Which metric do you think is the most important?

CANDIDATE: I would choose the number of newly uploaded files. Files not only drive engagement on a per-user basis, but it has a viral effect that draws in other Dropbox users, whether it is existing or new, into engaging with the Dropbox platform.

INTERVIEWER: Bingo. That is our engagement model, plain and simple.

Support Metrics for Dropbox

What metrics would you track if you were Dropbox's support manager?

Things to Consider

- Number of customer tickets
- Time to resolution
- First response time
- Contact volume by channel
- Tickets handled per support member
- Customer satisfaction with Dropbox support

Common Mistakes

- Drilling down too quickly on very specific issues such as sync errors or billing issues.

Answer

CANDIDATE: Just to make sure I understand: the support manager is someone who is in charge of the customer support team?

INTERVIEWER: Yes.

CANDIDATE: Can you give me some time to brainstorm?

Candidate takes one minute.

CANDIDATE: Here are a few metrics I would look at:

- **Number of customer issues per day, week, month, quarter, or year**. Not only does this help a support manager staff effectively, but also it could be an indicator of product quality, especially after a new release.
- **Requests that are about the same issue, ranked by frequency.** I want to see if we have unresolved issues that affect large groups of customers. This could help prioritize product development initiatives.
- **Summary of categories by ticket count.** This could help determine general problem areas.
- **Average and total response time.** If we do not have enough customer service agents, our customers may wait longer than they would like.
- **Resolved vs. unresolved tickets.** This tells me how many outstanding issues are out there. It also indicates how efficient we are in resolving the queue of incoming issues.
- **Net promoter score.** This is one of my favorite customer satisfaction metrics.
- **Customer mood at the beginning and end of the call.** Agents' perception of the customer's mood, especially at the end of the call, could indicate satisfaction.
- **Number of tickets handled per team member.** This could indicate a team member's efficiency.
- **Number of re-opened or unresolved cases per team member.** Indicates an agent's effectiveness in getting issues resolved the first time or in general.
- **Most requested features**. The support team can share this feedback with the product development team.

INTERVIEWER: Which one would you say is the most important?

CANDIDATE: While ticket resolution may seem like the most important thing, based on my personal experience, I found that response time was the most important metric.

Customers wanted to know that someone was working on their problem immediately. The attention made them feel respected.

In addition, when support team members interact immediately with the client, it gave customers a chance to vent and release their frustration. Sometimes venting ventured into vicious verbal abuse. As much as I did not like that, I understood that allowing customers to vent improved our overall satisfaction metrics.

INTERVIEWER: Thank you.

Success Metric for UberPool

What should be the main success metric for UberPool?

Things to Consider

- # of UberPool requests
- # of UberPool matches
- # of UberPool trips, given a time period
- # of active UberPool users
- Reduction in city congestion, due to UberPool usage

Common Mistakes

- Choosing vanity metrics such as visitors and visits to UberPool web page

Answer

CANDIDATE: Hmm, UberPool is the one where you are carpooling with multiple people right? For one ride? And each rider is being picked up from different locations and going to different pickups?

INTERVIEWER: Yes.

CANDIDATE: Hmm, I would split potential metrics into:

Adoption

- Number of people that have taken at least one UberPool ride
- Percent of all UberX riders that have also taken at least one UberPool ride

Usage

- Mix of UberPool rides vs. non-UberPool rides
- Number of times Uber app users that first selected UberPool but then selected a non-UberPool class of service such as UberX

217

- Average number of people per UberPool
- Average price per UberPool ride vs. non-UberPool ride

Retention

- Average rating differences between UberPool and non-UberPool rides
- Average number of UberPool trips per month by repeat users

Monetization

- Revenue from UberPool
- Revenue per UberPool hour

Driver Metrics

- Number of Uber drivers who accepted UberPool rides
- Earnings per hour for an UberPool driver vs. non-UberPool driver
- Changes in vehicle occupancy due to UberPool

There are a lot of interesting metrics here, but if I were to only choose one, I'd pick the number of Uber users who have taken at least one UberPool ride, followed by the average number of UberPool rides per month for those who have taken at least one.

INTERVIEWER: Why is that?

CANDIDATE: This is a newer service for us, so adoption should be our number one objective. We want to gauge customer reaction to sharing an Uber with a stranger. We're also fundamentally changing the value proposition of Uber once again. The original Uber is an alternative to black car service. UberX is an alternative to a taxi service. UberPool is an alternative to public transit. The key hypotheses we are trying to determine include:

- Are users willing to save money to have longer trips? This is unique because the prior value proposition was not saving money. It was speed and convenience.
- Are users willing to substitute public transit with UberPool? This is unique because previously those who did not want to take the bus or subway would either have to walk, drive a car, or on occasion take a taxi.

INTERVIEWER: Thanks for the long list of metrics and the thoughtful response.

Metrics for Uber Pick-up

What metrics should we track if we wanted to improve the Uber pick-up experience?

Things to Consider

- Number of people opening the request page
- Number of people making a ride request
- Number of requests that are fulfilled

- Time to fulfill request
- Post-trip satisfaction

Common Mistakes

- Focusing too much on low value-add items such as whether the driver offers water to its riders or whether the driver is a good conversationalist.

Answer

CANDIDATE: When you mean pick-up, do you mean just the waiting period, or do you count the finding a driver part of the experience?

INTERVIEWER: I mean the whole experience.

CANDIDATE: Okay, I would track the following:

Before a Pickup

- How long does it take someone to get a ride after opening the app?
- How many times did surge pricing happen? Frequent price surges indicate higher rider fares and a driver shortage.

Pickup

- How long does it take the driver to arrive at the pickup location?
- How often did the driver or rider have to initiate a call or text to find one another?
- How often did a driver leave before picking up the passenger?

After the Trip

- Average driver rating

INTERVIEWER: That is a good list. Which one would you pick if you could only pick one?

CANDIDATE: If we were concerned with the whole experience, then I'd pick how long does someone wait to get a ride after opening the app. Nobody is going to wait an hour for an Uber to show up.

If we're concerned specifically with the pick-up experience, I would track the number of times the driver left without picking up the passenger. If that happened, something drastically wrong occurred. I'd want to investigate why that happened and fix it immediately.

INTERVIEWER: Thank you.

Slow Download on Kindle

How would you troubleshoot a slow download of content on a Kindle device?

Things to Consider

- Large Kindle files

- Slow user connection
- Slow Amazon connection
- Slow server performance
- Slow user device performance

Common Mistakes

- Not considering non-Amazon issues, such as slow Internet connectivity.

Answer

CANDIDATE: I would first determine if this is a global problem or a country or regional problem. If it's a country or regional problem, it could be our infrastructure or the Internet in that area.

If it were a global problem, I would think about our devices. Is this on a specific model?

If that is not it, then maybe it's our distribution servers. Judging from the phrasing of this question, I am going to assume not, because I am sure Amazon has checks in all these critical parts. So if there were a failure, we would know instantly.

I would content type next such as book or videos. Does the issue affect all content types?

Then I would look at content categories. Maybe it's a specific category of movies or videos over a certain length.

Pinterest Metrics

Imagine you are a Pinterest's VP of Product. What metrics would you track?

Things to Consider

- Visitors and visits
- eCommerce conversions and revenue
- Images saved onto a Pinterest board. This includes from the web, the user's home feed, and other users' Pinterest boards

Common Mistakes

- Using the wrong terminology, such as calling a pin or save a retweet.

Answer

CANDIDATE: Can I get some time to brainstorm this?

Candidate takes one minute.

CANDIDATE: I am thinking of these metrics:

- **Number of users.** We want to drive user growth, including international growth and new customer segments.
- **Daily, weekly and monthly active users.** These are good engagement measures.

- **Pins.** I want to see how many people are pinning content every day. Nobody wants to use a pinning with a small or outdated selection of images.
- **Most pins.** What is the most pinned content on our website? This is the most interesting content. I would also dissect this by user-type (based on their search and uploads) so I can see what kind of content is considered the most desirable by these groups.
- **Re-pins.** Re-pins can indicate popular and quality content. I would also want to track the ratio of new pins vs. re-pins. If the re-pin ratio is too high, it may indicate that we do not have enough fresh content.
- **New pins per day.** How often are we getting new images per day?
- **Number of searches per day.** How many people are actually searching on Pinterest? This is the same idea with uploads per day, except for people who only use Pinterest for finding content.
- **Average search time.** How quickly does someone find something he or she is satisfied with? If it takes too much time for users to find what they're looking for they might seek out alternatives on competitor websites.
- **Conversions.** Of the times we showed buyable pins, what percent turned into a purchase?
- **Revenue.** How much money did we generate due to advertising on Pinterest?

Rehabilitation in Irish Prisons

How would you measure the rehabilitation rate in Irish prisons?

Things to Consider

- Rehabilitation, as defined by Wikipedia, is the "re-integration into society of a convicted person."
- Some metrics to consider include:
  - % arrested after reintegration within a defined timeframe
  - % arrested by offense type such as drug trafficking, fraud or robbery
  - Sentence type and length for rehabilitated persons arrested

Answer

CANDIDATE: What do you mean by rehabilitation?

INTERVIEWER: I mean, former Irish prisoners who are no longer committing crimes and are capable of taking care of themselves.

CANDIDATE: I would check:

- How many of them are no longer in prison?
- How many of them have a job?
- How many are actively looking for jobs?
- How many of them have been arrested for a new crime?
- How many of them are mentally healthy?
- How many of them are suffering from an addiction such as drugs and alcohol?

INTERVIEWER: I find it interesting that you want to track mental health. Why?

CANDIDATE: Some prisoners are depressed or have trouble controlling their anger. Poor mental health may increase the probability of someone committing a crime. Improved mental health may indicate someone who has successfully rehabilitated.

Go-To-Market and Success

How would you measure the success of a go-to-market strategy?

Things to Consider

- As a starting point, think about all the key pieces of the marketing funnel: awareness, interest, trial, and purchase.

Common Mistakes

- "Go-to-market" can have differing interpretations. Many candidates assume that they share a common understanding with the interviewer.
- Not mentioning a complete set of go-to-market metrics.

Answer

CANDIDATE: Hmm, this is an open-ended question. Let me first describe what a go-to-market is and then share my success metrics.

INTERVIEWER: Sounds good.

Go-to-market can probably be best explained as a marketing process. When you start, you should think about your customers. Who are they? Are we targeting consumers or businesses? What kind? Once we identify a target segment, we can think about what marketing campaigns can target this segment most effectively. For example, if we are targeting businesses, a direct sales effort is more effective, especially since business products are a high involvement process. Then we need to think about how they can purchase our service. Going back to the business example, they can sign contracts with us, or they can sign for our service on their own, using a credit card like a software-as-a-service business like Salesforce. Our account managers can then serve as the first point of contact should our business customers encounter any problems.

INTERVIEWER: What success metrics would you look at?

CANDIDATE: I would measure various metrics:

- **Reach.** How many customers did we reach?
- **Conversion rate.** Of those that we contacted, how many purchased our service or product?
- **Customer acquisition cost.** How much are we spending to market our products and goods? I would like to compare this by product line, geography, and sales channel.
- **Revenue and profit.** Most tech companies care about revenue because tech companies have significant fixed costs such as R&D labor that can't be easily assigned to a single P&L. However, it would be best if we can track profitability. Numerous companies have incorrectly sustained poor performing businesses because they allocated costs incorrectly.

- **Market share.** Market share is most critical for winner-take-all markets such as two-sided marketplaces like Airbnb, Uber, and eBay.
- **Word-of-mouth.** How many customers come to us because of other customers? We can track this using the industry measure for virality, the K-factor.

Chapter 19 Hypothetical: Opinion

Creating Product Roadmaps

How do you define or create a product roadmap?

Things to Consider

- It is difficult to improvise an answer to this question, especially if you have not put together a product roadmap recently.
- Plan what you are going to say so that you don't provide an incomplete or unsatisfying answer.
- An important part of roadmaps is the sequence of features, which imply tradeoffs and an understanding of critical path dependencies.

Common Mistakes

- Failing to draw the roadmap template one would use, especially since product roadmaps are innately visual.
- Poorly explaining the feature prioritization.

Answer

CANDIDATE: When I create roadmaps, here's my approach:

1. **Goals**. What are we trying to achieve? More customers or revenue? Or decreased churn?
2. **Brainstorm**. Create a giant list of every possible feature that I'd want to add. Creativity is a weapon. And one of the best ways to get groundbreaking, creative ideas is to brainstorm as much as possible.
3. **Prioritization**. Which combination of features will help us meet those goals, considering effort, cost (both labor and financial), and risk? Which ones have dependencies?
4. **Visual communications**. I'd put the roadmap on a slide so it is easier to communicate and get buy-in across audiences.

INTERVIEWER: Can you elaborate on how you would prioritize?

CANDIDATE: Sure, I would use a prioritization matrix. Here's an example:

| | Benefit | | | Cost | | | Overall | |
	Increase revenue	Customer value	Strategic value	Implementation effort	Operational costs	Risk	Score	Rank
Native iOS App	5	3	4	5	3	3	68	3
Referral Feature	3	4	4	3	2	3	84	1
New Dashboard	1	4	2	2	4	1	72	2

Source: Inspired by ProductPlan.com

INTERVIEWER: Can you draw out your roadmap?

Acme X Roadmap	2016 Q4			Q1			Q2			2017
	October	November	December	January	February	March	April	May	June	July
Maximize Revenue										
Referral Feature										
Native iOS App										
New Dashboard										

CANDIDATE: I'd recommend we start building the referral feature in November. It's our most important feature, and it's expected to drive significant customer acquisition at low ongoing operational cost. The native iOS app work should start in January. I know the iOS app is ranked third in our list, but our Los Angeles engineering team has the bandwidth to take it on then. They're also talented iOS developers. Lastly, the new dashboard work should start in March. We have a functioning dashboard today. It's not the most user-friendly dashboard in the world, and it has some awkward manual workarounds. But I think we'll live if we have to wait three to four extra months.

Product Roadmap Best Practices

What are some product roadmap best practices?

Things to Consider

- A satisfactory best practice and interview answer makes the interviewer feel smarter after hearing your response.
- A strong best practice example is also novel and new.
- An anecdote, featuring a best practice insight from a recent book, article or workshop, can work well. It shows that you keep up with the industry and indicates that you have a propensity for self-improvement.

Common Mistakes

- Answering the question by offering only a definition when the interviewer is expecting best practices.

Answer

CANDIDATE: I would be happy to share product roadmap best practices, but can you provide more details on what you are looking for? Are you looking for general advice, product roadmap templates, or something else?

INTERVIEWER: Ah, sorry. I'm looking for a product roadmap template that I can use for my executive presentation next week.

Candidate is momentarily perplexed but quickly regains composure.

CANDIDATE: When I put together roadmaps in the past, I've used three different format types: timelines, roadmap without dates, and Kanban. Would you like me to walk through these three types and discuss the pros and cons of each?

Interviewer nods eagerly.

INTERVIEWER: Yes, please.

Candidate draws on the whiteboard.

Timeline

Q1			Q2				Q3		
Jan	Feb	Mar	Apr	May	Jun	Jul	Aug	Sep	

User Interface (UI)
- Conduct user interviews
- Interactive UI improvements
- React framework

Application Programming Interface (API)
- Define API specifications
- API Beta
- Rollout production-ready API

Storage
- Agree on storage vendors
- Move entire product lines to new storage vendors
- Performance improvements

Other Services Integrations
- Narrow down integration partnerships
- Complete integrations before EOY
- Rollout first 5 integrations

Screenshot / ProductPlan.com

This format shows how initiatives relate to one another in the context of time. The advantage of this format is that it's clear when things happen, but the disadvantage is that it doesn't emphasize strategic importance.

Candidate draws on the whiteboard.

Roadmap Without Dates

People
- Increase staff
- Split groups in special task forces
- Onboarding & training

Technology
- Define SLA
- Rollout three 9s
- Increase to five 9s
- Migration Plan
- Migration implementation

Security
- Agree on security plan
- Rollout must-haves
- Meet production goals

Roadmap Without Dates

People

Increase staff		Split groups in special task forces

Onboarding & training

Technology

Define SLA	Rollout three 9's

Increase to five 9's

Migration Plan	Migration implementation

Security

Agree on security plan	Rollout must-haves

Meet production goals

Screenshot / ProductPlan.com

This format shows initiatives relative to strategic priorities. In the example above, the strategic priorities are clearly people, technology, and security. The disadvantage is the opposite of the previous example: the strategic priorities are clear, but it's not clear when these initiatives will start or end.

Candidate draws on the whiteboard.

Kanban

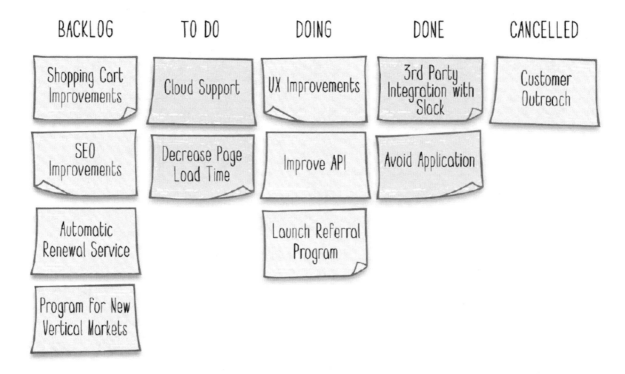

A Kanban-style roadmap indicates the status of individual initiatives, something the other two formats do not do. This format has two disadvantages:

- Start and end dates are not clear
- Strategic priorities are not clear

INTERVIEWER: Which one do you use?

CANDIDATE: I personally like the timeline method. I find that by having clear start and finish dates, we can be more goal-oriented in our approach. The best-performing companies, including Google and Intel, have a time-based, goal-oriented approach.

Prioritizing Requests

How would you prioritize feature requests, if you could not do them all?

Things to Consider

- What are your criteria?
- How do you tradeoff between two requests that appear to be equally important?

- Giving a non-committal answer and implying that "one can do it all" by simply working longer hours.

Answer

CANDIDATE: Prioritization is all about tradeoffs. Tradeoffs start with our intended objective, which may differ based on the product and its maturity cycle.

Did you want me to take about how I would prioritize generally? Or did you want me to focus on a specific company's product?

INTERVIEWER: The general case is fine.

CANDIDATE: Here are my top criteria for determining which priorities to handle first:

- **Revenue Impact.** Which requests have the greatest estimated revenue?
- **Customer Satisfaction.** Satisfaction can lead to positive word-of-mouth marketing. It could also lead to higher usage, which increases the likelihood of renewals or incremental purchases if the product is sold on a subscription or a la carte basis.
- **Number of Customers Affected.** The magnitude of impact is important.
- **Time to Resolution.** Sometimes there are simple product fixes that don't take a long time to address. Here I am thinking of short-term ROI. A minor fix may receive due consideration, especially if a burning issue may take a long time to resolve.
- **Technical Feasibility.** There is no point in addressing an issue if the fix is not technically possible.

INTERVIEWER: Your list makes sense. Let's say a vocal minority disagrees with your priorities or your prioritization criteria. How would you handle that minority?

CANDIDATE: When that happens, here's what I tend to do:

- **Allow the vocal minority to make their case.** Most people get upset when their requests are rejected without any consideration.
- **Explain why another feature received higher priority.** People get upset and alienated when they feel that decisions are made arbitrarily.
- **Provide evidence.** Some feel better when there is evidence that accompanies a decision. Sometimes the data can be quantitative in nature. Other times, it can be qualitative like customer complaints.
- **Share detailed reasoning.**

INTERVIEWER: That's a good approach. Thank you.

Good vs. Bad Product Managers

What are three characteristics of successful product managers? And what are three characteristics of bad product managers?

Things to Consider

- Use the Rule of Three
- For additional characteristics of good vs. bad product managers, refer to the following resources:
    - Ben Horowitz's famous essay, "Good Product Manager, Bad Product Manager."
    - Ian McAllister's Quora answer, "What distinguishes the Top 1% of Product Managers from the Top 10%?"

Common Mistakes

- Narcissistic responses.
- Answering the question by redirecting the interviewer to read another work such as, "Good product managers? You should read the essay that X wrote."

Answer

CANDIDATE: Successful product managers have three characteristics:

- **Ship products.** Some product managers obsess over details too much. As a result, their products take longer to ship than necessary. While making the perfect product is admirable, good PMs know how to balance time and quality.
- **Metric-centric.** Good product managers should have strong opinions. However, the best can analyze those opinions objectively and acknowledge contrarian viewpoints when necessary. Good product managers aren't obsessed with protecting their ego. They can let the data and metrics do the talking. And when it doesn't work, they are open to trying something else.
- **Motivate the team.** A good product requires a high performing team. Good product managers know how difficult and long it takes to make or improve a product. Sometimes teams will lose sight of the goal, but not teams with good product managers. Good product managers keep dreaming about the product; they will motivate the team to keep marching. Nothing is impossible. They bring the burning ambition that fuels the team.

Bad product managers have the following characteristics:

- **Attempt to use authority.** Product managers manage the product, not the people. And product managers usually have limited authority. Even if they do have authority, using authority to get things done is a sign of weakness. Better product managers get things done through influence, usually through domain knowledge, data analysis and a proven record of accomplishment.
- **Married to their ideas.** Bad product managers grow attached to their ideas and will not let go, even if the data suggests otherwise. Good product managers take ownership of the product but never to a specific idea. Bad product managers don't understand this; they become offended whenever their ideas are rejected.
- **Have no goal.** Bad product managers don't have a goal or vision for their product. They get lost. They also have trouble articulating the roadmap toward the goal. They get distracted and jam everything into the product, confusing the team and delaying the schedule in the process. Bad product managers don't gather feedback and incorporate the feedback into the product. Their product becomes a cacophony of chaos.

Challenges for a PM

What are some of the challenges for a PM?

Things to Consider

Most common challenges for PMs include:

- Articulating product vision
- Convincing the team on a certain course of action
- Figuring out ways to help the team do more in less time

Common Mistakes

- Complaining about unsexy tasks, such as taking notes and scheduling meetings.
- Complaining about being responsible even when the product is bad, marketing is poor, resources are limited, or the engineering team is incompetent.
- Complaining about unclear executive priorities or not having enough time in the day.

Answer

CANDIDATE: A PM has a few challenges she needs to look out for:

Convince your team effectively

As a PM, you have no official authority, so if you want the team to work on your ideas you need to use influence skills. This can feel frustrating because you may feel you know what is best and influencing others can take a lot of work. Being patient, accepting that influencing is necessary, and knowing that building bridges now with key stakeholders will be better than reacting to their concerns later.

Strive to understand why

Whenever someone tells you something cannot be done the way you wanted it to be or that they do not understand your ideas, you need to empathize. You need to see from their point of view why they do not agree and see if you can address their needs to convince them. I have found that often it is simply a misunderstanding. This is why you need to dig at the why. If you do not know the underlying reason, how can you fix it? This goes for both working with a team and designing a product.

Beware of falling in love with an idea

As a PM, you may have many ideas in your head. Unfortunately, not all of them will be good. That is why getting your team's feedback helps.

Getting feedback is part of the design process. So don't feel depressed. If an idea does not work, don't force it. See if you can think of something better.

Mobile vs. Desktop Design

What are the differences between mobile vs. desktop design?

Things to Consider

- Use the Rule of Three.
- Backup your thinking with evidence.
- Further illustrate your point with examples, anecdotes or diagrams.

Common Mistakes

- Getting flustered.
- Giving up on answers and asking for a pass because one is not a designer.

Answer

CANDIDATE: Can I brainstorm for a bit?

Candidate takes 30 seconds.

CANDIDATE: I can think of a couple of things:

Space

Let's start with the most obvious: mobile phone screens are smaller, so you can't fit as much information onto a mobile app.

Desktop computing, especially those connected to external monitors, have more screen real estate.

Pointing devices

One's fingers control mobile devices whereas a mouse or trackpad controls the cursor for a desktop device.

On the one hand, fingers are wider than the tip of a cursor. As a result, the tap areas need to be sufficiently large on a mobile device. On the other hand, multiple fingers can be used for innovative gestures such as pinch-to-zoom, which is not something that can be replicated with a cursor.

Pressing fingers across a glass surface invoke a user's own mental model on how their fingers interact with non-digital windows such as swiping, holding, or pulling gestures.

One last thing: hovering over a button, doable with a cursor, is not doable on a mobile device.

Keyboard devices

Desktop keyboards are larger and more comfortable for human fingers.

Mobile keyboards are significantly smaller and not suited for human fingers. As a result, keyboarding can be error-prone and tedious. Mobile users may prefer to input with voice. Or they may frown upon UX elements that require typing such as search boxes.

Intermittent usage

Mobile devices are often used for short, sudden periods of activity. Desktops are more often used for tasks for a longer duration such as drafting a document or editing a spreadsheet. It's likely why mobile user interfaces provide information at a glance such as push notifications. Twitter, with its 140-character limitation, is also particularly ideal for on-the-go glances.

On-the-go usage

Desktop devices are most comfortably used when sitting down. It's hard to imagine someone using a desktop while waiting for a bus to come.

Different screen orientations

Most desktop monitors are placed in landscape mode whereas mobile devices are often in portrait mode.

Also, mobile devices are more likely to switch between portrait and landscape mode than desktop devices.

Emerging Technology

Talk about an emerging technology that you are tracking.

Things to Consider

- Research emerging technologies beforehand, if you haven't already; Time Magazine's annual Best Inventions issue is an excellent starting point.
- Save time in learning about the latest technology trends by using the following Google search query: "emerging technologies in <industry> <current year>"
- Prepare to educate others on a few emerging trends by organizing your talking points in advance.

Common Mistakes

- Picking a cliché technology, which induces boredom.
- Picking your own product or technology, which reveals a lack of preparation.
- Not explaining what the technology is or how it works.
- Making a feeble attempt on why the technology is groundbreaking.

Answer

CANDIDATE: Recently, I've been tracking screenless display technology. Screenless technology, as the name implies, allows a computer to transmit visual information from a visual source without the use of a screen. Today, there are three categories of screenless technology: holograms, retinal displays, and synaptic interfaces.

Holograms are self-explanatory. Retinal displays project images directly onto the retina usually with contact lenses. Synaptic interfaces bypass the eye and transmit images directly to the brain.

Here are three reasons why I'm excited about screenless technology, especially bionic lenses that provide retinal displays to the visually impaired:

- **Potential Market Size.** The large market size is very attractive. Think about how many people wear glasses today. Billions! Visually impaired individuals would never need glasses again. Glasses are a terrible annoyance. They can get lost, slide off the face easily, and bounce around during physical activities.

- **Utility & Convenience.** Think of how useful it is to track everyone based on his or her eyes. Imagine walking around and have billboards display ads that are relevant to you. Sure, some might be concerned with privacy. But are smartphones not already tracking our every move? This isn't that different. Also, think about convenience. You no longer need to wait in line at the airport, and you can even have bionic lenses tie to your payment information so you can just hop on the train or grab a meal without pulling out your wallet.
- **Health & Safety.** Having this technology would improve safety and well-being. Nearsighted individuals would minimize the number of accidents that happen when they can't see well.

To summarize, I am a big fan of bionic lenses because of the market size, utility, and contribution to health and safety.

Impact of Self-Driving Cars

What will be the impact of self-driving cars?

Things to Consider

- Better responses consider how the technology will create new industries and destroy old ones.
- Brainstorm an exhaustive list of things to consider such as the environment, urban planning, government agencies, customers, and competitors.
- To better illustrate the impact, compare and contrast how the situation would be different under traditional vs. self-driving cars.

Common Mistakes

- Limiting your answer to a few ideas. Interviewers expect many.
- Stating only obvious, commonplace answers such as taxi driver unemployment will go up.
- Not structuring the answer, making it hard to follow.

Answer

CANDIDATE: I can think of a few things:

- **Transforming what "driving" means.** By definition, the driver of a self-driving car won't be driving. This means they can spend their car time doing other things, which creates opportunities to change what it means to spend time in a car. Passengers can work, sleep, or relax.
- **Decrease in Car Ownership.** If cars are self-driving, then it should be even simpler to summon one. Driver commissions are 20 to 25 percent of Uber's costs. It's safe to assume that self-driving cars should make a self-driving Uber even cheaper. If this is the case, then it might become even cheaper to rent a car, allowing for higher utilization, reducing maintenance costs, and eliminating parking fees.
- **Reduction in Parking Real Estate.** Expanding on the point above, if cars are being utilized at a higher rate then the need for parking goes down. This means space that is currently used for parking, both indoors and outdoors, can be repurposed.
- **Driver Unemployment.** If drivers are no longer needed, then paid drivers will lose their job. Those affected include taxi, truck, bus, and other commercial drivers.

- **New Jobs Created.** On the flip side, the new category of self-driving vehicles will create new jobs for skilled workers to design, monitor, repair, clean, and sell them. Many of those jobs will be opportunities that are hard to imagine today.
- **Change in Competitive Differentiators.** Cars have been traditionally been evaluated based on top speed, horsepower, and fuel-efficiency. The evaluation criteria for self-driving cars might be different; buyers may consider autopilot technology, utilization optimization algorithms, and the number of available applications to be top buying factors. Thus, companies that are leading the self-driving car industry might look radically different from the ones that are currently leading the car industry.

Favorite Android Apps

Tell us about your favorite lesser-known Android applications. Why?

Things to Consider

- The prompt is asking for lesser-known apps so stay away from popular apps like Yelp and Facebook.
- The reason this question is being asked: interviewers want to be inspired and learn something new.
- Interviewers also want to know you are curious about new products; it's an indicator of a product-centric product manager.
- Don't forget to explain what the product is and why it's your favorite. Describing how it works is optional.

Common Mistakes

- Not explaining what it is or explaining poorly.
- Giving lukewarm reasons on why an application is your favorite.

Answer

CANDIDATE: I can think of three:

Unified Remote

It turns your Android device into a PC remote, making it easy to start music or TV shows.

More people are "cutting the cord" and consuming shows or music on their computers instead. The computer doesn't have the convenient interface of a wireless TV remote. This application mimics the TV remote feeling with a simple app on the phone.

Given how much time we like to spend on the couch, fiddling with our phones, it's a fantastic opportunity to push advertising.

RunPee

This app lets you know when it is a good time to step outside for a bathroom break depending on the movie you are watching. It is a useful app because movie theaters, unlike the Netflix app, do not have pause buttons.

Hooked

This app is fast food news, focused on college towns. For college students who are looking for deals and don't want to eat pizza again, the app surfaces discounts and shares information about new restaurant openings.

There's an intriguing business model here. Loyal users may open the app as often as three times a day; it's ripe for local, contextually targeted ads from restaurants, local businesses, and e-retailers focused on young adults.

Product Management Definition

What does product management mean to you?

Things to Consider

- Answer by using the Rule of Three. It gives your answer depth; it also makes it easy to follow.
- Your hypothetical answer, in the best-case answer, would only take 30 seconds.
- I would recommend that after the first 30 seconds to offer an actual example where you behaved in accordance with the three principles outlined in your hypothetical answer.

Common Mistakes

- Giving a meandering, hard-to-follow response. This commonly happens when the candidate is trying to think and articulate their answer at the same time.
- This is a nit-pick, but many candidates unnecessarily stall by saying, "Great question." It is a filler phrase.

Answer

CANDIDATE: When I think about the role of a product manager, I think of three main pillars:

- **Serve as a team leader.** The PM serves as the hub for the entire team. Product development is becoming more and more complicated, and it's not strange for a team to have multiple departments within. The PM serves as the interface between all the teams and customers. This person routes resources, plans the steps and fixes problems. The PM also ties the team together and marches forward toward the goal with them. Lastly, the PM brings consensus and mobilizes execution and success.
- **Define the goal**. The PM figures out the goal and the needs for the product. Which market are we targeting? What features do we need? Who are our customers? These are all answers the PM must answer. In essence, the PM is there to figure out the true north for the product, and this person is there to guide the team. Whenever anyone is lost, the PM is there to remind that person what the true north is. This person builds expectations and drives the vision.
- **Explain the vision or game plan**. The PM needs to figure out why we are doing this product this way, and why. This person needs to figure out the prioritization of these features and why they are done in this order. The PM doesn't do this through sheer mental power. The PM also looks and pokes around the data and presents it to the team so they understand why. This person makes sure the team understands his point of view and addresses their questions or concerns.

Can I give you an example where I demonstrated all three pillars?

INTERVIEWER: Sure, we have some time.

CANDIDATE: Back in January of this year, I was in charge of the Amazon Web Services (AWS) Ireland project. We wanted to launch a new UI portal, and I was in charge of 20 service teams to get it released. In this role, I served as the team leader, determined the goal, and explained the game plan to the team.

First, I determined the goal. We wanted to launch the new portal in four months, and I defined the key performance indicators (KPIs) for the project including service uptime, service availability, and cross-team employee satisfaction.

Then, I communicated the process that included:

- Establishing a framework
- Streamlining work with our vendor teams
- Publishing documentation for the team's reference

Lastly, I prioritized our team's work items. I looked at several criteria including:

- Customer impact
- Urgency
- Strategic importance
- Critical path dependencies

I am proud to announce that the UI portal launched two weeks ahead of time. Andy Jassy, the Amazon SVP who heads up AWS, congratulated our team for a job well done. He told my boss that my leadership and communication skills impressed him.

INTERVIEWER: Thank you.

What Do You Bring

What would you bring to the team that nobody else would?

Things to Consider

- Use the Rule of Three.
- Highlight personal attributes that reinforce your personal brand; that is, characteristics that make you special versus others.

Common Mistakes

- Choosing general, undifferentiated attributes like working hard and getting along with others.

Answer

CANDIDATE: There are three things I'd bring to the team:

- **Telemetry.** With project teams getting bigger and bigger, it's becoming increasingly hard for team members to understand what is going on around the company. As a PM, I would bring telemetry to the table. It's one of the core functions of the PM to interface with every team. I would route resources, plan the next step, and sync with everyone to make sure everyone knows what they need to push the product forward. My job is to get our team focused on the most important priorities throughout the journey.

- **Well-roundedness.** As a PM, my background and experience is well rounded. Engineering, product design, project management, user experience, and business are just some of the skills I can bring to the table. I also like to think deeply about each person's motivation. That knowledge allows me to tap into their self-interest to get consensus more quickly.

- **Motivation & Teamwork.** Building a product is hard. Teams can run into roadblocks and get frustrated easily. It's important that I try to motivate them, as PM. I would explain that it is okay to run into problems they cannot seem to fix; the team exists to help one another. Working together, there is nothing we cannot fix. We cannot do our best work if we are feeling discouraged. My job is to keep our team's morale high.

Would you like me to tell you a time when you shared these three traits at work?

INTERVIEWER: No, that's not necessary. I'd like to move onto the next question.

CANDIDATE: Okay.

What Do You Like About Being a PM

What do you like about being a PM?

Things to Consider

- Use the Rule of Three.
- Acknowledge some of the keys traits of the role (design, product, and engineering), which preferably coincides with your strengths.
- Be thoughtful.

Common Mistakes

- Not having a good explanation of why you chose or transitioned into PM.
- Revealing character flaws that indicate not being suited for a PM role, such as a preference for working alone.
- Being overly enthusiastic, bordering on being pretentious.

Answer

CANDIDATE: There are a couple reasons why I like being a product manager:

- **Intersection of Design, Product, and Engineering.** As a PM, I feel lucky being able to stand at the intersection of design, product, and engineering. The PM role allows me to get involved in all three on a day-to-day basis, which is an absolute dream to me.
- **Teamwork.** It feels great to build a product with a team. The togetherness builds camaraderie and fulfills my sense of community.
- **Continuous Improvement.** When we iterate and improve a product, I get a sense of progress and improvement. We deliver our work, collect feedback, and repeat. There are new challenges every day.

Unlike other roles, I do not feel like I am doing the same thing over and over again, using the same solutions day-in and day-out.

- **Customer Interaction**. I spend time interviewing customers as a product manager. It reminds me of whom I am building for and why I am building it. Customer interaction reinforces my sense of purpose, and it makes me happy when my products make their lives easier.

Challenges for a PM

What are some of the challenges for a PM?

Things to Consider

- Use Rule of Three.
- Be excited, not demoralized, by challenges.

Common Mistakes

- Only listing one to two challenges and unable to mention more, even when asked.
- Suggesting challenges that sound naïve such as too many meetings or too much politicking.

Answer

CANDIDATE: There are many challenges I can think of:

- **No Authority.** The PM manages the product, not the people. A PM doesn't have direct authority over anyone. I can't ask someone to do something if he or she doesn't agree with me. Sometimes I imagine it would be easier if I could make everyone do everything the way I want. But remember, even if I had authority, using it is a sign of weakness. Proposals and suggestions that need to be forced down may indicate that they weren't good suggestions to begin with. Deep down I know my ideas will not encounter success without feedback. Don't take negative criticism personally; it's a gift.
- **Letting Go.** Sunk cost thinking can cloud my judgment. I think about the time, energy, money, and prestige associated with an existing or in-progress feature that I can't let go of. In those times, I have to remember that there is a bigger growth opportunity that is more deserving of time, energy, and resources.
- **Giving Up.** It sounds contrary to the previous point, but there is a risk of giving up too early. The world is filled with innovative features and products led by product managers who quit, only seeing other product managers, take the same exact concept, through the finish line.
- **Doing the unglamorous dirty work.** There is a lot of dirty work associated with product management: taking meeting notes, getting buy-in, logging bug requests, and cleaning up the backlog. It can feel tedious at times, but I have found that paying attention to these small details can make a difference in team performance.
- **Getting overwhelmed.** As the product development leader, a product manager can feel like they are responsible for millions of to-do items. Tracking and completing them can feel overwhelming.
- **A never-ending list of required skills.** Some product managers take on roles and responsibilities that engineers, designers, marketers, sales, and support staff normally perform at other companies. It can be frustrating and difficult to deliver high-quality engineering, design, marketing, and sales results when a product manager hasn't been properly trained to do so.

Handling Client Feedback

How would you make sure all client feedback is gathered and acted upon?

Things to Consider

- Since this is a hypothetical question, the first part of your response should be a hypothetical answer.
- Apply the rule of three in your hypothetical answer.
- Ask the interviewer if they'd like an example where you handled client feedback in accordance with the process you indicated.

Common Mistakes

- Giving answers that are short, ambiguous, or vague.

Answer

CANDIDATE: First, we need to understand client feedback comes from different channels such as forums, email, and social channels. We could also get feedback for different products like our web or mobile application.

Next, we need to think about organizing feedback. We can group feedback by type. Categories could include praise, complaints, requests for help, and all-encompassing "everything else" bucket.

Then we need to prioritize based on urgency. We may determine urgency based on revenue or PR impact. Synchronous communication channels, such as phone calls and live chat, may feel more urgent than asynchronous ones like email.

It is useful to then subgroup into symptoms and problems. Client feedback can refer to symptoms, not problems. For instance, a single problem may explain one customer's observation that "nothing shows up on my screen" and another's complaint that "I click and the screen does nothing."

Then we can consider the investment required to fix. Some issues are just questions that we can answer immediately. Some may have workarounds that users can implement on their own. Other problems may take hours, days, or even weeks to fix. When considering fixes, we need to consider our development schedules. It may not be prudent to ask our developers to forgo their responsibilities and react to customer complaints instead.

Lastly, we need to figure out how we would respond to customers. Ideally, we would love to report that the issue is fixed, but that is far from realistic. At the very least, in our response, we should aim for a quick acknowledgment that we are working on the issue with an estimated time to resolution.

INTERVIEWER: How would you track the effectiveness of your responses to clients?

CANDIDATE: I would implement a 1 to 5-star rating as well as a "Was your problem solved?" question from an account manager, business developer, or customer service representative. I would also track the success rate by feedback. On a separate note, I understand that some problems may not have a solution or that some solutions may take time to implement.

INTERVIEWER: I see.

CANDIDATE: Did you want me to give you an example of when I applied this client feedback process?

INTERVIEWER: Thanks for the offer. We are short on time, so let us move on to the next question.

Chapter 20 Hypothetical: Problem Solving

Amazon and CEO of Lighting Company

Let us assume you are now in an elevator with the CEO of a lighting company, what would you say to convince her to list products on Amazon?

Things to Consider

- Displaying products on Amazon can improve awareness.
- Having products on Amazon expands the pie. That is, the lighting company will likely have greater overall profit, even if the company offers a unit discount on Amazon. (Increase in unit sales could offset decreases in unit price.)

Common Mistakes

- Not utilizing emotional appeals. They could be as important, perhaps more important, than rational appeals.

Answer

CANDIDATE: Are there any specific reasons why she doesn't want to list her products on Amazon?

INTERVIEWER: She's concerned that listing her product on Amazon will cannibalize other distribution channels.

CANDIDATE: Does she sell online?

INTERVIEWER: She sells it primarily through her own brick-and-mortar shop. She also sells through home improvement stores like Lowe's and Home Depot.

CANDIDATE: I can see why she's afraid of cannibalization. She probably doesn't want to anger channel partners like Home Depot and Lowe's. And when selling through her brick-and-mortar store, she doesn't have to share margin with Amazon.

Therefore, there are a few ways I can approach this:

Amazon's Market Share

I understand she makes most of the profit from her brick-and-mortar shop. However, with Amazon's global reach, brand recognition, and reputation for customer service, she's missing out on Amazon's incredible reach and popular marketplace. She'll likely benefit from increased demand and make more money even if she makes less on each purchase.

Different buyers

The people who buy from her brick-and-mortar shop are not the same as those who buy from Amazon. She will unlock a new global market. Granted, some of her local customers may showroom her products and choose to order on Amazon instead.

An incremental channel

She already has a multi-channel strategy, which includes Lowe's, Home Depot and her own shop. It doesn't hurt to have another channel, especially one that is as impressive as Amazon. Natural cannibalization must already exist with the three channels. Fears of cannibalization are likely to be overblown; the more important issue is whether she has bandwidth and resources to manage another distributor relationship.

An emotional appeal

Emotional appeals can be effective. In this case, I can emphasize the fear of missing out. That is, if she doesn't join Amazon, a competitor will establish and gain first-mover advantage. For instance, first-movers get higher placement in the Amazon search results, which we'll assume is based on sales performance.

INTERVIEWER: Good points. So what's your final recommendation?

CANDIDATE: I'd start with a one-year pilot on Amazon's marketplace. She can assess whether the benefit of incremental sales outweigh the risks of cannibalization and increased coordination costs. If all goes well, she can continue her distribution partnership with Amazon. If not, terminate the agreement.

Kindles on Christmas

You have 100,000 Kindles. There are three weeks until Christmas. These vendors typically sell the following numbers of Kindles per week:

Best Buy	20K
Walmart	10K
Staples	1K
Fred Meyer	2K
Amazon	50K

How would you allocate the 100K Kindles that you have?

Things to Consider

Profit should be the main consideration, but other considerations that may come into play including channel relations, transportation contingencies, and customer perception.

Common Mistakes

Allocating without a logical, profit-focused framework

Answer

CANDIDATE: I have four criteria when considering how I'd allocate Kindles. I'd consider:

- **Total profit impact**

- **Customer perception.** If Kindles are available at one of our channel partners but not on Amazon.com, customers may find that odd and buzz about it on social media.
- **Channel relationships.** Some channels may retaliate, such as dropping our product from their shelves completely, if they don't get their requested allotment.
- **Transportation considerations.** It may be easier to get our inventory to some channel partners vs. others. Geographical distance and coordination complexity are two issues we'd have to consider.

INTERVIEWER: Let's focus on total profit impact and set aside the other considerations. How would you do that?

CANDIDATE: I'd take the estimated demand, leading up to Christmas, and multiply it by the incremental profit.

INTERVIEWER: Go for it.

CANDIDATE: First, I wanted to check if I can assume the weekly run rate you gave me earlier would hold true going into the last three weeks of Christmas.

- For the brick-and-mortar stores, are we expecting demand to ramp-up, as we get nearer to Christmas?
- And for Amazon, are we expecting demand to ramp-down, especially as free Super Saver and Prime shipping deadlines (for Christmas delivery) pass?

INTERVIEWER: Those are good observations, and yes, we do see those trends in our own internal data. But for the purposes of this discussion, assume that the historical sales figures will hold for the last three weeks.

CANDIDATE: Got it. Do you have information about the unit economics?

INTERVIEWER: What do you mean?

CANDIDATE: When I refer to unit economics, I'm thinking about the revenue Amazon generates on each Kindle they sell into the channel minus the cost of each Kindle unit.

INTERVIEWER: You can assume that it's $10 per unit.

CANDIDATE: Are there any volume discounts for Best Buy and Walmart? And does the Amazon.com team get preferred pricing?

INTERVIEWER: The Kindle team has a transfer pricing agreement with Amazon.com. The Amazon.com team does not get the units free; doing so would lead to perverse marketing behaviors that would ultimately harm our channel partnerships. Amazon.com, along with Best Buy and Walmart, do qualify for the 20 percent volume discounts, per unit.

CANDIDATE: A 20 percent discount means a $12 unit profit at Walmart, Best Buy, and Amazon.com.

INTERVIEWER: Correct.

CANDIDATE: If that is the case, we should soak up all possible demand at Staples and Fred Meyer, since they have the highest unit profit. From there, we can choose to allocate the remaining units to Best Buy, Walmart, and Amazon.com. Assuming everything else is equal, we should be indifferent to whether we get our $12 unit profit from any of those three.

INTERVIEWER: Can you summarize the # of units you would allocate across the five?

CANDIDATE: Sure.

Candidate draws the following for the interviewer.

	Unit Profit	Estimated 3 Week Demand	Proposed Allocation	Expected Total Profit
Best Buy	$12	60K	23K	$720K
Walmart	$12	30K	11K	$360K
Staples	$15	3K	3K	$450K
Fred Meyer	$15	6K	6K	$90K
Amazon.com	$12	150K	57K	$1.8M

INTERVIEWER: How did you come up with the 11K, 23K, and 57K allocations?

CANDIDATE: On the one hand, Best Buy had twice the estimated demand of Walmart. On the other hand, Amazon.com had five times the estimated demand of Walmart. Therefore, each company received an allocation that's roughly proportional to estimated demand.

INTERVIEWER: Makes sense. You mentioned we could be indifferent on which one of three sells the Kindle. Why not give the entire (remaining) amount to Amazon.com? That team has more than enough demand. We would help our sister organization.

CANDIDATE: We could. However, Best Buy and Walmart are valuable channel partners. I want to preserve those relationships. They may retaliate by not carrying our products next season.

INTERVIEWER: Let's say the Amazon.com team comes back with evidence that each Kindle they sell leads to $10 incremental purchases, across the Amazon.com site, with a contribution margin of 25%. What would you do then?

CANDIDATE: If that's the case, then Amazon.com's unit profit increases from $12 to $14.50. From a pure profit perspective, I would take Best Buy and Walmart's entire allocation and give it to Amazon.com.

INTERVIEWER: What happened to preserving channel relationships?

CANDIDATE: I'd be transparent with Best Buy and Walmart about the situation. If they are sensible, they'd understand. And I'd give both companies an opportunity to improve their unit economics by cross-selling Amazon gift cards, Amazon Echos, and products from our AmazonBasics.

INTERVIEWER: The AmazonBasics team would be thrilled if you could get their products on Walmart and BestBuy's shelves.

CANDIDATE: You never know unless you try.

Overstocked Books at Amazon

Let us assume we don't have a system that tracks and manages our inventory levels (we do).

How would you approach the challenge of overstock books?

Things to Consider

- Did you show your understanding of why overstock books are a problem for Amazon?
- How can you turn overstock inventory into cash?
- How can you turn overstock inventory into non-monetary value?

Common Mistakes

- A small number of suggestions with limited rationale.

Answer

CANDIDATE: Just to be clear, we suddenly received a lot of overstock books, and you want to know what I would do to get rid of them, right?

INTERVIEWER: Yes.

CANDIDATE: Do we have books of all different genres and types such as textbooks or novels? Or is there an overstock of a particular type?

INTERVIEWER: You have a mixture.

CANDIDATE: Okay, can I get some time to brainstorm?

Candidate takes one minute.

CANDIDATE: I can think of a few ideas.

- **Discounts.** Reduce the price of the book to generate incremental demand. A sale would also attract some new users, both new to Amazon and those new to buying books on Amazon.
- **Bundling.** We do a bundle where you buy two books and get the third one free.
- **Giveaways.** We can give the book away the book for free, perhaps conditioned on a purchase.
- **Charity.** We could donate the books to charity and generate positive PR.
- **Marketing.** We could increase buzz, excitement, and demand for the books by featuring them in Amazon's newsletters.
- **Goodreads.** We can promote the books on Goodreads, a social network for readers.
- **Find alternate distribution channels.** We can try to sell the books to either our competitors or inventory liquidators.

INTERVIEWER: Which one would you recommend?

CANDIDATE: Discounts. It attracts both existing and new Amazon customers (that is, those that haven't bought books before). It can also drive impulse buys on the way toward checkout. Discounts may sacrifice per-item margin, but as you can see, there can be some long-term positives in doing so.

INTERVIEWER: How would you implement this?

CANDIDATE: To start, I would need some data regarding our profit margin on the books. I want to see how low I can sell the books without taking a loss. I would also want to see data on complementary products. That'll give me an idea about which books to pair with which items. I would pair popular items with not so popular books or books that are overstocked. This way I can get rid of them faster.

INTERVIEWER: Thank you.

Vendor Failure during Holiday Season

How do you deal with a vendor's failure to deliver on a large contract during the holiday season?

Things to Consider

- What is the impact?
- Who is affected and to what degree?
- Why did this happen?
- How do we prevent this from happening again?

Common Mistakes

- Not holding the vendor accountable.
- Not suggesting a backup plan.
- Not planning for this potential risk.

Answer

CANDIDATE: It depends. Does the vendor supply prominent products during our holiday season?

INTERVIEWER: What do you consider a prominent product?

CANDIDATE: Perhaps it is a hot toy like a Sony PlayStation.

INTERVIEWER: Okay. Let's assume the vendor is supplying prominent products.

CANDIDATE: That's a big problem.

INTERVIEWER: Why?

CANDIDATE: The problem does not just stop at missed sales of an unavailable product. It ripples across our business. Consider the following:

- **People want to buy product X**. If it's out of stock, it's missed revenue, disappointed customers, and possibly negative publicity.
- **People who buy product Y and Z because they go well with product X**. In other words, these are missed sales of complementary products.
- **People who didn't intend to purchase product A and B at the retailer but did so because they were buying product X**. The retail industry calls these discretionary purchases. That is, they weren't planning to buy AA batteries, but walking through the retailer's virtual aisles reminded the customer that they should stockpile for a rainy day.

INTERVIEWER: That's a good analysis. How would you handle these problems?

CANDIDATE: I can think of a few solutions:

- **Don't discount product X.** Fewer people will buy product X due to the higher price. It'll allow us to hold more inventory before a stock out. Some will be disappointed with higher prices, but it'll be better than not being able to buy the product at all. Not a perfect fix, but better than empty shelves.
- **Don't promote product X.** Similar to the previous solution. For example, let's not feature it on the home page. Less attention means fewer buyers; fewer buyers means we can hold onto more product before it goes out of stock.
- **Limit purchases per account.** By limiting the purchase quantity to one or two per account will give more customers a chance to buy at least one. This rationing strategy reduces hoarding and stockouts.
- **Hold the vendor accountable.** Push back on the vendor and insist that they fulfill their promise to provide inventory. Different ways of driving accountability could include continuous follow-up, executive escalation, or legal action. The retailer could also threaten the vendor. That is, we may not carry their product next season. Or they may get less co-op marketing dollars for next season.
- **Find an alternate vendor or encourage other resellers to sell on the site.** See if others can offer identical or nearly identical products. Sometimes it could be an alternate manufacturer if it is a quasi-commodity like AA batteries. Other times it can be another reseller, such as an electronics boutique, for a hot product like Sony PlayStation.
- **Suggest alternative products.** Sometimes dissimilar products can serve the same need. For example, customers looking for a Japanese massage chair recliner may be satisfied with a massage stick that costs $2,500 less.
- **Purchase from other retailers.** It's an odd tactic, but I once heard Jeff Bezos commanded Amazon employees to stock their toy department with the 100 hottest products from Toys 'R Us. Doing so is unlikely to lead to positive margins, but it minimizes negative publicity, drives customer traffic, and creates cross-selling opportunities.

INTERVIEWER: That's a good list. Now let's say our marketing team has promoted our upcoming sale in a direct mail campaign that was sent last week. Customers are anticipating this product for a certain price. What should we do?

CANDIDATE: I would stop promoting it right now and definitely not promote it on the website. I would also limit the purchases by account. While it will minimize the bad user experience, it won't completely solve the problem.

As a customer, I've encountered this situation before, and it's frustrating. Limiting purchases is disappointing. But it's better than not offering the product at all or selling it at a higher price than advertised.

INTERVIEWER: Of these solutions, which one would you propose?

CANDIDATE: I'd start with holding the vendor accountable. Next, I'll look for alternative suppliers and resellers. And lastly, I'd keep an eye on incoming demand and adjust our advertising, promotional discounting, and product rationing limits appropriately.

Not Hitting a Deadline

You have to do feature X or launch product Y, which requires 10 engineers to finish on time. You only have five. What do you do?

Things to Consider

- Can you get more resources?
- Can you change scope?
- Can you gain more time?

Common Mistakes

- Not developing a structured framework that is easy to follow.

Answer

CANDIDATE: Can I get some time to brainstorm?

Candidate takes one minute

CANDIDATE: Anytime I face a tight deadline, I use the following six-point framework to consider my options:

1. **Recruit Engineers Externally.** Recruit more engineers externally to fulfill our requirement.
   - **Pros:** Solves the problem completely.
   - **Cons:** Might take time to recruit. Takes time for new engineers to get comfortable. And if we don't need the extra engineers after the deadline, it's difficult to terminate them.
2. **Recruit Engineers Internally.** Recruit more engineers, internally, to work on this project.
   - **Pros:** Solves the problem completely.
   - **Cons:** Might take time to recruit. Might not have engineers on standby. Takes time for new engineers to get comfortable. Other project leaders may not be happy when we take away their resources.
3. **Change Implementation.** Maybe our approach is too complex. We can search for a simpler implementation.
   - **Pros:** Might discover new solutions when reassessing.
   - **Cons:** Users or decision makers might not like our alternate approach. Perhaps it is wiser to invest in the long-term fix than to waste resources on a short-term solution.

4. **Change Scope.** Maybe we should implement a partial fix so that we can focus on features that are more critical. When we have more time, we can come back and complete the project.
    o   **Pros:** Rather than spend time to perfect it, get a partial solution in customers' hands. From there, we can use their feedback to guide future work.
    o   **Cons:** Customers may be unhappy with the partial fix. Rather than launching the feature once, we are launching twice. That would require extra effort from other teams such as marketing and support.
5. **Push Deadline Back.** We can ask for more time.
    o   **Pros:** Resolves the time crunch.
    o   **Cons:** The delay may create an opportunity for competitors. Or it may affect other projects, especially if our project is a critical dependency.
6. **Overtime.** We can ask the team to work overtime.
    o   **Pros:** Fixes the problem completely.
    o   **Cons:** Bad for team morale. Team will not be happy. It'll also create a bad precedent.

INTERVIEWER: It's interesting you mentioned overtime. That's a very touchy issue for a PM to bring up to your team. How would you approach this?

CANDIDATE: I would first not tell the team about this. I want to approach the higher-ups first. Ask them if the team commits to overtime (I would estimate the overtime needed), could the team get some additional vacation time after the deadline? If the higher-ups agree, I will then ask the team if they want to do this. If they say yes, I'll communicate back to the higher-ups.

INTERVIEWER: What if the higher-ups say no to vacation time and just want you to work extra hours?

CANDIDATE: I would have to assess the situation. Although feature delivery is very important, losing team morale is not a consequence I take lightly. Think about it. They could retaliate. They could quit.

INTERVIEWER: So you would tell the higher-ups that it's not doable?

CANDIDATE: It's hard to answer because there is no win-win situation, so I have to pick a side. In most scenarios, I would side with my team. Besides the reason above, my team would also lose trust in me. I can't do my job properly as a PM if my team no longer trusts and respects me.

INTERVIEWER: You are saying you would give in every time your team makes a request?

CANDIDATE: No, I would not. I had to pick a side, and after careful consideration, I concluded that was the better solution.

INTERVIEWER: But situations like this happen a lot. Are you going to do this every time? How can the company trust you as a liaison between upper management and the team?

CANDIDATE: If they trust me to be the liaison, they should trust my judgment. I get where they are coming from. I really do. However, sometimes we have to consider team morale and make sacrifices. Overtime is something that happens a lot, but who caused this anyway? Was this a project estimation error? We need to perform an analysis on what went wrong so we can prevent this next time. But for this current situation, we need to move forward and hit our goals.

INTERVIEWER: Let us say after the analysis, your peers concluded you were the one most responsible for what happened. What would you tell the team?

CANDIDATE: I would own up to my mistake. There is no point in deflecting blame. They will find out anyway, and you should be honest toward your own teammates. If you aren't going to do that, then how can they trust you?

User Problems

Half the users have one problem. The other half has another problem. How would you resolve this?

Things to Consider

- What is the issue?
- Which issue is more important?
- Are there opportunities to resolve both with a single solution?

Common Mistakes

- Not demonstrating a willingness to investigate the issue deeply and instead, just reacting.
- Showing poor prioritization judgment.

Answer

CANDIDATE: I would start by seeing if these two problems are connected. Maybe they are different symptoms for the same root cause.

I would then understand the customer population. Perhaps one set uses Windows PC, and the other set uses Mac. Perhaps their problems are related to their operating systems.

If there are no distinguishing characteristics between the two user populations, then I can exclude those factors.

INTERVIEWER: Let's say these two customer populations are unrelated. Why would they see different problems?

CANDIDATE: Here are some potential reasons:

- One is using mobile, and another is using desktop.
- They are using different operating systems such as iOS vs. Android.
- They are using different browsers such as Chrome vs. Edge.
- They are whitelisted for a special A/B test experience.
- They are doing different things. Perhaps one is trying to buy a game, and another is trying to buy electronics.
- They are in different countries such as Japan vs. the US.

- They are using different languages such as Japanese vs. English.
- They are using different payment options such as credit cards vs. PayPal.

INTERVIEWER: That's a good list of things to explore. Thank you.

Kindle Date Slip

It is March. You are on the Kindle Team, and the engineers tell you that the new Kindle due in September will not ship until January. What do you do?

Things to Consider

- If your first thought is freak out, you're not the only one. Resist the urge to start blabbing; instead, use your fight or flight impulse as a reminder to take a moment to calm your nerves and think about the situation before answering.
- Consider using the Five Whys technique to investigate the root cause of the delay.
- Many candidates become so preoccupied with the analysis that they forget to issue a recommendation.

Common Mistakes

- Not issuing a recommendation.
- Not going deep enough on the potential reason for the delay.
- Not suggesting a satisfactory solution.

Answer

CANDIDATE: I'm going to take a minute to collect my thoughts.

Candidate takes one minute.

CANDIDATE: I would first start asking him the reason why they are delaying it.

INTERVIEWER: They believe the product is not feature complete. If it launches in September, they believe it'll disappoint customers.

CANDIDATE: I would ask what features do they think are missing?

INTERVIEWER: Whispersync. It lets you synchronize your audiobooks with your regular books.

CANDIDATE: Is this a new feature or a feature carried over from the previous version?

INTERVIEWER: Does it matter?

CANDIDATE: Well, if it's a pre-existing feature, then customers will feel that Amazon is taking a step backward, especially if it's an important feature.

INTERVIEWER: It's a brand new feature.

CANDIDATE: Is there any reason why we never included it in the original spec?

INTERVIEWER: The team thinks that only a small percentage of users would find this useful, so they didn't feel it was necessary to include it the first time around.

CANDIDATE: So what is the reason for including it now?

INTERVIEWER: The team researched the market again and realized it is a feature requested by 40 percent of the users surveyed.

CANDIDATE: How many users did the team survey?

INTERVIEWER: Around 50,000.

CANDIDATE: I am assuming the holiday shopping season is the reason why we decided to ship this new Kindle in September. If we delay it until January, we'll miss out on holiday demand. How many Kindles are we expecting to sell in the first month?

INTERVIEWER: Around four million.

CANDIDATE: Is this a software feature or a hardware feature? Meaning, can we patch this feature in after the Kindle has shipped?

INTERVIEWER: It is a software feature. We can patch it in after it has shipped.

CANDIDATE: Have we announced this new feature?

INTERVIEWER: Yes, it was announced recently.

CANDIDATE: Then I would suggest we do not delay the launch. I'd rather sell the units now so that we can take advantage of holiday demand. We can tell customers that we intend to release the new feature in an upcoming software release. While this isn't ideal, I'm hoping that we lose no more than 10 percent of our anticipated demand.

I would share the plan with the engineering team. That is, we'll launch the Kindle in September and then add the new feature in a software update in January.

INTERVIEWER: Let's say you have this meeting with the engineering lead. He agrees with your revenue motivations, but he thinks we are disappointing a lot of our users and this will hurt our branding.

CANDIDATE: Here's how I'd explain it to the engineering leader: our PR team will spin the situation as wanting to get the new Kindle to our users earlier. Not all users will understand, but in the end, we will end up selling more units. To help alleviate the engineering leader's concerns, I'll share examples of companies that have successfully sold well-received products with software updates, such as Tesla.

Chapter 21 Strategy: New Market Entry

New Markets for Amazon

Let us pretend you are a brand new Product Manager at Amazon. Tell me how you would determine the next big thing for us and then walk me through your idea for it.

Things to Consider

- Start with Amazon's core competencies.
- Factor in customer needs.

Common Mistakes

- Getting defensive when the interviewer asks clarifying questions or pushes back on an idea.

Answer

CANDIDATE: I would start with Amazon's core competencies. Ideas that start with a company's strengths are more sustainable in the long-term.

Here is a list of the Amazon products I can think of:

- **Amazon.com**. E-commerce. Lots of high-income customers with a propensity to spend. Good fulfillment infrastructure, selection, and customer service. Only limited to the Internet though.
- **Amazon Fresh**. Grocery purchasing.
- **Amazon Digital Services**. Lots of digital goods on Amazon including games, books, and music.
- **Amazon Prime Video**. TV shows and movies-on-demand. Original content too.
- **Amazon Fire TV**. A digital media player that allows you to stream video and audio content to a TV.
- **Amazon Web Services**. Server infrastructure. Lots of enterprise customer relationships.
- **Amazon Advertising**. Sell ads to other companies on both Amazon.com properties and possibly third-party sites too.
- **Twitch**. Game streaming website with a large user base. Opportunities to show ads and host tournaments.
- **Kindle**. Physical products and platforms for books, apps, music, games, movies, etc.
- **Alexa**. Web traffic data and analytics.

Let me know if I missed any major products.

INTERVIEWER: That looks like a pretty decent list.

CANDIDATE: I am going to first think about Amazon's strengths. Building something new is easier when we're building on top of strength. Then we'll think about opportunities, especially if there are marketplace gaps not well served by our competitors or us. Lastly, I'll outline some potential threats and highlight past mistakes that should be avoided.

Can I have some time to brainstorm?

Candidate takes one minute.

CANDIDATE: Okay, let's first go over Amazon's strengths as a company:

- **Vast Resources and Scale.** Amazon is one of the world's biggest companies, so we already have resources such as employees, customers, capital, and proven distribution channels. We've also got all of these at scale, which means we can think big.

- **Risk-Embracing Culture.** Amazon has a culture of experimenting with bold ideas and accepting that some of them will fail. For example, the Kindle was a success while the Amazon Phone wasn't. The opposite could have turned out to be true, but the only way to know was to launch these products.

- **Competitive, Business-Savvy DNA.** As one of the few tech companies that embraces MBA's and a CEO with a Wall Street background, Amazon understands that a great product alone is insufficient to win. Great products must be coupled with sound business strategy and defensible moats for lasting success.

- **Focus on the Customer.** Amazon is a customer-centric company. They provide an exceptional shopping experience and world-class support. They also build loyalty by passing savings to the end-user. Amazon continually focuses on delighting their customers.

Does this sound right for you?

INTERVIEWER: Yes, it does, please go on.

CANDIDATE: Great. Now, here are some markets where Amazon is already successful in:

- **eCommerce.** Amazon is the largest online retailer in the world. Not only has it pioneered the field with features such as Prime and 1-Click ordering, but also it is relentlessly innovating with products such as Amazon Fresh and Drone Delivery.

- **Cloud Infrastructure.** AWS is one of the leading cloud-based computing providers, rivaled by only a handful of competitors. This is a market that is still expanding, and AWS is well-positioned to be a major long-term player.

- **E-books.** The Kindle is the most popular e-reader. Nearly all titles published electronically are available on Kindle. Amazon's dominance from physical to digital book sales wasn't something they could take for granted; I'm impressed they successfully defended Apple's attack in that space.

As for gaps in this market, I don't know too much about AWS offerings, so if it's okay with you, I'd like to set that aside in this discussion. E-books are interesting, but the potential is smaller than e-commerce's.

INTERVIEWER: What e-commerce opportunities would you consider?

CANDIDATE: I can think of a few ideas:

- **Amazon Games.** We need something to attract developers to develop games for the Amazon platform, including Amazon Fire TV. Phones didn't succeed because not enough developers adopted it, meaning not enough content. Fire TV is doing okay; developing games for it would help. With so many games sold on Amazon.com already, this would be a great natural fit. Twitch would also contribute by streaming games and hosting tournaments. This might seem trivial today, but video games keep increasing in popularity. With ever-more immersive VR experiences, combined with Twitch's distribution platform, 10 years from now, professional gamers might be considered in the same breath as professional athletes.

- **Amazon Browser.** Google is a major threat to Amazon. Its search engine and browser dominance mean that Google can subvert a user's journey toward Amazon. Just imagine, Google can distract Amazon customers with product offers and competitive alternatives. Amazon is doing a good job building customer awareness that commercial searches should start with Amazon; a recent study showed that over 50% of purchase-related searches start on Amazon, not Google. By having our own browser, we further protect ourselves. A browser improves our understanding of user intent and Internet usage behavior, which can improve analytics and ad targeting. And any information we collect is less information that Google collects. We can start by making our Amazon browser the default on Kindles.

- **Amazon Capital.** We mentioned before that Amazon is a company with deep business roots. Given the number of merchants that sell on Amazon.com and startups that host their products on AWS, these customers may be tomorrow's leading businesses. Amazon could use their performance data, on either Amazon.com or AWS, to signal which companies have the best prospects. From there, Amazon can provide equity or debt financing.

Is there a specific opportunity you want me to expand on?

INTERVIEWER: Why don't you walk me through Amazon Capital in more detail?

CANDIDATE: Of course. There are two main ways Amazon could invest in companies:

- Loan money for expansion
- Invest in exchange for equity

It's hard to predict which one would work best, so I'd experiment with both to start. Over time we'll see which one has the bigger payoff.

Although the concept is new to Amazon, it's not totally unproven. Google has an investing arm called CapitalG; some of their most successful investments include Uber, Lyft, Airbnb, and SurveyMonkey.

Amazon's culture is even more business-oriented than Google's. I don't see why we wouldn't have a shot at this market. Also, Amazon as a company has been successful in managing multiple distinct businesses, such as Amazon.com, AWS, and Zappos. In other words, history has shown that Amazon isn't easily distracted with seemingly dissimilar businesses.

INTERVIEWER: Interesting. But aren't there huge risks associated with startup investing?

CANDIDATE: Yes. The biggest risk is that a startup fails, and you lose your entire investment in that company. But here's the interesting thing: since Amazon's portfolio companies are likely to be Amazon customers. So whatever revenue Amazon generates from AWS or third-party merchant fees offsets any potential investment loss.

Another risk is adverse selection. Most investors do not have a clear and accurate picture of how startups are performing. This leads good money to chase after bad companies.

Amazon can audit a startup's Amazon services (e.g. AWS) data to verify whether a startup is performing as advertised. We can never completely remove all the risk associated with an idea, but it does seem that Amazon's unfair "data" advantage can help us become a successful investor.

INTERVIEWER: Thank you.

Dropbox in a New Market

Dropbox is planning a big launch in a new market.

What would you evaluate? What problems will you encounter?

Things to Consider

- Customer demand, technical capabilities, as well as sales and marketing capabilities.

Common Mistakes

- Not mentioning regulatory issues.
- Payment problems are also prevalent from country-to-country. Certain countries accept unique credit cards like Japan's JCB. Other countries or organizations may prefer check payments. Others may prefer post-paid vs. pre-paid billing.

Answer

CANDIDATE: Can I ask some clarifying questions?

INTERVIEWER: Sure, go ahead.

CANDIDATE: What is our primary goal in this market for the launch? I would assume market share, but I want to confirm this.

INTERVIEWER: Your assumption is correct. We want to grab as much market share as we can right now before a competitor enters the market.

CANDIDATE: What is the launch plan? We'd want to consider advertising, sales, technical infrastructure, business development, government relationships, office space, and other local partners.

INTERVIEWER: We have the standard launch marketing plan: blog post, press interviews, social media, online referrals, offline marketing, and appearances with government officials.

CANDIDATE: How's the technical infrastructure? I'm concerned primarily about latency and security.

INTERVIEWER: We are using Amazon's server infrastructure, and they have servers locally. We also performed a full security audit, and it passed our CIO's tests.

CANDIDATE: Are there any constraints in this market I should know before I proceed?

INTERVIEWER: What would you classify as constraints? Are you trying to get me to answer the question for you?

CANDIDATE: I wanted to know if there is anything specific that you wanted me to know before I start. But your concern is fair. I'll begin to share potential issues we should consider:

- **Number of Computers Owned.** How many people actually own computers?
- **Internet Access.** How many people actually have Internet? High Internet adoption is critical because Dropbox requires Internet access.
- **The Need for Cloud Syncing.** How many people actually need cloud synchronization? What's the best way to acquire those users?
- **Competitors.** Who are our competitors in the local market? Who are they targeting? And what is their value proposition? Do we go after the same users? And how do we make our value proposition differentiated?
- **Internet Infrastructure.** You assured me that our server infrastructure isn't an issue. However, we are dependent on the user's Internet service provider (ISP), which can impact the overall customer experience. An ISP with slow service or frequent disruptions can affect the Dropbox experience. We'd have to tailor our product to account for this.
- **Local Servers.** You mentioned that we're using Amazon's services, but there may be reasons why we would need a local server. Here are some reasons why a local server could help:
    - *Reduce bandwidth costs*
    - *Improve application performance* by reducing latency
    - *Improve application availability*, especially if there is a government-imposed firewall
- **Languages & Customer Service.** Our website, software, and customer service need to be localized. Certain countries, such as Malaysia and Belgium, use multiple languages.
- **Pricing.** We'll have to adjust pricing to adapt to local spending power. We may also have to consider local preferences. For instance, certain consumers may not like to pay for services on a monthly basis and would prefer to pay a one-time fee instead.
- **Payment.** Maybe the local market doesn't use credit cards or PayPal, for example, and we would need to work with carrier billing, prepaid cards or even cash payment. We may have to support both pre and post-pay models.

INTERVIEWER: That's a lot. If you had to pick, what would be your top three issues you'd address?

CANDIDATE: My top three would be:

- **Internet Infrastructure.** Knowing how it affects product performance, it'd be one of the first things I'd investigate.
- **Payment.** It would be terrible if people wanted to pay for our service but can't.
- **Languages & Customer Service.** Not taking the time to localize our service reinforces the customer's belief that:
    - Our service doesn't care to localize.
    - Our service didn't have time to localize.

- o Our service is foreign and exported from another country.
- o Our service is out of touch with local customs or their needs.

INTERVIEWER: That's a good prioritization. Thank you.

Selling on Amazon

Amazon started as a place in which you can "buy" stuff, and they were doing really well. At some point, they also decided to allow people to "sell" their stuff. It was a very risky decision; they could not anticipate if it was going to be successful. Do you consider it was a good or bad decision to do so? Why?

Things to Consider

- What is the cannibalization impact?
- How did this shape customer satisfaction?
- How did this affect competition?

Common Mistakes

- Hindsight bias

Answer

CANDIDATE: I want to point out that in reality, Amazon must have done a lot of market research and some initial testing before they decided to roll it out to everyone else. But to answer this question I would say it was a good decision because of these reasons:

- **More Traffic.** You mentioned Amazon is a place in which you can "buy stuff." Allowing people to sell would reinforce this benefit. Increasing product inventory (via "sell stuff") you'll increase buyer traffic too.
- **Diversification.** Increasing the number of sellers minimizes their supplier risk.
- **More Profit.** This opens a new revenue stream for Amazon. When people sell on Amazon, Amazon gets a commission. While sellers would like to list and sell items for free, Amazon sellers can't deny that Amazon's reach and brand as an eCommerce destination is well worth the commission they pay to the company.
- **Defensive & Offensive Play.** It takes time and effort to manage inventory across multiple marketplaces. By opening up Amazon to sellers, they reduced the likelihood that those sellers would sell on competitive sites like eBay.
- **Monitoring & Data.** By having these transactions occur under Amazon, not only can we gauge the latest price points (so we can reprice accordingly), we can also get valuable data on user buying habits. We can see what sells and what doesn't. We can identify product gaps and focus on supplier efforts.

INTERVIEWER: Wouldn't selling through a third-party seller minimize our revenue? That is, margins for first-party supplied products are often larger than third-party supplied products?

CANDIDATE: It can, but I think there are three good things about this:

1. **Increase market share**. Amazon has focused on gaining market share, often at the expense of lower margins. This third-party seller strategy is in-line with that spirit.

2. **Increase long-term revenue**. Offering more product options is likely to improve customer retention, which leads to higher long-term revenue.

3. **Reinforce the brand**. Customers have confidence that our marketplace is the "world's biggest store" with some of the most competitive prices. Confident in that belief, our customers are less likely to shop with our competition.

INTERVIEWER: What are some negative points you can think of?

CANDIDATE: Well, besides the one you mentioned, here are a few more:

1. **Weaken the Amazon Brand.** If third-party sellers provide suboptimal shopping experiences, customers will blame Amazon.

2. **Increase coordination costs.** We will incur significant overhead managing relationships with thousands and possibly millions of new third-party sellers. We'll also serve as the liaison between customers and third-party sellers, increasing the workload on our customer service teams.

3. **Confuse Amazon's customers.** Some customers may get confused when they see features targeted to sellers such as the "Apply to be a Seller" call-to-action. Although Amazon's current design has minimized this confusion, this was surely a problem the launch team pondered the initial rollout.

INTERVIEWER: Thank you.

Uber's Ultra High-End Service

Should Uber roll out an ultra-high-end taxi service? That is, should Uber offer ridesharing services using Rolls Royce, Bentley, and other super-luxury cars?

Things to Consider

- Is there enough demand?
- Will the new service cannibalize existing services?
- What are the challenges with super-luxury cars? Availability? Impact on insurance premiums?

Common Mistakes

- Unfairly dismissing usage of super-luxury cars due to preconceived notions of cost.
- Overestimating the surcharge customers are willing to pay for a super-luxury car.

Answer

CANDIDATE: I would consider the following:

- **Potential Market.** This would probably be city-specific. We can look at our data and see if there are people who might be interested in similar services. They could be people who are very wealthy. Popular locations could include New York, San Francisco, Dubai, and Hong Kong. Wealthy people live there and are probably the markets with the highest demand for this service. They may want the prestige associated with experiencing or showing up in a super-luxury vehicle. Since these cities have bad traffic, people may prefer to sit in a nice car but not drive themselves.

- **Enough Drivers with Super-Luxury Cars.** Uber drivers typically provide their own vehicles. So the question is: are there enough Uber drivers who own a super-luxury car? Would these people want to be Uber drivers in the first place? Money might not be a motivation for them. It could be other motivations like showing off their cars or meeting new people. I would also consider businesses that actually do this already and see if they might be interested in partnering with Uber.

- **Uber without the Driver, a new business model.** It's possible with ultra-luxury cars the passengers would rather be the driver. Why sit in a super-luxury car such as a Ferrari when you can drive it? Perhaps the Uber driver would deliver the super-luxury car for the Uber customer to drive. When the customer is finished, the driver will take the super-luxury car back.

- **Competitors.** I want to see if there are competitors. How they operate, how much profit margin they are making, and how much market share they own are things I would think about. It's good to learn from others' experiences.

- **Customer Confusion.** Brand extensions always create an opportunity for customer confusion. Uber already has a seemingly endless number of options, including UberX, UberPool, and UberBlack. Perhaps this is not a concern for the company, but it should be considered, especially the implications on the UI and not cluttering the user experience.

- **Customer Confusion.** This comes in two parts. Customers may be confused because we try to offer another service. Sure, it's similar to our core model, but would this add confusion to our story? It's something we need to be careful about as we implement. Another is the UI. We need to make sure it doesn't clutter up the UI and create too many choices for our users. They may not like it.

- **Test Launches.** We would want to test launch this in select cities. Assumptions and projections are nice, but nothing beats real data. This way we can be sure our pricing and margins are optimized before our rollout to the general public.

INTERVIEWER: You mentioned Uber drivers could be motivated for reasons other than money. Let's say we roll this out, and some drivers with really nice cars are using this to meet wealthy clients. Shouldn't we be worried that Uber drivers have hidden agendas? A wealthy client may not want to get pestered by a star-struck Uber driver.

CANDIDATE: I get where you are coming from, and I understand this is a touchy issue. Our rating system and driver policies can go a long way to minimize driver behaviors that annoy our customers. We can ban drivers that go too far.

INTERVIEWER: Thank you.

Next Country for Amazon Expansion

How would you determine the next country for Amazon expansion?

Things to Consider

- What are your criteria for country expansion?
- Why did you include certain criteria? Why did you leave out others?

- Not factoring shipping and fulfillment challenges.
- Not factoring in payment challenges.
- Not factoring in regulatory issues.

Answer

CANDIDATE: Did you want me to name a specific country? Or did you just want my criteria and thought process on how I would choose the next launch country?

INTERVIEWER: Please focus on the latter.

CANDIDATE: I can think of three major factors:

- **Potential Market**. How big is the potential market? Here are some sub-factors I'd consider:
    - **Market wealth**. What is the average income per capita?
    - **Growth**. How fast is income per capita growing?
    - **Spending habits**. Is the market a consumer-oriented economy?
    - **Competition**. How strong is the competition? Is it fragmented?
    - **Labor and real estate**. Are labor and real estate reasonable?
    - **Regulations**. Are the local regulations favorable to Amazon? Licenses, financial regulations, and taxes must be factored in.
    - **Supplier power**. Do retailers have significant negotiation leverage with suppliers in that home market?
- **Feasibility.** How feasible is it for us to expand right now? That would certainly limit some of our options. This breaks down to location (might be better to expand to Belarus when we already have a huge presence in Russia because it's close by), local talent (can't really expand if we have trouble setting up an office there), and budget (we might not be able to target large countries or countries with fierce competition if we don't have enough resources).
- **Opportunity Cost.** Is investing in that market better an alternate investment?

INTERVIEWER: For potential market, do you mean it's a bad idea to target a country if there is already a major competitor there?

CANDIDATE: It depends. On the one hand, we want to avoid countries with intense competition because it would be an uphill battle. It might be more effective (considering everything else is equal like wealth and spending habits) to target a country with little to no competition.

On the other hand, we may want to target markets with lots of competition. A good example is a market that serves as a competitor's cash cow. By striking there, we can distract and harm our competition, even though it may not be the most profitable opportunity for us.

INTERVIEWER: I've got another question for you. You mentioned earlier that Amazon should factor in a market's spending habits. Should we completely avoid markets that don't have a strong consumer-driven economy?

CANDIDATE: It really depends on the situation. While that's not ideal, it's possible that could deter our competition. So due to lack of competition, less consumer-oriented markets might actually be more profitable, even though total spending would be less.

INTERVIEWER: Makes sense. Thank you.

Google's Cable TV Service

Should Google build a Comcast-like TV cable service?

Things to Consider

- The phrasing is ambiguous, but this is a casual-sounding strategy question.
- When answering a strategy question, organize your discussion around a framework such as SWOT or a pros and cons list, at the very least.
- Conclude your answer with a recommendation.

Common Mistakes

- Not wanting to take a stand, afraid to take the wrong position.
- Not wanting to ask the question, given a lack of expertise in TV cable services.

Answer

CANDIDATE: So are we talking about actual TV content, with commercials and all that? We are not doing Internet-based TV?

INTERVIEWER: That is correct.

CANDIDATE: Let me brainstorm some ideas that utilize Google's strengths. Then I will analyze our market and decide if these ideas fit.

Candidate takes one minute.

CANDIDATE: I can think of a few ideas.

- **YouTube content delivery.** Google's new Comcast-like service can deliver YouTube content. The advantage: it could expand YouTube's fan base. The potential disadvantage: the users could already be YouTube consumers.
- **Original content delivery.** "Content makes the network" is what the industry insiders say. Original content is the reason why we can get users to choose us vs. our competitors. YouTube has some original content, but it doesn't have a reputation for original content like Netflix or Amazon Prime.
- **Streaming.** Streaming is another way to get endless content. YouTube is beginning to do a lot of streaming, although most of it is game related. This might be targeting the same crowd as YouTube.

I think the most promising feature is the YouTube content delivery, followed by streaming, and then original content delivery. Ideally, I want to have all three, but it might be more feasible to do just one to test. I want to make a note here that we are just porting YouTube over to a TV format. It would be easier if we were doing Internet TV.

I also want to say I left out traditional TV content because Google doesn't have any resources in that area. We can buy shows in the future if this kicks off.

INTERVIEWER: You described some problems before but didn't really go into detail. What are some challenges you think this will face if it is done this way? How would you solve them?

CANDIDATE: I can think of several challenges:

- **Cable TV is a dying business**. Over the last couple of years, everyone wants to "cut-the-cord." They can access their favorite content, either Netflix or YouTube, via the Internet. And they don't need cable TV to do so. They can watch it on their phone (via their wireless carrier's data plan), at work, or through publicly available Internet at the library or coffee shops.
- **Cannibalization of YouTube**. This will cause a dip in YouTube traffic. We might target the same people who are already using our services. We can't really solve this unless we have original content that is not available on YouTube. However, if we have these two distribution channels, why would we exclude one?
- **Lower Ad Revenue**. I mentioned cannibalization earlier, and it might seem like it won't matter when both networks are under us. The problem is YouTube allows for ad attribution, so any ads we run on there are going to do better. If some users are instead watching our TV network, ad attribution is harder, perhaps leading to lower ad revenue. On a side note, revenue from new users can mitigate loss from existing users. Also, some commercials that previously don't do well on YouTube might do well on the TV, which can bring our revenue up.
- **Setup costs and a steep learning curve**. It'll be hard to set up our service. I am not an expert on how to build a TV network infrastructure. I get the feeling that it is not something we can buy off-the-shelf.
- **Competition**. We are going to have to compete with traditional TV networks. With our lack of original content, this will be a challenge. Also, the Google brand may be a curse than a blessing. People know Google as a tech company, not as a TV network. I'd recommend we use YouTube's brand instead of Google's.

INTERVIEWER: What do you think of this idea overall?

CANDIDATE: If it were up to me, I would do an Internet-based TV box instead. I believe Google is already doing that with Android TV. It's a growing market, and our competitors' moves into that space validate the industry's enthusiasm for Internet-based TV boxes (Fire TV, Apple TV). It would still have some of the problems I described earlier, but it does not have the steep learning curve or setup costs of a TV network infrastructure.

Chapter 22 Strategy: Launch Plan

Expedia and Train Tickets

Let us say Expedia.com wants to enter a new category: selling train tickets. You are in charge of launching this new category. What would you do?

Things to Consider

- Do we know how to efficiently acquire customers?
- Does Expedia have relationships with train travel providers? If not, can it easily obtain relationships?
- How can they get the travel provider data? Will the data be fresh?

Common Mistakes

- Not appreciating how hard it is to get train data.
- Not appreciating how hard it is to get fresh and accurate data.
- Not appreciating how complicated is to calculate possible trip permutations.

Answer

CANDIDATE: Since Expedia.com operates globally, I would start by focusing on countries with high consumer train usage. The US is not one of them.

INTERVIEWER: Do you know which countries are?

CANDIDATE: Unfortunately, I do not, but we can research it later. The idea here is to come up with a plan. I would first pick a country Expedia already operates heavily in with a lot of consumer train usage and then do a launch there. From there, we can improve how we operate and open it up to the world country by country.

To pick such a country, we need to keep the following in mind:

- **Potential Market.** We're looking to maximize profitability and ROI. If the pilot country is a small market, that's okay, especially if our goal is to just learn about the opportunity. However, our subsequent rollout should be a larger market. It'll let us see if success from a smaller market can be repeated in a bigger market.
- **Competitors.** What's the competitive landscape like? If the competition is non-existent or fragmented, then that means we can use our scale and brand power to win market share quickly. If the competition is strong and organized, we might have to take a more measured approach to how we want to differentiate from the incumbent.
- **Ease of Operation.** How easy would it be to operate in the target country? Do we already have a local presence? Is the local market easy to enter from a regulatory, supplier and labor perspective? Is it easy for us to access the target customer via local advertising or perhaps through a partner channel?
- **Synergies.** Can we use our strengths to our advantage? For example, Expedia has a strong assortment of air, hotel, car, and cruise options. Can we construct a better end-to-end purchasing experience vs. competitors who focus strictly on rail?

INTERVIEWER: You mentioned competition. Would a strong competitor deter you from entering the market?

CANDIDATE: Competition wouldn't scare me outright, but I do think it's important to have first-mover advantage, especially when there isn't a significant product or service differentiation between companies.

I can give you an example. Uber didn't operate in China for a long time, giving an opportunity for other firms to pop up. When Uber decided to enter the Chinese market, Uber had to spend billions to mount an attack. Uber responded too late. Their competitor, not Uber, became the number one player.

Although Uber recently left the market by merging with their number one rival, it was worthwhile for Uber to give the Chinese market a shot. They shouldn't just give up the world's largest market without even trying.

INTERVIEWER: Okay, keep going.

CANDIDATE: I'd consider customer scenarios next. Here's a list:

- **Holiday vs. Commuter Travel.** Some Expedia users will be train commuters. Other users might consider train travel only for holidays.
- **Discounts and Deals.** Yield management is a big concern since train seats are perishable. We'll have to manage discounts carefully to help train operators maximize revenue.
- **Long vs. Short Distance.** Consumers traveling a short distance place a higher value on being on time. Consumers traveling a long distance may be slightly more lenient about arriving on time.

INTERVIEWER: Can you tell me more about yield and revenue management?

CANDIDATE: Sure, every train has a set of operational costs when it makes a journey. It includes labor and fuel. There are other fixed costs such as:

- Depreciation
- Cost of capital
- General and administrative costs
- Insurance
- Marketing expense
- Trainyard operations
- Maintenance costs for trains, railway structures, and signals

Since train operators incur these expenses, regardless of how many passengers travel, every single passenger ticket a train operator can sell will help pay for these upfront costs. Discounts are an effective way to generate revenue (and pay off these costs) because the incremental cost of carrying and servicing an additional passenger is close to zero, as long as the train is below capacity.

INTERVIEWER: Would Expedia have these costs? They sell the tickets. They aren't the train operator.

CANDIDATE: You are correct. The train operator, not Expedia, would have these concerns. However, Expedia needs to understand their suppliers' business and attendant complications. If they neglect the train operator's challenges with high operational costs and perishable services, Expedia's lack of empathy would lead to inferior solutions for critical suppliers.

INTERVIEWER: Fair enough. How would you address the holiday travel scenario?

CANDIDATE: The problem with this is that there are simply too many people wanting to use trains during a short time window. In some countries, I've seen scalpers purchase multiple tickets and attempt to resell them at a higher price. I propose these solutions:

- **Reactive Pricing.** As soon as the tickets become available, people who buy them as soon as possible will get the best price. As time goes on, the prices will increase. The price increases will help us manage yield. And yes, we'll attach fees for canceling or rescheduling, minimizing the likelihood of empty trains.
- **Limited per Person.** Limit ticket sales per government-issued identification card. This will stop people from purchasing multiple tickets and reselling them at a higher price.
- **Season Pass.** A season pass will give us the flexibility of collecting revenue upfront and minimizing demand risk. As an extra benefit, season pass holders can pick trips and seats earlier than those who don't have a season pass.

INTERVIEWER: Which idea is your favorite?

CANDIDATE: The season pass one is my favorite. We get to collect revenue upfront. And for season pass holders who don't show up, we can resell their seat to someone else, effectively selling the seat twice.

INTERVIEWER: Thank you.

Launching Uber in New City X
How would you go about launching Uber in a new city X?

Things to Consider

- Is there sufficient driver supply? Customer demand is important, but driver supply is a bigger problem.
- What is the marketing plan?
- How will you manage tricky PR issues such as passenger safety and driver employee relations?

Common Mistakes

- No thoughtful plans.
- Disorganized discussion.
- Missing critical dependencies such as driver availability.

Answer
CANDIDATE: I would do several things:

- **Potential Market.** What's the market for this city? Do we have enough customers? We have to consider the city's traffic patterns. That is, when is rush hour? Where are the popular commute regions? How much demand is there for each region? How much are the consumers willing to pay? Finally, will consumers be comfortable with this form of transportation?

- **Product.** What parts of the default Uber mobile app can we keep? What parts should we add or remove? Potential things that can be localized include different forms of:
    - Payment
    - Transportation
    - Computing infrastructure (e.g. allow the app to work when there's limited or no connectivity)
- **Driver Supply.** Do we have a sufficient supply of Uber drivers? Are there people interested in being Uber drivers? How does working for Uber as a driver compare with alternative jobs? Do prospective drivers have their own vehicles?
- **Competitors.** How we price the product, relative to the competition, affects our demand. Also, studying the competition can help us understand effective driver recruiting tactics, challenges working with the city, and marketing best practices. Studying our competition can flatten our learning curve.
- **Payment.** What are the acceptable forms of payment in the local market? Unlike the United States, many places around the world do not use credit cards. For example, citizens in developing countries are more familiar with pre-paid cards or carrier billing as forms of payment. Other alternative forms of payment include Alipay and WeChat Payment in China.
- **Pricing.** On the one hand, we will have to determine a price that is acceptable to prospective customers, factoring in market rates and cost of living. On the other hand, we have to maintain an acceptable margin given our operational costs.
- **Legal.** We will consider regulatory issues, including licenses and taxes.
- **Public relations.** Uber is a new form of transportation for many parts of the world. As a result, Uber's arrival can threaten the status quo. Taxicab drivers reacted negatively when Uber entered Brazil and France. We also need to consider consumer reactions; many have heard about Uber's business practices or alarming headlines about passenger safety.

INTERVIEWER: You mentioned localizing the Uber app. Wouldn't the customizations increase our operational overhead?

CANDIDATE: It would, but different places have different habits. If we don't adjust our product accordingly, our product would not meet the local market's needs. If we don't meet the local market's needs, then we will hand our competitors an opportunity to serve our customers better. When that happens, we lose market share.

INTERVIEWER: How would you decide whether we should launch Uber as-is vs. waiting to launch with a more localized, customized version of Uber?

CANDIDATE: I would do a gap analysis. As part of the gap analysis, I would see how the gaps affect revenue and profit. For example, what is the point of launching Uber in China, if the expected forms of payment, such as Alipay, are not available?

INTERVIEWER: Would you refrain from entering a market where there is a large and successful competitor?

CANDIDATE: That's a hard call. On the one hand, we want to be efficient with our limited resources. If there is an untapped market with no competitors, it's hard to turn that down. But market size matters; we shouldn't give up a large, important market, just because it has an established competitor. We should act fast. Otherwise, it might harder to enter that large, competitive market and be successful if we delay.

INTERVIEWER: I'm not going to let you hedge like that. How would you make the decision?

CANDIDATE: I would build a spreadsheet model with an ROI analysis. The ROI analysis would include a 10-year pro forma analysis that includes:

- Potential revenue
- Costs, both fixed and incremental
- Cost of capital, to factor in opportunity cost

INTERVIEWER: Thanks.

Chapter 23 Strategy: Other

Cutting a Microsoft Product

If you were the CEO of Microsoft, what product would you cut?

Things to Consider

- Use the Rule of Three.
- Be prepared to defend the opposing viewpoint.
- Consider the goal. There may be considerations other than declining profits or revenue.

Common Mistakes

- Not taking a stand.
- Only having one reason.
- Taking a timid position such as cutting a universally hated or already deprecated feature such as Microsoft Clippy. Timid positions come across as underwhelming and cowardly.

Answer

CANDIDATE: Can you give me a minute to think about this issue?

Candidate takes a minute.

CANDIDATE: I'm sure many candidates have told you that Microsoft should cut Windows Phone. Or others have suggested cutting the Bing search engine, which appears to be in a losing war against Google. Or avoid the question completely by suggesting humorously that Microsoft should kill Clippy, the Office Assistant, if Clippy still exists.

But to make it interesting, I'm going to suggest a more controversial decision: Microsoft should kill Microsoft Project. I'm guessing not many interview candidates have asked you to kill off successful, decades-old products like Project. But here's my reasoning:

- Limited growth opportunity
- Keeping it impedes Microsoft's innovation
- Opportunity costs

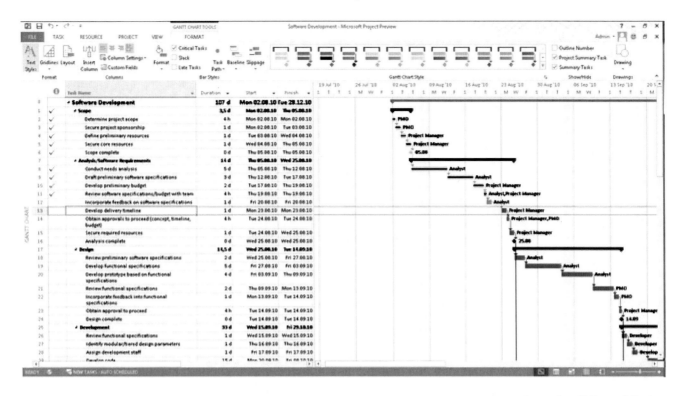

First, I'm not privy to your internal data, but I'm guessing Microsoft makes more than one billion dollars a year from Microsoft Project. While that seems attractive, as you can tell from the screenshot above, Microsoft Project's interface is optimized for waterfall project planning.

While waterfall is used by many industries such as construction and heavy manufacturing, the methodology is losing popularity over time. Agile methods have been more popular in the last 10 years, as more companies embrace lean innovation and production methods. Microsoft is probably seeing the impact from the shift from waterfall to Agile as competitors, like Trello and Asana, grab market share from Microsoft.

To summarize my first argument, Microsoft should not be putting resources in stagnant or declining projects. Microsoft Project is firmly rooted in an outdated trend: waterfall planning.

Second, while killing off a multi-billion dollar cash cow may not make sense, I would argue that keeping it around would be symbolically detrimental. Addicted to its revenue-generating potential and surrounded by Project employees who want to keep their jobs, Microsoft will likely fall prey to erroneously rationalizing the existence of Microsoft Project, even when consumers and competitors disagree.

I believe Microsoft CEO, Satya Nadella, would agree with me if I said Microsoft failed to take seriously the following trends: the rise of Mac after Apple's bankruptcy and the dominance of G Suite in enterprise. Had Microsoft weaned itself from the revenue dominance of Windows and Microsoft Exchange and Outlook sooner, Microsoft may have adapted to those threats more effectively.

Third, consider the opportunity costs associated with Microsoft Project. It may feel like Microsoft has infinite resources, both in terms of money and people. However, core businesses, such as Windows and Office, are under attack. They could use more resources, perhaps from the Project team, to defend the strategic Windows and Office assets.

Defending a Microsoft Product

Now you are the CEO of Microsoft and the board wants to cut the product you chose previously. Defend it.

Things to Consider

- Use the Rule of Three.
- It is okay to shift to the opposing position, but it's not a good idea to present contradicting logic or arguments.

Common Mistakes

- Withdrawing arguments or bashing logic that a candidate previously presented.

Answer

CANDIDATE: Ah, you tricked me! Okay, let's give this a shot. Give me a minute to brainstorm.

Candidate takes a minute.

CANDIDATE: I can think of three reasons why I would want to keep Microsoft Project. They are:

1. User convenience
2. Offline access
3. Perceived value benefits

User convenience

Having Microsoft Project included in the default Microsoft Office installation process makes it convenient for users. There's no need to first research project management software options, purchase, then set up and install. It sounds trivial, but users love the convenience of pre-installed software. Trello and Asana would be thrilled if their apps were pre-installed on a user's computer.

Offline access

Microsoft Project is desktop-, not cloud-based. In other words, Project is fully functional off-the-grid whereas cloud-based alternatives are not. I can think of many scenarios, including construction, where a project manager may not have access to the Internet.

Perceived value benefits

Including Microsoft Project in the Microsoft Office bundle increases the bundle's perceived value. The additional value, even if the customer doesn't use Project, may increase purchase conversions, leading to more revenue. It may sound counterintuitive, but consumers value the option of using Project in the future. Cutting Microsoft Project from Office would decrease its perceived value, possibly hurting Office bundle sales.

Dropbox in US vs. EU

What are the differences between acquiring new Dropbox users in the United States and Europe (EU)?

Things to Consider

- Don't give up on this question if you're not familiar with the geographic regions.
- Talking about unfamiliar geography naturally makes one feel uncomfortable.
- Good leaders routinely are in uncomfortable situations, and they have to courage to feel that discomfort and trudge forward.
- This is also a test of customer empathy. Let's say you're unfamiliar with European users. Can you accurately guess how their behavior might be different?

Common Mistakes

- Pushing the interviewer to explain Dropbox's European usage, making the interviewer feel that he or she is answering the question for the candidate.
- Begging the interviewer to move on to the next question.

Answer

CANDIDATE: Can I take some time to brainstorm?

Candidate takes one minute.

CANDIDATE: I can think of several factors:

- **Language localization.** There are many languages in the EU while English is the dominant language in the US.
- **Population.** There are more people in the EU compared to the US.
- **Infrastructure.** The server infrastructure could be different. Western Europe tends to have more advanced infrastructure when compared to Eastern Europe.
- **Favorite Software.** Software preferences may vary in each European country, while US software preferences have less variation. This could affect what type of files are usually stored.
- **User Habits.** The two biggest potential variations that come to mind include the types of files and storage needed.
- **Pricing.** Even though most EU countries use the Euro, spending habits are different in each country. A single Euro may have more purchasing power in a particular country.
- **Business Relationships.** I am not sure if Dropbox is dependent upon local providers, but it's possible that the ones Dropbox works with in the United States may not have a presence in Europe.
- **Customer acquisition.** What might work in one country may not be appropriate in another. We'd have to tailor our marketing message and acquisition tactics appropriately.

INTERVIEWER: Can you prioritize the top three issues we should focus on, based on your list?

CANDIDATE: I would go with acquisition, localization, and infrastructure. For customer acquisition, I am most concerned with finding effective customer acquisition tactics and providing support. For languages, we need to tailor our software to local languages and customs. And for infrastructure, we'll have to address concerns around slow Internet speed.

Microsoft Product Strategy

How would you characterize Microsoft's product strategy? Should we wait to release a perfectly finished product and risk delays, or should we ship an unfinished product to meet deadlines, and make updates as we go? Can you cite some examples of products that fit either of these categories and would you call them successes or failures? Lastly, how does your recommendation compare with your personal philosophy?

Things to Consider

- This question tests your ability to weigh tradeoffs between getting things right vs. getting things done.
- A good response objectively weighs both points of view, using examples to illustrate.

Common Mistakes

- Choosing poor examples.
- Not objectively weighing both points of view.

Answer

CANDIDATE: Wow, that's four questions! Give me a second to jot them down.

Candidate takes 15 seconds.

CANDIDATE: One more clarifying question, do you have a specific department in mind or just in general?

INTERVIEWER: In general.

Candidate takes another 5 seconds to think.

CANDIDATE: The answer is that it depends. I personally believe it's better to make updates and changes as we go. Like Mark Zuckerberg, I believe perfect is the enemy of finished. And thanks to client-server models, we can push out a release – whether it's a web product or mobile app feature – and easily update the server (or release a new mobile app) faster than before.

Just imagine back in the 1990s, if Microsoft accidentally launched a buggy version of Windows OS, think about the headache involved. They'd have to alert their OEMs, Dell and HP, to issue a recall. Then they have to reach out to consumers as well as IT managers to download and apply patches for a critical bug.

Microsoft can adopt an "update and change" philosophy for its web and to a lesser extent, mobile products. However, Microsoft must be careful with its hardware and shrink-wrapped software products. Hardware and shrink-wrapped software updates are tedious. It could take months or possibly years for the ecosystem to fix a bug.

In addition to the hassle, shipping unfinished shrink-wrapped products can affect PR. For example, consumers and press perceived Windows Vista as unusable and unfinished. Microsoft patched Vista, but the negative PR backlash didn't go away. Many users stayed away from upgrading to Windows Vista, choosing a more cautious approach to stay on Windows XP. Not only did this delay significant upgrade revenue for Microsoft, but it also coincided with the rebirth of Apple's Mac OS.

Windows 10 is a product that I would consider launch complete. It's been on the market for a while, and the perception has been very favorable. I would also consider the Microsoft Office suite as well as Xbox as two other products that I would consider as finished.

App for Apple TV

Should Microsoft build an app for the Apple TV?

Things to Consider

- Question asks the candidate to defend their position, so use a pros and cons analysis.

Common Mistakes

- Misinterpreting the question as to *what* app should Microsoft build? vs. *should* Microsoft build an app? If there is any uncertainty, clarify with the interviewer.

Answer

CANDIDATE: Do we know what type of app Microsoft is thinking of building?

INTERVIEWER: What would you recommend?

CANDIDATE: I'd start by tapping into Microsoft's strong video game brand and adapt legendary Xbox games, such as Halo and Forza Motorsport, for Apple TV.

INTERVIEWER: Anything else?

CANDIDATE: Skype is the only other consumer app that comes to mind. Skype would be suitable, especially if Apple TV has a Kinect-like camera. However, I'm not sure Apple would be a big fan of having Skype since they have Facetime.

INTERVIEWER: If Apple was open to having Skype on Apple TV, what do you think their reasoning would be?

CANDIDATE: FaceTime doesn't have as much cross-platform support as Skype. So having Skype on Apple TV could make Apple TV more useful since Skype could tap into a larger audience.

INTERVIEWER: Bingo. So let's shift back to video games. Walk me through the reasons why Microsoft would want to adapt its video games for Apple TV.

CANDIDATE: Here are my reasons:

- **Big Market.** Despite the rise of non-TV devices, such as computers, smartphones, and tablets, consumers continue to spend a lot of time-consuming media on a TV. According to the latest Nielsen stats, Americans, for example, are watching five hours of TV a day. Having a foothold in this market is key. With TV continuing to attract strong usage, there's an opportunity to sell additional digital media and services through the TV platform.
- **Additional Distribution Channel.** Microsoft didn't have to worry about this before when Windows was the dominant computing platform. However, now that Microsoft failed to build market share with smartphone operating systems, Microsoft understands the importance of adapting its applications to as many distribution channels as possible.
- **New Customer Segment.** Even if consumers are using the Xbox and Apple TV for similar use case scenarios, our audiences are likely to be different. Xbox owners are more likely to be hardcore gamers. Apple TV users are more likely to be casual gamers. By building applications for the Apple TV platform, we tap into a new customer segment that will experience Microsoft's new products and services.
- **Growing Market.** Digital media players have more potential to grow. The last figure I saw showed 25% ownership among TV owners.
- **Customer Demand.** Consumers really enjoy video games, and it's just a matter of time that they'll play more games on their digital media players.

INTERVIEWER: If our app turns out to be popular, wouldn't that promote Apple TV?

CANDIDATE: We could live in fear of helping Apple. And this issue could be particularly sensitive for both companies. While Microsoft's Xbox is a video game console first, Xbox is trying to establish itself as the living room hub as a digital media player.

However, we have to believe that competition is ultimately healthy for not only the market, but also Microsoft. Building an app allows us to dip a toe in the water. If it happens to gain popularity, we will be prepared to compete. Our involvement might also lead us to consider whether we should get into the standalone digital media player business too.

INTERVIEWER: Thank you.

Microsoft's Threats

What do you think will be the main threats to Microsoft's continued success in the future and why?

Things to Consider

- What are key consumer trends that can affect Microsoft?
- Consider trends on Internet and mobile. Don't forget about virtual and augmented reality either.

- Focusing on Microsoft's most recognizable sources of income, Windows and Office, and forgetting other businesses such as Windows Server, SQL Server, Exchange, Xbox, or Bing.
- No mentioning less obvious threats such as government regulations, distribution access, customer loyalty, and network effects.

Answer

CANDIDATE: Can I brainstorm for a bit?

Candidate takes one minute.

CANDIDATE: I can think of several threats to Microsoft.

- **Browser**. Microsoft is losing the browser war; I read that Chrome's market share worldwide is somewhere between 42 and 52 percent. This is terrible news for Microsoft, given that entered the browser market 13 years before Google. The browser is a very important platform for Microsoft. While the traditional OS is still strong, the browser is emerging as a very important platform, given that many Internet applications are OS independent. By losing out in the browser fight, several of Microsoft's online products, which rely on the browser, will be affected. This includes Bing.com, online advertising, and Outlook.com, formerly known as Hotmail.
- **Mobile**. Microsoft's Windows Phone is not doing well. Its market share is in the single digits. Mobile is a very powerful platform; it's the only computing device that we carry with us wherever we go. Mobile app revenue is growing; Google and Apple get a lucrative 30% commission anytime a developer sells an app through their app stores because they are the default app store on Android and iOS platforms respectively. Microsoft, by not owning a dominant platform, misses that revenue opportunity.
- **Console**. Microsoft is slowly losing against Sony in the current generation of console wars. Aside from the profit implications, Microsoft's Xbox plays a critical role in introducing the Microsoft product family to young adults, beyond just video games. Xbox helps build the perception that Microsoft can be hip, when they are generally not perceived as such.

Overall, Microsoft is losing out in the platform war on multiple fronts. While it remains strong in the OS race, Microsoft struggles to be relevant in fast-growing, emergent markets.

Buying OfferUp

Should Facebook buy OfferUp?

Things to Consider

- Does OfferUp utilize Facebook's core competencies such as the social graph or the Audience Network?
- What synergies can Facebook unlock so that the resulting value is greater than the purchase price?
- Did you organize your thoughts in a framework so your answer is satisfying, comprehensive, and easy to follow?

Common Mistakes

- Not citing the benefit of faster time to market.
- Not mentioning how acquiring OfferUp might distract Facebook from its core business.

Answer

CANDIDATE: Just to clarify, OfferUp is Craigslist on mobile, right?

INTERVIEWER: Yes, it is.

CANDIDATE: We have two options: buy them outright or build our own OfferUp-like solution. I know that they recently concluded their series B at around $20 million. So buying them outright could probably cost us around $200 million.

To figure out if it's worth spending $200M, we'll have to consider how much it would cost to build an equivalent solution on our own. Assuming a team of one PM, three engineers, two designers, one marketer, and one data scientist, it would probably take us about three to six months to build it. I'll be conservative and go with six months. With an average annual salary of $150,000, it would be around 8 * $150,000 / 2 = $600,000.

But that's not all! We have to think about marketing expenses such as cost per install (CPI). Let's shoot for about one million users, with an average CPI of $3, which is $3M.

Even with $3M, we can get new installs overnight. It'll probably take us six months to do so, which we'll continue to pay salaries for our core team of eight. So that's another $600K. In total, that's 12 months at $3M for marketing and another $1.2M for salaries, which brings us to a total cost of $4.2 million.

After a quick run of the numbers, let's think about some qualitative pros and cons:

Buying

- Pros:
  - Saves time
  - Pre-existing user base
  - Don't need to recruit a new team
- Cons:
  - Costly
  - Might have features we don't want
  - Integrating a new team may be difficult, especially if there are cultural differences

Building

- Pros:
  - Cheaper
  - Can build it exactly the way we want it
  - Tighter integration with Facebook assets such as prominent placement in the newsfeed and cross-promotion on WhatsApp and Instagram
- Cons:
  - Takes time

- o No existing users
- o Need to recruit our own team
- o Facebook doesn't have eCommerce experience
- o Success is not guaranteed

This is not a clear-cut decision. There are benefits and risks to each approach. However, if I were asked to choose, I would choose to build vs. buy. Assuming my back-of-the-envelope calculation is reasonable, I'd much rather pay $4.2M, or even 10X that, than to part with $200M.

iPhone Exclusive Partnership

Do you think allowing AT&T to be the exclusive Apple iPhone carrier, at launch, was a good or bad idea?

Things to Consider

- What were the benefits of exclusivity to AT&T?
- What were the benefits of exclusivity to Apple?
- What were the potential outcomes if Apple did not grant exclusivity?
- Are there non-exclusivity examples from other countries? That is, based on outcomes elsewhere, we may infer what could have occurred if Apple did not grant AT&T exclusivity.

Common Mistakes

- Defending the exclusive partnership as being best, even though the alternative is unknown.

Answer

CANDIDATE: That was a while ago, no? I don't remember the details. Can you remind me?

INTERVIEWER: Sure. When the iPhone originally launched in January 2007, AT&T was the exclusive and sole provider in the United States. That agreement expired. Today, consumers can purchase iPhones from any wireless carrier in the US.

CANDIDATE: Got it. Okay, let me collect my thoughts.

Candidate pauses to think for 20 seconds.

CANDIDATE: I'm sure Apple received a healthy fee in exchange for exclusivity. And exclusivity sounds like a closed ecosystem, a control-focused maneuver that Steve Jobs would have preferred. He hated it when third-party companies messed up his beautiful products.

However, I'm not in favor of the deal. And I can almost argue that since no one carrier has iPhone exclusivity anymore that it's Apple acknowledgment of their mistake. But I'll be a little bit more thoughtful than that:

Reduced Market Share

I believe it was important for Apple to prioritize market share first. By doing so, it would have given Apple more customers to sell complementary goods and services like accessories (such as headphones and smartphone cases) and App Store purchases (where Apple gets a 30% cut) later.

This is called the razor-and-razorblade model. You've probably heard of this term. It's when companies sell a platform for a low price and generate profits later by cross-selling complementary goods. Platform examples include the Windows OS, PlayStation video game consoles, HP printers, razors and of course, the Apple iPhone.

Giving AT&T exclusive distribution rights limited Apple's initial market share. In the US, there are four major wireless carriers: AT&T, Verizon, Sprint and T-Mobile. If each carrier had an equal share of the market, AT&T would have 25 percent. However, I feel that AT&T was one of the market leaders, so let's assume that AT&T had a 35 percent market share.

While 35 percent sounds substantial, it prevented Apple from accessing the remaining 65 percent of the market. Apple would like to think that users could freely switch from competing carriers to AT&T, attracted by Apple's compelling smartphone offering. However, back in 2007, multi-year customer contracts prohibited short-term mobility between carriers.

Encouraging Anti-Apple Activity

Losing customers to AT&T couldn't have sat well with competitive carriers like Verizon. Verizon, and others, probably fought with vigor. This probably meant millions of marketing dollars to promote Android phones. Furthermore, it was not likely that they spoke favorably about the iPhone in their advertising campaigns.

Increased Freeloading

Since AT&T was the only way customers could get the iPhone, AT&T may have been lazy with its sales and marketing efforts. That is, thanks to the exclusive partnership, why would AT&T invest additional sales and marketing dollars when the coveted phone sold itself?

INTERVIEWER: I recently read that Apple has less than 10% smartphone share around the world, but they have 90% of the smartphone industry's profits. Isn't that evidence that Apple made the right decision?

CANDIDATE: That's survivorship bias.

INTERVIEWER: What do you mean?

CANDIDATE: There's nothing to indicate that Apple wouldn't have had even *better* results had they decided against being exclusive.

INTERVIEWER: Good point. Would you say all exclusive deals are bad?

CANDIDATE: I believe that all exclusive deals are bad. Both consumers and businesses benefit from competition.

INTERVIEWER: That's a strong statement. There's no instance where an exclusive deal is helpful?

CANDIDATE: Okay, you've pushed me to think harder about the issue. Let me think about it.

Candidate takes 10 seconds.

CANDIDATE: Giving it more thought, some exclusive deals could be a win-win. In business school, we learned that some companies would award exclusive distribution or retail rights, especially when there are significant upfront costs.

For example, a small business owner wants to license a McDonald's franchise in a particular location. To start a McDonald's store, the small business owner would have to invest roughly $1M to $2.2M. That's a large sum. If McDonald's allowed another small business owner to start a franchise one block away, the initial small business owner would be very unhappy. It'll impact that small business owner's sales, affecting the ROI and payback period of her startup investment. Had she had known that McDonald's would be so unpredictable in awarding franchise rights, she wouldn't have bothered to invest.

Her decision would have affected McDonald's immensely. McDonald's would miss out on franchise fees and monthly service fees. McDonald's store footprint would be smaller by one store, which reduces opportunities for increased brand awareness.

And one last point, here's the critical difference between McDonald's and Apple: McDonald's, on the one hand, was faced with an all-or-nothing scenario. That is, if McDonald's didn't award exclusive rights, small business owners wouldn't open franchises, given the sizable upfront investment. Apple, on the other hand, wasn't in an all-or-nothing scenario. They wouldn't have been deterred from selling the iPhone without exclusive rights. Carriers had already set a precedent of selling and promoting phones without exclusivity.

INTEVIEWER: I learned something new today. That's a fascinating bit of business history. Thank you.

Chapter 24 Technical

Load Balancer for google.com

Design a simple load balancer for google.com. What data structures would you use? Why? Define access/delete/add order of complexity for each data structure and explain your choices. Design an algorithm to add/delete nodes to/from the data structure. How would you pick which server to send the request? Why? Why not?

Things to Consider

- Clarify definitions if they are unfamiliar to you.
- Inquire about goals and constraints.
- To get going, work out a simple example.

Common Mistakes

- Not being familiar with queue data structures
- Not understanding order of complexity concepts

Answer

CANDIDATE: Hmm, my understanding is google.com is a global website. So let's say you are using google.com in the US. It would be logical to first select the closest server group for you based on your region (e.g. California), then pick a server that has available computing power. It might be more tiered than this (based on city), but that's the general idea.

I am also guessing if, in the event that the entire California cluster is full, I would have no choice but to reroute the request to a nearby cluster like Nevada. It is a bad user experience, but better than waiting until an empty "slot" opens up in California.

Based on this, I would say this probably needs a round-robin or some variation of it. Based on my understanding, round-robin uses a queue. So how it works is that envision we have 10 available slots (a slot would be a node in the queue) from 1-10.

1,2,3,4,5,6,7,8,9,10

When user 1 comes, the load balancer grabs the first available slot for him. Since we are using a queue, the dequeue would give him 1, because it's FIFO:

2,3,4,5,6,7,8,9,10

Then user 2 comes, and he would get 2:

3,4,5,6,7,8,9,10

Let say user 1 is done, and node 1 becomes available again. It would get enqueued:

3,4,5,6,7,8,9,10,1

So if we are going by the double-tiered system I described earlier (states->individual slots), we would have two queues. The first queue would be states. The second queue would be individual server clusters.

But remember for our states, we need to pick the closest states if your current state isn't available. The round-robin algorithm, in that case, would be weighted. Meaning the queue would be sorted each time so that available servers in your closest states would show up first when you need it.

The complexity for access is O(1), since the closest available server is always on the head.

The complexity for delete is O(1), since it's dequeue.

The complexity for add is O(1), since it's enqueue.

The algorithm is quite simple. A queue is basically a list where you only have three functions:

peek(); enqueue(node newNode); and dequeue();

peek() returns the current head of the list: return list.head;

enqueue(node newNode) adds the newNode at the end of the list: list.end.next = newNode;

dequeue() returns the current head of the list and deletes it off the list:

     node headNode = list.head;

     list.head = headNode.next;

     return headNode;

Something we have to note is that there is a switch in the round-robin algorithm. The slot becomes available again after some set amount of time even if the process is not complete. So if user 1 takes too long with slot 1, slot 1 stops working on the process and goes back to being available again (enqueued). The next available slot (slot 3 in the above example) is used to continue the job. This prevents starvation, which is where a task is continually denied access to a resource. In this case, it's when a request is continuously denied because there are no server slots left each time it requests.

A more complex model would probably be using Level 4 and Level 7 load balancers. I've heard of them but have not really delved any deeper. I know they balance based on network and application layers, respectively, instead of just based on physical location like my simple version.

Dictionary for Scrabble

How would you design a dictionary lookup for Scrabble?

Things to Consider

- What's the optimal data structure to store this data?

283

- How would one indicate if a sequence of letters is a valid word?

Common Mistakes

- Picking the wrong data structure.
- Suggesting inefficient algorithms or algorithms that find duplicate words.

Answer

CANDIDATE: Are we using English?

INTERVIEWER: Yes.

CANDIDATE: I am imagining using a Trie. It's a data structure built perfectly for the English language. When we think about this, we are thinking we got a "rack" of letters (e.g. A, B, E, E, G, S, X). There are a few attributes I am seeing:

- We can have repeated letters.
- This is out of order.
- We might have anagrams.

Let's keep these in mind and brainstorm our solution. An ideal function in Java would probably look like this:

String[] lookup(char[] letters) {};

What this does is that it takes an array of letters and returns an array of strings. These strings hold solutions to the problem. It could also return an empty array when there are no solutions. Let's explain this with an example. If letters are {A, E, S, T}, we can get this as our string array:

Seta, tea, sea, set, east, …

Ideally, it should return points associated with each word, but that's the easy part.

So how should we do this with a trie? Let's try a naïve approach. What if we just add all letters of the alphabet into a trie? It doesn't sound so bad when you realize the longest word in Scrabble is 8 letters. Even if we play with an extended board or something, there is a max length.

So here is what each node in the trie looks like:

```
Class trieNode {
    char letter;
    boolean endOfWord;
    List<trieNode> children;
};
```

- letter denotes the current letter (e.g. A)
- endofWord denotes if this is the end of the word in the trie
- children is the list of trieNodes that come after

What does this trie look like? The head would be a random symbol that is not a letter, e.g. ^, which represents the empty string, then the head would have the children A-Z, while its children A would have the children A-Z, and B would have the children A-Z, etc. We do this up to depth 8. In total, we have 26^8+1 nodes, and each node has relatively little memory but it does get up there.

Can we improve this? Yes. There are certain paths down the tree that doesn't make any sense because they don't contain words, and we can prune those out. For example, aaa is not a word, so we can prune out the entire branch. We only have to do this one time and output the result to a file that we can use next time. We can just look up a dictionary database somewhere.

Once this trie is done, given a rack of letters, we can input it into the function and go through the rack of letters. Going back to example {A, E, S, T}, we can:

- Lookup A, then see if E, S, and T exist as branches.
- You are now at AE, see if S and T exist as branches.
- You are now at AS, see if E and T exist as branches.
- …
- Lookup E, then see if A, S, and T exist as branches.
- …

Each word lookup requires $O(N^2)$, where N is the length of the word. Space complexity wise, it's 26^8+1 node, with each node essentially being 2 (char) + 1 (boolean) + 8 (object reference) = 11 bytes in the worst-case scenario. The average case scenario is probably small enough to fit into memory.

Statistical Frequency Analysis

What is statistical frequency analysis?

Things to Consider

- Clarify if you do not understand the question.

Common Mistakes

- Confusing correlation with causation.
- Forgetting that data analysis is about meaning or decision-making rather than just extracting and presenting data.

Answer

CANDIDATE: You just wanted me to give you a definition? Or did you have some raw data that you wanted me to analyze?

INTERVIEWER: No. This is a general question. Do you know what frequency analysis is?

CANDIDATE: Yes.

INTERVIEWER: Can you describe it to me?

CANDIDATE: It's basically where you get a lot of data, and you are trying to make sense out of it. So maybe you are trying to find some sort of pattern, so you begin separating all the data into elements. Then you see which elements show up the most frequently and least frequently to get a sense of what this data is and what results we can gather from this.

INTERVIEWER: Can you give me an example?

CANDIDATE: Sure, so cyphers use frequency analysis a lot. For example, if I give you a paragraph of English, the most frequent letters are probably going to be A, E, T, and O. The least frequent letters are going to be Q, X, and Z. So let's say instead I give a modified paragraph (e.g. cypher, I switched A to B, and B to C, and C to D, etc.), I can find the most frequently occurring letter. It's probably going to be either A or E. It may not be those two, but it gives me a really good starting point. I can do the same with the least frequent letters as well. I can test different matches and see which ones end up displaying a coherent English paragraph.

INTERVIEWER: You're assuming the cypher is English.

CANDIDATE: Well, it's most likely going to be one of the spoken languages we know or perhaps even Morse code. We can try out each language. As long as we have the frequency analyzed, it gives us a starting point. We'll first do frequency analysis on the language we want to try matching to, then do the same thing I described earlier. If this language doesn't work, we try another one. Eventually, we'll find one.

INTERVIEWER: That doesn't sound very efficient.

CANDIDATE: It feels that way, but this is more deterministic than guessing blindly.

INTERVIEWER: You're right. I'm just being tough on you.

Candidate smiles.

Google Search Service

Design the Google search service including the essential pieces and logic. Also explain key design decisions and tradeoffs.

Things to Consider

- Step 1. You'll need a web crawler to collect web pages and follow links.
- Step 2. You'll have to store a copy of those web pages.
- Step 3. Show relevant results, based on a user query.

Common Mistakes

- Waste time specifying non-software requirements including the need for servers, firewalls, load balancers, and an Internet connection.
- Avoiding a detailed discussion by telling the interviewer that one would use an open-source package like Nutch, Scrapy, and Heritrix and modify it from there.

Answer

CANDIDATE: When a user types a query in Google search, Google will try to understand the search string first to get an idea of what type of websites it should look for in the results. If there are misspellings or similar searches (e.g. "that blue social network" -> "Facebook") it would also find that. Then it will find all the results (in the form of website pages) and rank them based on the most relevant one for this search query.

Another essential thing is the user account. I can think of five parts:

1. If the user has searched for similar things before, it will be taken into account.
2. If the user has searched for related things before (e.g., he searched about programming before, so when he asks about C, he's probably talking about the language, not the letter), it'll be taken into account.
3. If the user has watched a lot of strategy game videos on YouTube or similar things on other Google services and if he's searching about Terran, he's probably talking about StarCraft.
4. If the user lives in Mountain View or is searching from Mountain View (based on his current location), and he's searching for "nearby restaurants," it's best to show up restaurants near Mountain View.
5. If the user has data showing he likes hamburgers, and he's searching for restaurants nearby, we should show up ads related to burger joints nearby.

There are probably many more, but these are the ones I can think of right now. The point of all of these is to provide context. This allows:

- Searches to be more accurate. Better user experience, obviously.
- Searches to be more pertinent. Better user experience since the user can find what he or she needs in the shortest amount of time.
- Ads to be better targeted. More revenue if a user clicks on an ad that he finds relevant.

Google search also has other essential pieces that have to do with context. For example, if a user writes a string like, "3*5+10" Google will pop out a calculator showing the result. If the user writes a string like, "What is the population of the US?" Google will tell you 323 million.

After the server receives the search string and context, it looks for the "correct" results. It then ranks them based on multiple criteria. I don't know the criteria, but I am guessing it has to do with:

- **Number of times someone entered a similar search string and clicked on this link**. This is also known as the clickthrough rate (CTR). We can also check the clickback rate. That is, after clicking on one link, did the user go back and click a second result? If so, it may indicate that the user was unsatisfied with the webpage suggested from the first click.
- **Number of follow-on queries**. We want to reduce the time it takes the user to find what they want.
- **Time**. An example of this is if someone typed "best TV shows," the webpage that talks about the latest TV shows will come up first (due to webpage timestamp and recent traffic) instead of a webpage about the best TV shows from 10 years ago. More relevant information means a better user experience.
- **Ads**. Let's say if you type "buy flowers," advertisers that purchase Google ads will show up first. This means more revenue.
- **Google affiliates**. Let's say you type "map," you'll see Google Maps, not Bing Maps. Google would much rather send traffic to a sister property than to a competitor.

Another dimension is filtering. There are many reasons why Google may want to filter results:

- Offensive results, including bad language
- Illegal results, such as sites that violate the country's hate speech laws
- Malicious results, including phishing sites and those that install malware
- Sexually explicit material, especially for users under the age of 18
- Spam results that are irrelevant or inappropriate to the query

The last intriguing topic is the inclusion of ads. Many think that Google's ads clutter the website, but it's a necessary sacrifice for a free service. However, like any computer-based algorithms, the Google search results algorithm is not perfect. Human intervention is necessary to fine-tune results. Google's ads provide that opportunity for humans, outside of Google, to offer their opinion on what (paid) results deserve to be on the search results page. The inclusion of ads is one of those rare business decisions where it's a win for the user (more relevant results) and a win for Google (paying for what is seemingly a no-cost service).

All-in-all, these decisions lead to a more complex and resource-intensive algorithm. However, all of it serves to provide Google better search results and a better user experience.

Bayesian vs. AI

When are Bayesian methods more appropriate than artificial intelligence techniques for predictive analytics?

Things to Consider

- What is the Bayesian method?
- Which artificial intelligence method is the interviewer referring to? Machine learning? Rules-based?

Common Mistakes

- Quitting due to one's lack of familiarity with either Bayesian or AI methods.
- Not coming up with plausible, cohesive reasoning on why Bayesian is better.

Answer

CANDIDATE: Let's start with a definition, just so we're on the same page:

- **Bayesian methods** use statistical methods to predict probabilities based on existing information. Compared to artificial intelligence (AI), which I am assuming, in this case, involves machine learning, Bayesian is faster because its methods are simpler.
- **AI**, which I assume, involves machine learning. This means the AI algorithm tries to gather enough information to formulate a scenario and match with pre-existing patterns so it can know what to do next. Machine learning AI tends to be more complex.

With these thoughts in mind, I can think of three scenarios where Bayesian is more appropriate than AI:

- **We don't have enough data**. Thus, using the more complex machine learning method would not increase predictive power dramatically.
- **We want to avoid overfitting**. This happens when we try "too hard" to figure out a pattern because we have so much data that we end up corrupting our results with noise.
- **We don't have enough experience**, with machine learning AI. Sometimes the best tool for the job is the tool one knows how to use.

Reducing Bandwidth Consumption

How would you reduce global bandwidth consumption for Google search?

Things to Consider

- How does website complexity and content affect bandwidth consumption?
- What repetitive pieces of information can be left out?
- What information can be obtained from a non-Google source?

Common Mistakes

- Suggesting solutions that Google has already implemented, such as code minification.

Answer

CANDIDATE: Hmm, when I think about the largest file types, three come to mind:

- **Videos**. They occupy the largest amount of space, in general. I do not believe Google Search stores any videos: cached or otherwise. They usually let third parties store the videos and then link to them. If there is video storage, at most, I believe Google stores thumbnail images to these third-party videos.
- **Images**. Images occupy a fraction of what videos consume space-wise. However, images can be quite large, usually exponentially larger than text files. I am not sure if Google caches third-party images on their website, but it would make sense to do so since serving would be more reliable than using a third-party server, given Google's extensive, scalable server infrastructure. The same infrastructure also provides a much faster user experience, which Google emphasizes.
- **Text files**. Google's likely to have text-like files such as HTML, CSS, or JavaScript content. They're also likely to store cached versions of third-party web pages, which means more HTML and CSS.

I have a few solutions in mind:

- **Cache Policies.** If we detect the user is from a certain country, we ask their browsers to cache more data. Good targets would include users that are:
  - Far from Google servers.
  - Originating from countries that are known to have limited last-mile bandwidth.
- **Cache Settings.** Require or encourage client browsers to turn on their cache settings.
- **Smaller Result Sets.** If we find that users only look at the top X results, we can then eliminate the ones below X.

- **Less Detailed Results.** We can show less detail for each result. Display smaller snippets, show preview images and videos at a lower resolution, and turn off, by default, lesser-used featured such as the "See Cached Page" button.
- **Improve file compression**. I imagine Google is already using file compression, but there's always an opportunity to improve. I had always thought image compression couldn't be improved further, but I was impressed by Google's recent compression breakthroughs, using computer vision and machine learning techniques.

INTERVIEWER: Which one would you recommend?

CANDIDATE: I like *Cache Policies* and *Smaller Result Sets*. Here's why: the engineering effort required is minimal, but it will make a big impact.

I would discourage the elimination of longer snippets or removal of the "See a cached version" button. Instead, I would simply turn off these features by default. And for power or legacy users who want to see longer snippets or download cached versions, they can turn on that classic experience by adjusting their settings.

Racing 15 Horses

You have 15 horses that run various speeds. You also own a racetrack where you can race the horses; this track holds a maximum of 5 horses per race. If you have no stopwatch or other means of telling exactly how fast the horses are, how many races would you need to run between the horses to be absolutely sure which horses are first, second, and third fastest?

Things to Consider

- Work out the base cases.
- Divide the problem into small pieces to solve the overall problem.

Common Mistakes

- Not taking into consideration that horses from one heat can be faster than another.

Answer

CANDIDATE: Let's label our 15 horses as horse 1 through horse 15. I would first do three races with five horses each. So the races would be as follows:

- Race 1. Horse 1 thru 5.
- Race 2. Horse 6 thru 10.
- Race 3. Horse 11 thru 15.

Let's say the finish order is 1 to 5, 6 to 10, and 11 to 15.

We can observe some things about each of these 3 races:

- If a horse is #1, it may be in the top 3 spots. Up to 2 other horses (#2 and #3) from its race can be in the top 3 as well.

- If a horse is #2, it may be in the top 3 spots. Up to 1 other horse (#1 from the race) from its race can be in the top 3 as well.
- If a horse is #3, it may be in the top 3 spots. No other horses from its race can be in the top 3.
- If a horse is #4 or #5, we can eliminate them completely.

We can now eliminate these horses: 4, 5, 9, 10, 14, and 15 because of the last observation. We are now left with 9 horses.

Then I would race 1, 6, and 11 on one track. This is our 4th race. Let's say the results are: 1, 6 and 11.

We can now safely eliminate these horses:

- 8, because 6 is #2 in this race. Only 7, which was 2nd place in the race between 6-10, can be in the top 3.
- 12 and 13, because 11 is #3 in the race. None of the horses in its race (between 11-15) can be in the top 3.

We are now left with these 6 horses: 1, 2, 3, 6, 7, and 11. We only need one last race to determine this, because we do not need to racehorse 1. It's already confirmed to be #1.

We race 2, 3, 6, 7, and 11. Let's say the result is in this order as well. We now know the top 3 horses are: 1, 2, and 3.

The last race could turn out differently, let's say: 6, 11, 7, 2, 3. Then the top 3 horses would be: 1, 6, 11.

The point is it doesn't matter how the last race turns out. The first 2 spots in the last race will always be 2nd and 3rd place.

This took a total of 5 races.

Racing 16 Horses Instead

Follow up to the previous question, now you have 16 horses. How many races would you need to conduct to find first, second, and third?

Things to Consider

Check your solution for 15 horses. See if there's an extra racing slot where you can put the extra 16th horse.

Answer

CANDIDATE: Still 5 races. In race 4, I only had 3 horses in the race. We can just add horse 16 in there. Then let's say the result is: 1, 6, 11, and 16. We can just eliminate 16 because it's number 4. There is no way it can be in the top 3.

If horse 16 comes in any place but last, then we eliminate the last place horse (either horse 1, 6 or 11) and instead include horse 16.

Chapter 25 Traditional

Why Amazon

Why Amazon?

Things to Consider

- The interviewer is evaluating whether you are passionate about the company.
- The hiring manager is afraid that, you, if hired, will leave for a better paycheck.
- Using the Rule of Three can convey credibility and sincerity.

Common Mistakes

- Getting lazy and not customizing a response for each employer.
- Applying inadequate thought into the question.
- Failing to see the company's future, fixating on what happened to Amazon in the past and present.

Answer

CANDIDATE: Why Amazon? I've got a couple of reasons:

Innovation

Amazon is one of the most innovative companies today. Its successes have been breathtaking; I immediately think about how Amazon has transformed retail ("the everything store"), pioneered cloud services (AWS), or invented a new class of home electronics (Echo). Then there are lesser-known innovations including third-party fulfillment (Fulfilled by Amazon) and drone delivery.

I want to be part of a company that has the best record of innovating in tech today.

Hands-on culture

I'm very happy that Amazon's culture has a bias for action. I can't stand it when bureaucracy or laziness impedes progress and improvement.

Customer obsession

I'm a customer-centric product manager, and I love empathizing with customers. Amazon's philosophy of "working backward from the customer," doing things like writing the press release for a new product feature, is something I can relate to.

Amazon's customer focus has paid off. Every year, Amazon is named consumers' favorite brand in America.

Willingness to make big bets

Recently Amazon spent $13.7 billion to purchase the American supermarket chain, Whole Foods. There were no shortage of naysayers on the acquisition including:

- **The brands are incompatible**. Consumers recognize Whole Foods for having high prices whereas they see Amazon for having low ones.
- **The employee culture is different**. Whole Foods lavish employees with benefits whereas Amazon does not.
- **The retail experience is dissimilar**. Whole Foods' spacious, relaxed shopping experience is nothing like Amazon's cramped, in-and-out brick-and-mortar bookstore experience.

But despite all the naysaying, Amazon's executive team has a vision on how the Whole Foods distribution channel could reinforce Amazon's core strategies including convenient delivery and a point-of-trial for Amazon's electronics including Echo, Kindle readers, and Fire tablets. Reflexively, Amazon's expertise in logistics and supplier negotiations could help Whole Foods lower their prices.

Chapter 26 Behavioral

Most Difficult Interaction

Tell me about the most difficult interaction you had at work.

Things to Consider

- Use the DIGS Method™.
- The listener must feel tension in your story. It increases appreciation and listener engagement.
- Establish a villain. It makes the story easier to follow. You, of course, should be the hero in your story.

Common Mistakes

- Not taking responsibility for one's actions.
- Answering with a shallow breath, indicating stress and tension.

Answer

CANDIDATE: Back in November, the CEO, Ines, told me that our investors weren't pleased with our progress. They wanted our company to switch from building casino games to building sports games. I was shocked. Casino and sports games were completely different. There would be almost no code reuse whatsoever. I protested, but Ines said we had no choice. The investors would withhold a $2M investment if we didn't do what they asked. Ines left the meeting saying that I had three days to figure out how I would break the news to the engineering team.

As I went back to my desk, I evaluated my options:

1. Drop the news without warning
2. Pretend that creating a sports game was no different from creating a casino game
3. Have them warm up to the idea

Options one and two were equally bad; it would have either damage morale or insult the team. That left me with option three. So here's the plan I concocted:

I implemented a team bonding exercise that day called *Game of the Day*. *Game of the Day* split up the engineers into small teams of three. Each team played and evaluated a randomly chosen sports game. As part of the evaluation, they wrote down things they liked and didn't like. Lastly, they would then present their findings with the rest of the team.

They liked *Game of the Day*. It broke the monotony of regular work, fostered community, and helped them keep up with new industry trends. And most importantly, after two days, they started to appreciate the sports game genre. I also met privately with team members one-on-one and asked how they felt about building a sports game on a trial basis. Thanks to the team exercise, several were open to building a sports game.

On the third day, I made the announcement. I explained that our investors wanted us to start building sports games. Their reception went smoother than expected. They admitted that were disappointed, but they were excited to build a sports game of their own.

Helping a Customer

Walk us through a time when you helped a customer through a difficult process. What did that look like?

Things to Consider

- Did you dramatize the situation so that the process came across as difficult?
- Did you give the customer a name so the story is easier to follow?
- Did you provide an elegant and clever way of helping the customer through that process?

Common Mistakes

- Declaring that one has not had the experience of helping a customer through a difficult process.
- Responding with an example that's not perceived as difficult enough.

Answer

CANDIDATE: Three months ago, a customer, Willie, complained that he didn't receive the in-game currency he paid for, and it happened multiple times. This occurred before we set up our customer support dashboard, so we didn't have access to the in-game log unless we pulled from the database. That was during the New Year, so all of our developers were on vacation. However, this guy spent a lot of money. We didn't want to lose him, so we needed to move fast.

It was hard to understand the nature of his requests. Willie said that sometimes he saw the in-game currency he purchased; other times he didn't. Through our limited backend, I could see he did indeed pay multiple times, but I wasn't 100 percent sure.

At first, I asked him for his purchase dates and times. It could help me pinpoint abnormal transactions. Willie said he didn't remember because he had several transactions, in quick succession.

I then told him that Apple sends email receipts, and I asked him to check his email. Willie replied that he did not remember his password. I then assisted him with password recovery, using the "Forget Password" function. Willie logged in and started digging through his inbox.

Next, I asked him to filter his email to just Apple's, and there were still a lot. Apparently, Willie makes a lot of in-game purchases! I helped Willie filter just our game and asked him to work patiently through all 20 transactions. He determined which ones he didn't get currency for. I double-checked against our database and confirmed that the ones he flagged were failed transactions.

Surprisingly, he apologized for wasting my time. I told him that I was happy to get to the truth and rewarded him with free in-game currency for his understanding and sympathy.

Handling a Busy Situation

Describe how you would handle a busy situation where three people are waiting for your help.

Things to Consider

- Propose a three-step process, with at least three-steps, so it sounds substantial.
- Provide an example, if time allows, proving your ability to get a positive result.

Common Mistakes

- Claiming that you would "do it all." The interviewer is evaluating your judgment on what you think is important vs. what is not.
- Sharing an example that's underwhelming.

Answer

CANDIDATE: The people that need my help: are they requesting it in-person, email or live chat?

INTERVIEWER: Let's go with live chat.

CANDIDATE: I would first reply with a "Hi {NAME}." I want to acknowledge their presence, so they don't feel ignored. Then I would then ask them what's wrong. Based on what they say, I would prioritize requests based on:

1. Severity
2. Customer importance
3. Estimated time to resolution

If I were time-constrained, I would see if there's anyone else on my team who can assist. If not, I would keep those who are waiting with clear visibility on when they could expect a response. I might say something like, "Give me 30 minutes to research the issue. Can I call you when I'm ready with a fix?"

INTERVIEWER: Would you solve issues simultaneously? Or would you solve them one at a time?

CANDIDATE: I'm comfortable multitasking.

INTERVIEWER: What if a single request requires your undivided attention?

CANDIDATE: I'd tackle it one at a time, prioritizing based on criteria I specified above. I would apologize for the situation for those who are waiting and got upset. And if necessary, I would provide a peace offering to soothe them.

After the near-term crisis was over, I'd figure out how I'd prevent such issues from happening again. It could involve a mixture of the following:

- **Setting expectations** so that my availability isn't taken for granted
- **Implement a request process** and clarifying that all requests require at least a one week lead time
- **Collaborate with my boss** and get his input on my top priorities

INTERVIEWER: Thank you.

Risk and Failure

Give me an example of when you took a risk and failed.

Things to Consider

- Did you use an example where the listener said, "Wow, that's a big career risk I wouldn't have taken?"
- After hearing your story, would someone have said, "Geez, I knew that's exactly how it would unfold, and I wouldn't have done that if I were in your shoes?"

Common Mistakes

- Selecting an underwhelming example, such as moving to a new state or taking a new job.
- Choosing an example with limited consequence. For example, sharing a time when a candidate was disappointed that he or she did not get a promotion initially but got it eventually.

Answer

CANDIDATE: In 2011, I decided to be an entrepreneur. Back then, Groupon and Living Social were popular, so I decided to build a daily deals company. After nine months, the daily deals space burst, so I decided to pivot my company into an up-and-coming trend: local meal delivery. After nine months, the local meal delivery business started to consolidate, and we went out of business. I was embarrassed. I fired more than 50 people, and the company lost five million dollars. Some of that was my own, but some belonged to investors including family and friends. Needless to say, there are some family members who still won't talk to me today.

I took a step back to analyze when went wrong. After some deep reflection, I made the following conclusions:

- **No plan**. I impulsively jumped into two business opportunities without research or a clear plan.
- **No commitment**. I didn't commit myself, often quitting after nine months in. I never fully believed in the mission of either company.
- **No customer understanding**. I didn't take time to understand customers and their needs, choosing to simply copy competitors, on the mistaken belief that I could out-execute or out-market them.

I vowed to not make the same mistakes. So I started my third entrepreneurial venture with extensive customer research, a three-year plan, and an unwavering 30-year personal commitment to the mission.

In 2014, I started my new company, a competitor to Craigslist, with an emphasis on mobile devices. It was a daunting task, fraught with competitors and lots of tough times. 18 months later, we had 10 million listings and completed over $10 billion in transactions. We sold the company for 1.3 billion dollars. After taking a nine-month break, I'm energized and ready to tackle my next adventure.

Overcoming an Obstacle

Tell me a time when you overcame an obstacle and delivered results.

Things to Consider

- Is your dilemma clear?
- How did you approach the situation?
- Was there a happy ending?

Common Mistakes

- Using an example where you overcame an obstacle, but did not deliver tangible results.

Answer

CANDIDATE: During my time as a student, I was a part of a group of four engineers who had to implement an e-commerce website using MySQL, Java, JavaScript, and HTML. We had two weeks to do it. Unfortunately, two of my teammates dropped the class and the other one had multiple final exams. I figured that if we had any chance of completing this project, I would have to step up.

First, I took the time to sit with my remaining teammate and discuss how we could split up the project. Because he didn't have much time, I started by understanding his strengths. Then I suggested tasks and goals appropriate to his strengths. That person had already done some front-end web development, so they said they could handle the JavaScript and HTML. I suggested finding and adapting e-commerce templates, which would save us the work of designing our e-commerce website from scratch.

Then, I set up a GitHub repository to share and store our code. GitHub allowed us to see each other's progress. I also included a clear list of tasks to be completed in our GitHub readme section.

The next two weeks were intense, and I gave myself daily goals that I had to complete. Piece by piece, I got the back-end of our e-commerce site working. I also set check-in meetings with my teammate every other day. Each week, I attended office hours with our teacher to discuss our biggest problems. The professor helped us get unstuck; it also showed our professor that I cared about having a final project that met all of her requirements.

When it came time to put everything together, things went more smoothly than I had imagined. Even though my partner didn't do as much as I would have hoped, he did a good job on the tasks he did do. I was glad we had taken the time to sort everything out at the very beginning.

When it came time to present, everything worked as intended. Some teams had been overly ambitious about what they could accomplish; they had features that were buggy or half-implemented. Other teams had less impressive sites because they did the same work twice.

That was a big takeaway for me: our constraints had forced us to think through what the core features of the product should be. Not only did it focus our efforts but also it created some natural "to do" tasks for our team.

In the end, our team ended up with an A- for the project. It wasn't a perfect grade, but it was well above the average and higher than what I originally expected when half of our team left, and the remaining team member could barely commit any time to the project.

Creating an Innovative Product

Tell me a time when you created an innovative product.

Things to Consider

- Why did you believe the product could be improved?
- What was your innovative solution, and what other alternatives did you consider?
- What business impact did your innovation create?

Common Mistakes

- Suggesting an improvement that comes across as a routine, incremental change.
- Making it hard to determine if the candidate or the team was responsible for the innovation.

Answer

CANDIDATE: Previously, I was a product manager for a global company. Since our company builds multiple apps from Finland, it was sometimes hard to keep track of which product was using which ad network. After talking to a colleague in marketing, I asked the other product managers on the team if creating a platform to organize all of this, along with the proper permissions, would be useful. This way, all three teams – product, marketing, and engineering – could track what was going on.

After getting a few nods, I ended up working with our in-house developer to implement this product in one month. It was easy-to-use and easy-to-customize. It took time for everyone to get used to it, and we became proficient.

Both the marketing and product team could add new products and ad networks easily, reducing our update time by 30 percent. And more importantly, we no longer had to pester our junior team member, Tony, for ad network information.

Learning Outside of Work

How do you find the time to stay inspired, acquire new knowledge and find innovation for your work?

Things to Consider

- Use the Rule of Three. E.g. "Even with my busy schedule, here are three things I do to find time to stay inspired outside of work. First, _____. Second, _____. Third, _____."
- The interviewer is expecting to "feel smarter" after hearing your response, so come up with some inspiring ideas.

Common Mistakes

- Short responses, especially ones that are less than 30 seconds. It leaves the interviewer unsatisfied.

Answer

CANDIDATE: Outside of work, I seek new knowledge in three main areas:

- Insights to be a better product manager

- Technologies my team uses
- New product innovations

Over time, I've learned that I do my best when I structure my own learning from everything available online. As a result, my favorite resources to stay inspired, acquire new knowledge, and learn about new innovations include Quora, Coursera, and Product Hunt.

Quora is a goldmine of insights from experienced PMs and entrepreneurs. By reading answers from top tech managers, I learn directly from industry veterans whose would otherwise be difficult to access. On Quora, I've read about how product managers at Facebook, Google, Uber, and other tech giants have thought through the challenges PMs face including:

- How to tradeoff between shipping quickly and staying true to long-term company objectives
- How to create team dynamics that push people to excellence
- How to deal with product launches that didn't go as planned

Coursera helps me stay up to date with our team's technology. Coursera offers a variety of topics, and I've been pleased with the tech ones. For instance, while I'm not a software developer, I've learned enough HTML, CSS, and JavaScript, through Coursera, to make small front-end changes. Thanks to my newfound knowledge, I'm no longer reliant on limited engineering time to get changes on our production servers.

Product Hunt helps me keep abreast of new product innovations. Every day, new products are posted and upvoted across multiple categories. Product Hunt allows me to try apps early, see which ones become hits and which ones don't. Each product page also includes a comment section. The creators usually chime in, allowing me to learn more about their product development processes.

INTERVIEWER: Thank you.

Diving Deep into Data

Tell me about a time when you had to dive deep into data and the results you achieved.

Things to Consider

- Demonstrate your analytical experience. Experienced folks know that analyzing data is just 10 percent of the problem. The other 90 percent is getting access to the data and cleaning the data.
- Good data analysts have a clear hypothesis they're trying to test.
- Your story should have clear, actionable insights.

Common Mistakes

- Not going into specific details, thinking that the interviewer won't understand.
- Sharing a data analysis story that does not have a recommendation or clear, actionable next steps.
- Using an example where the data set is not sufficiently complicated such as reviewing Google Analytics or AdWords data.

Answer

CANDIDATE: For one of our games, we had two hard currencies with six purchasing tiers each. Hard currencies are currencies you need to purchase with real money. We also had two hard currencies that players could only purchase when they ran out of money. That meant we had 14 different ways to purchase.

Given all the possibilities, there were optimization opportunities. I had to also segment our optimization by player type. Some players like to purchase a lot, and some do not. Some purchase only when they have to.

To build my optimization recommendations, I started by analyzing the data. I first extracted all the purchasing habits over the last month during our soft launch and created different views when looking at purchase data. Some of these include checking purchases based on country, player level, and a player's last action. Patterns began to emerge. It was getting clearer how likely purchases would be given a certain set of customer behaviors.

With this insight, I created a series of hypotheses. I validated these hypotheses with a series of tests. I experimented with different bundles and price discounts to small subsets of players. I recorded my conclusions based on what converted and what didn't.

After a month's worth of data, I rolled out new pricing and bundles on our platform, leading to a revenue increase of about $120K.

Connected ROI

Tell me about a time when you observed two business opportunities to improve ROI, and how did you determine they were connected?

Things to Consider

- If you can't think of a good story, you might have trouble with memory recall. Take time to reflect on what happened in your career. Go through your resume and jot down all your experiences, good and bad. Assign a label such as "data analysis" or "data mining" to indicate which type of behavioral question could use that story.
- Details are important. They convey credibility.
- Using details doesn't mean your response should have more words. For instance, "I went to a liberal arts college in New England" is wordier and less precise than "I went to Harvard."

Common Mistakes

- Using corporate jargon that only your co-workers (and not lay people) can understand.
- Displaying nervous signals including: playing with a pen, stroking hair, or not smiling.
- Failing to project your voice.

Answer

CANDIDATE: When we decided to launch our game in Taiwan, I realized we could either integrate a SDK of a local third-party app store, or we could integrate carrier billing. It was then I realized the two were related.

First, for the local third-party app store, it was true that while they did have their own inventory, a lot of it stems from the fact that they have their own prepaid cards that were located in local convenience stores. This was related to carrier billing. What I noticed was that a lot of paying users were people below the age of 18, and they did not have access to credit cards. It then became mandatory to allow them to pay through other methods, and both methods were popular alternatives.

When I found out both were related, our objective then became, "Which method do we want to integrate first?" instead. We ended up implementing both, which increased our Taiwan revenue by 60%.

Earning the Trust of a Group

Tell me a time when you earned the trust of a group.

Things to Consider

- How did you add value to the group?
- Did you rush to impose your will? Or did you assess the group's needs first?
- How did you continue to earn the group's trust going forward?

Common Mistakes

- Most interviewers do not like stories where a candidate lost the group's trust by making a mistake and earned it back by apologizing. Some may appreciate a good apology story, but most prefer that candidates not make mistakes in the first place.
- The same goes for stories where a candidate loses a group's trust by lying, gossiping or playing office politics. Most interviewers prefer that the candidate not do those things period.

Answer

CANDIDATE: When I started as PM for my current company, I inherited a project with an upset partner team in Madrid. The US team wanted to make some changes to the user experience because the product was originally successful in Spain. However, American users tend to have a different user experience when compared to Spanish users. The Madrid team didn't trust us because they never worked with us before.

To influence my Spanish counterparts to cooperate, I wrote a report for them. The report included:

- Analysis of metrics they felt were important, based on their target goals
- Suggestions for new UX improvements
- Estimated impact of those UX improvements
- Citations and inspirational sources for my UX suggestions

The report was very thorough, and the Madrid team loved it. Obviously, they weren't going to trust me based on a report alone, so I sat down with the product manager in Madrid and reviewed, line-by-line, what features and improvements we should do. In the end, we decided to soft launch the product with a few additions. We decided that we could always make additional changes after the soft launch, as needed.

We started to implement changes that I proposed. I made sure to show commitment by being responsive and apolitical. I also worked hard and tried to be accommodating. When they visited our offices, I offered to take them to dinner and show them around town when other colleagues preferred to go home to rest and relax.

After two to three of months working together, the product changed radically for the better. I had earned their trust, and in turn, they trusted my process and judgment. The pinnacle happened when my company awarded the Madrid partner team and me the Internal Excellence Award; it included a $5,000 cash bonus for each team member.

Next Steps

Thanks for taking the time to read the book. Now I'd love to hear from you! Please:

- Review the book on Amazon
- Join my community to find interview practice partners: bit.ly/PMInterviewGroup
- Move up the PM career ladder by mastering the six proven skills from the ESTEEM Method™, featured in *Be the Greatest Product Manager Ever* by Lewis C. Lin bit.ly/bgpm-lewis-lin
- Send any questions, comments, edits, or feedback to: lewis@impactinterview.com

Acknowledgments

The Product Manager Interview would not have come to life without the incredible contributions from the special people below.

I owe the biggest gratitude to my co-author, **Teng Lu**. We communicated every day and as a result, forged a special bond. He showed incredible grit, heart, and tenacity as he researched questions and prepared initial drafts. I have nothing but the highest respect for Teng, and I hope I get another chance to collaborate with him. His fortitude is in the top 1% of all the people I've worked with in my career.

Joseph Watabe showed similar grit. I'm fortunate to have him review each draft. **Elisa Yuen** contributed her keen eye for detail as she read the voluminous drafts and asked tough questions.

Tim Beiko was our most recent reviewer and made significant contributions to the version you see today. He provided copious comments, made countless suggestions, and updated answers to be current, comprehensive, and easier to understand.

Finally, there is a long list of advisors, giving input and feedback along the way. I have included them here. Any omissions are purely unintentional.

Abbie Austin	Phillip Scavulli
Ankit Roy	Saurin Shah
Bobby Liu	Sebastian Sabouné
Daniil Lanovyi	Shravan Rajagopal
Fahad Quraishi	Timothy Tow
James Routledge	Tyler Sanchez
Jamie Hui	

Made in United States
North Haven, CT
07 September 2023

41239951R00183